THE ROUGH GUIDE

PORTUGUESE

PHRASEBOOK

Compiled by

LEXUS

ROUGH
GUIDES

www.roughguides.com

Credits

Compiled by Lexus with Norma de Oliviera Tait
Lexus Series Editor: Sally Davies
Rough Guides Reference Director: Andrew Lockett
Rough Guides Series Editor: Mark Ellingham

First edition published in 1996.
Reprinted in 1998.
Revised in 1999.
Reprinted in 2004.
This updated edition published in 2006 by
Rough Guides Ltd,
80 Strand, London WC2R 0RL
345 Hudson St, 4th Floor, New York 10014, USA
Email: mail@roughguides.co.uk.

Distributed by the Penguin Group.

Penguin Books Ltd, 80 Strand, London WC2R 0RL
Penguin Putnam, Inc., 375 Hudson Street, NY 10014, USA
Penguin Group (Australia), 250 Camberwell Road, Camberwell,
Victoria 3124, Australia
Penguin Books Canada Ltd, 10 Alcorn Avenue, Toronto,
Ontario, Canada M4V 1E4
Penguin Group (New Zealand), Cnr Rosedale and Airborne Roads,
Albany, Auckland, New Zealand

Typeset in Bembo and Helvetica to an original design by Henry Iles.
Printed in Italy by LegoPrint S.p.A

British Library Cataloguing in Publication Data
A catalogue for this book is available from the British Library.

ISBN 13: 978-1-84353-631-4
ISBN 10: 1-84353-631-5

The publishers and authors have done their best to ensure
the accuracy and currency of all information in The Rough
Guide Portuguese Phrasebook however, they can accept no
responsibility for any loss or inconvenience sustained by any
reader using the book.

Online information about Rough Guides can be
found at our website www.roughguides.com

CONTENTS

Introduction

The Rough Guide Portuguese phrasebook is a highly practical introduction to the contemporary language. Laid out in clear A-Z style, it uses key-word referencing to lead you straight to the words and phrases you want – so if you need to book a room, just look up 'room'. The Rough Guide gets straight to the point in every situation, in bars and shops, on trains and buses, and in hotels and banks.

The main part of the Rough Guide is a double dictionary: English-Portuguese then Portuguese-English. Before that, there's a section called **Basic Phrases** and to get you involved in two-way communication, the Rough Guide includes, in this new edition, a set of **Scenario** dialogues illustrating questions and responses in key situations such as renting a car and asking directions. You can hear these and then download them free from **www.roughguides.com/phrasebooks** for use on your computer or MP3 player.

Forming the heart of the guide, the **English-Portuguese** section gives easy-to-use transliterations of the Portuguese words wherever pronunciation might be a problem. Throughout this section, cross-references enable you to pinpoint key facts and phrases, while asterisked words indicate where further information can be found in a section at the end of the book called **How the Language Works**. This section sets out the fundamental rules of the language, with plenty of practical examples. You'll also find here other essentials like numbers, dates, telling the time and basic phrases. In the **Portuguese-English** dictionary, we've given you not just the phrases you'll be likely to hear (starting with a selection of slang and colloquialisms) but also many of the signs, labels, instructions and other basic words you may come across in print or in public places.

Near the back of the book too the Rough Guide offers an extensive **Menu Reader**. Consisting of food and drink sections (each starting with a list of essential terms), it's indispensable whether you're eating out, stopping for a quick drink, or browsing through a local food market.

boa viagem!
have a good trip!

Basic Phrases

yes
sim
seeng

no
não
nowng

OK
está bem
shta bayng

hello/hi
olá

good morning
bom dia
bong dee-a

good evening/good night
boa noite
boh-a noh-it

see you!
até logo!
ateh logoo

goodbye
adeus
aday-oosh

please
se faz favor, por favor
si fash favohr, poor favohr

yes please
sim, por favor
seeng

thanks, thank you
(said by man/woman) obrigado/
obrigada
obrigadoo

no thanks, no thank you
não obrigado/obrigada
nowng

thank you very much
muito obrigado/obrigada
mweengtoo

don't mention it
não tem de quê
nowng tayng di kay

not at all
de nada
di

how do you do?
muito prazer
mweengtoo prazayr

how are you?
como está?
kohmoo shta

fine, thanks
(said by man/woman) bem,
obrigado/obrigada
bayng obrigadoo

pleased to meet you
(said to man/woman) muito
prazer em conhecê-lo/
conhecê-la
mweengtoo prazayr ayng kon-
yisayloo

excuse me
(to get past) com licença
kong lis**ayn**sa
(to get attention) se faz favor
si fash fav**ohr**
(to say sorry) desculpe
dishk**oo**lp

(I'm) sorry
tenho muita pena
tayn-yoo mw**ee**ngta p**ay**na

sorry?/pardon (me)?
(didn't understand) como?
kohmoo

what did you say?
o que disse?
oo ki dees

I see/I understand
percebo
pirs**ay**boo

I don't understand
não percebo
nowng

do you speak English?
fala inglês?
ingl**ay**sh

I don't speak Portuguese
não falo português
nowng f**a**loo poortoog**ay**sh

can you speak more slowly?
pode falar mais devagar?
pod fal**a**r mīj divag**a**r

could you repeat that?
podia repetir?
pood**ee**-a ripit**eer**

can you write it down?
pode escrever isso?
pod shkriv**ayr ee**soo

I'd like ...
queria ...
kir**ee**-a

can I have ...?
pode dar-me ...?
pod d**a**rmi

do you have ...?
tem ...?
t**ay**nq

how much is it?
quanto é?
kwantw**eh**

cheers!
saúde!
sa-**oo**d

it is ...
é ...; está ...
eh; shta

where is ...?
onde é ...?; onde está ...?
ohnd**eh**; ohnd shta

is it far?
é longe?
eh lohnj

9

Scenarios

1. Accommodation

is there an inexpensive hotel you can recommend?
▶ pode recomendar-me um hotel não muito caro?
[pod rikoomayndarmi oong ohtel nowng mweengtoo karoo]

---

sinto muito, todos parecem estar totalmente cheios ◀
[seentoo mweengtoo tohdoosh paresayng shtar tootalmaynt shay-oosh]
I'm sorry, they all seem to be fully booked

---

can you give me the name of a good middle-range hotel?
▶ pode dar-me o nome de um bom hotel de preço médio?
[pod darmi oo nohm doong bong ohtel di praysoo mehd-yoo]

---

deixe-me ver; deseja ficar no centro? ◀
[dayshmi vayr disayJa fikar noo sayntroo]
let me have a look; do you want to be in the centre?

---

if possible
▶ se possível
[si pooseevil]

---

importa-se de ficar um pouco fora da cidade? ◀
[importasi di fikar oong pohkoo fora da sidad]
do you mind being a little way out of town?

---

as long as it's not too far out
▶ desde que não seja demasiado longe
[dayJdi ki nowng sayJa dimaz-yadoo lohnJ]

---

where is it on the map?
▶ onde está no mapa?
[ohnd shta noo mapa]

---

can you write the name and address down?
▶ pode escrever o nome e a morada para mim?
[pod shkrivayr o nohm ee a moorada para meeng]

I'm looking for a room in a private house
▶ procuro um quarto numa casa particular
[prookooroo oong kwartoo nooma kaza partikoolar]

2. Banks

bank account	a conta bancária	[**koh**nta bankar-ya]
to change money	trocar dinheiro	[troo**ka**r deen-**ya**yroo]
cheque	o cheque	[shehk]
to deposit	depositar	[dipoozi**ta**r]
euro	o Euro	[**ay**-ooroo]
pin number	PIN	[peen]
pound	a libra	[**lee**bra]
to withdraw	levantar	[livan**ta**r]

can you change this into euros?
▶ pode trocar isto por euros?
[pod troo**ka**r **ee**shtoo poor **ay**-ooroosh]

como quer o dinheiro? ◀
[**koh**moo kehr oo deen-**ya**yroo]
how would you like the money?

small notes	big notes
▶ notas pequenas	▶ notas grandes
[**no**tash pik**ay**nash]	[**no**tash grandsh]

do you have information in English about opening an account?
▶ tem informação em inglês sobre como abrir uma conta?
[tayng infoormas**ow**ng ayng inglaysh sohbr **koh**moo abreer **oo**ma **koh**nta]

sim, que tipo de conta deseja abrir? ◀
[seeng ki **tee**poo di **koh**nta dis**ay**Ja ab**ree**r]
yes, what sort of account do you want?

I'd like a current account
▶ gostaria de abrir uma conta corrente
[gooshtar**ee**-a dab**ree**r **oo**ma **koh**nta koorr**ay**nt]

o seu passaporte, por favor ◀
[oo **say**-oo pasa**po**rt poor fav**oh**r]
your passport, please

can I use this card to draw some cash?
▶ posso utilizar este cartão para levantar dinheiro?
[**po**soo ootili**za**r aysht kart**ow**ng para livan**ta**r deen-**ya**yroo]

precisa ir ao caixa ◀
[pris**ee**za eer ow k**ī**sha]
you have to go to the cashier's desk

I want to transfer this to my account at Banco Totta & Açores
▶ desejo transferir isto para a minha conta no Banco Totta & Açores
[diz**ay**Joo transhfir**ee**r **ee**shtoo para **mee**n-ya **koh**nta noo bankoo t**o**ta-yas**oh**rish]

está bem, mas vamos ter de cobrar a chamada telefónica ◀
[shta bayng maJ **va**moosh tayr di k**oo**brar a sha**ma**da telef**oh**nika]
OK, but we'll have to charge you for the phonecall

3. Booking a room

shower	o duche	[doosh]
telephone in the room	o telefone no quarto	[telefohn noo kwartoo]
payphone in the lobby	o telefone público no hall	[telefohn pooblikoo noo hall]

do you have any rooms?
▶ tem quartos vagos?
[tayng kwartoosh vagoosh]

para quantas pessoas? ◀
[para kwantash pisoh-ash]
for how many people?

for one/for two
▶ para uma pessoa/para duas pessoas
[para ooma pisoh-a/para doo-ash pisoh-ash]

sim, temos ◀
[seeng, taymoosh]
yes, we have rooms free

▶ para quantas noites?
[para kwantash noh-itsh]
for how many nights?

just for one night
só uma noite
[saw ooma noh-It]

how much is it?
▶ qual é o preço?
[kwal eh oo praysoo]

90 Euros com casa de banho e 70 Euros sem casa de banho ◀
[noovaynta ay-ooroosh kong kaza di ban-yoo ee setaynta ay-ooroosh sayng kaza di ban-yoo]
90 euros with bathroom and 70 euros without bathroom

does that include breakfast?
▶ o pequeno almoço está incluido?
[oo pikaynoo almohsoo shta inklweedoo]

can I see a room with bathroom?
▶ posso ver um quarto com casa de banho?
[posoo vayr oong kwartoo kong kaza di ban-yoo]

ok, I'll take it
▶ sim, fico com este
[seeng feekoo kong aysht]

when do I have to check out?
▶ quando tenho de fazer o check out?
[kwandoo tayn-yoo di fazayr oo check out]

is there anywhere I can leave luggage?
▶ há algum lugar onde posso deixar a bagagem?
[a algoong loogar ohnd posoo dayshar a bagaJayng]

4. Car hire

automatic	automático	[owtoomatikoo]
full tank	depósito cheio	[dipozitoo shay-oo]
manual	manual	[manwal]
rented car	carro de aluguer	[karroo daloogehr]

I'd like to rent a car   por quanto tempo? ◀
▶ queria alugar um carro   [poor kwantoo taympoo]
[kiree-a aloogar oong karroo]   for how long?

two days   I'll take the ...
▶ dois dias   ▶ fico com o ...
[doh-iJ dee-ash]   [feekoo kong oo ...]

is that with unlimited mileage?   sim ◀
▶ é com quilometragem ilimitada?   [seeng]
[eh kong kilomitrajayng ilimitada]   it is

posso ver a sua carta de condução, por favor? ◀
[posso vayr a soo-a karta di kondoosowng poor favohr]
can I see your driving licence please?

e o seu passaporte ◀
[yoo say-oo pasaport]
and your passport

is insurance included?
▶ o seguro está incluído?
[oo sigooroo shta inklweedoo]

sim. mas tem que pagar os primeiros 100 euros ◀
[seeng mash tayng ki pagar oosh primayroosh sayng ay-ooroosh]
yes, but you have to pay the first 100 euros

pode deixar um depósito de 100 euros? ◀
[pod dayshar oong dipozitoo di sayng ay-ooroosh]
can you leave a deposit of 100 euros?

and if this office is closed, where do I leave the keys?
▶ e se o escritório estiver fechado, onde posso deixar as chaves?
[ee s-yoo shkritor-yoo shtivehr fishadoo, ohnd posoo dayshar ash shavsh]

pode depositá-las naquela caixa ◀
[pod dipoozitalash nakehla kīsha]
you drop them in that box

5. Communications

ADSL modem	o modem ADSL	[modem a-de-ehs-**ehl**i]
at	arroba	[ar**roh**ba]
dial-up modem	modem telefónico	[modem telefo**ohn**neekoo]
dot	ponto	[**pohn**too]
Internet	a Internet	[intirn**eht**]
mobile (phone)	telemóvel	[tele**mov**il]
password	senha	[**sayn**-ya]
telephone socket adaptor	adaptador da tomada de telefone	[adapta**doh**n da toomada di tele**fohn**]
wireless hotspot	hotspot sem fios	[hotspot sayng **fee**-oosh]

is there an Internet café around here?
▶ há um Internet café aqui perto?
[a oong intirn**eht** kaf**eh** ak**ee** p**eh**rtoo]

can I send email from here?
▶ posso enviar e-mails daqui?
[**po**soo aynv-yar emailJ dak**ee**]

where's the at sign on the keyboard?
▶ onde está o arroba no teclado?
[ohnd shta oo ar**roh**ba noo tikla**doo**]

can you switch this to a UK keyboard?
▶ pode mudar para o teclado britânico?
[pod moo**da**r paroo tikla**doo** brita**ni**koo]

can you help me log on?
▶ pode ajudar-me a iniciar a sessão?
[pod a**Joo**darmi a inís-yar a sis**ow**ng]

can you put me through to ...?
▶ pode ligar-me a ...?
[pod ligarme a ...]

I'm not getting a connection, can you help?
▶ não estou a conseguir a ligação, pode ajudar-me?
[nowng shtoh a konsig**eer** a ligas**ow**ng pod a**Joo**darmi]

where can I get a top-up card for my mobile?
▶ onde posso comprar vitaminas para o meu telemóvel?
[ohnd **po**soo komprar vítame**ee**nash paroo **may**-oo telemovil]

zero	five
zero	cinco
[**zeh**roo]	[**seen**koo]

one	six
um	seis
[oong]	[saysh]

two	seven
dois	séte
[doh-ish]	[seht]

three	eight
três	oito
[traysh]	[**oh**-itoo]

four	nine
quatro	nove
[kwatroo]	[nov]

6. Directions

hi, I'm looking for Avenida do Brasil
▶ olá, estou à procura da Avenida do Brasil
[oola shtoh a prookoora da avineeda doo brazeel]

desculpe, nunca ouvi falar desta avenida ◀
[dishkoolp noonka ohvee falar dehshta avineeda]
sorry, never heard of it

hi, can you tell me where Avenida do Brasil is?
▶ olá, pode dizer-me onde fica a Avenida do Brasil?
[oola pod dizayrmi ohnd feeka avineeda doo brazeel]

também sou um visitante aqui ◀
[tambayng soh oong vizitant akee]
I'm a stranger here too

hi, Avenida do Brasil, do you know where it is?
olá, Avenida do Brasil, sabe onde fica?
[oola avineeda doo brazeel sab ohnd feeka]

where?
onde?
[ohnd]

which direction?
em que direcção?
[ayng ki direhsowng]

▶ fica ao virar a esquina
[feeka ow veerar ashkeena]
around the corner

▶ à esquerda no segundo semáforo
[a-shkayrda noo sigoondoo simafooroo]
left at the second traffic lights

▶ depois é a primeira rua à direita
[dipoh-ish eh a primayra roo-a-dirayta]
then it's the first street on the right

à direita [a-dirayta] on the right	em frente [ayng fraynt] opposite	mais longe [mīj lohnj] further	saída [sa-eeda] turn off
à esquerda [a-shkayrda] on the left	em frente de [ayng fraynt di] in front of	perto [pehrtoo] near	sempre em frente [saymprayng fraynt] straight ahead
ali adiante [alee ad-yant] over there	logo a seguir a [logoo a sigeer a] just after	próximo [prosimoo] next	voltar [voltar] back
depois do ... [dipoh-ish doo ...] past the ...		rua [roo-a] street	

18

7. Emergencies

accident	o acidente	[asidaynt]
ambulance	a ambulância	[amboolans-ya]
consul	o cônsul	[kohnsool]
embassy	a embaixada	[aymbishada]
fire brigade	os bombeiros	[bombayroosh]
police	a polícia	[poolees-ya]

help!
▶ socorro!
[sookohrroo]

can you help me?
▶ pode ajudar-me?
[pod aJoodarmi]

please come with me! it's really very urgent
▶ por favor, venha comigo! é realmente muito urgente
[poor favohr vayn-ya koomeegoo eh r-yalmaynt mweengtoo oorJaynt]

I've lost (my keys)
▶ perdi (as minhas chaves)
[pirdee (aJ meen-yash shavsh)]

(my car) is not working
▶ (o meu carro) não está a funcionar
[(oo may-oo karroo) nowng shta a foons-yoonar]

(my purse) has been stolen
▶ (a minha carteira) foi roubada
[(a meen-ya kartayra) foh-i rohbada]

I've been mugged
▶ fui assaltada
[fwee asaltada]

como se chama? ◀
[kohmoo si shama]
what's your name?

preciso de ver o seu passaporte ◀
I need to see your passport
[priseezoo di vayr oo say-oo pasaport]

I'm sorry, all my papers have been stolen
▶ desculpe, roubaram-me todos os documentos
[dishkoolp rohbarowngmi tohdooz ooJ dookoomayntoosh]

8. Friends

hi, how're you doing?
▶ olá, como estás?
[oola kohmoo shtash]

bem e tu? ◀
[bayng ee too]
OK, and you

yeah, fine
▶ estou bem
[shtoh bayng]

not bad
▶ menos mal
[maynooJ mal]

d'you know Mark?
▶ conheces o Mark?
[kon-yehsiz oo mark]

and this is Anna
▶ e esta é a Anna
[ee ehsht eh a ana]

▶ sim, conhecemo-nos
yeah, we know each other
[seeng kon-yisaymoonoosh]

where do you know each other from?
▶ de onde se conhecem?
[dohnd si kon-yehsayng]

conhecemo-nos na casa do Manoel ◀
[kon-yisaymoonooJ na kaza doo manoo-ehl]
we met at Manoel's place

that was some party, eh?
▶ foi uma festa de arromba, não foi?
[foh-i ooma fehshta darrohmba nowng foh-i]

não podia ser melhor ◀
[nowng poodee-a sayr mil-yor]
the best

are you guys coming for a beer?
▶ querem beber uma cerveja?
[kehrayng bibayr ooma sirvayJa]

▶ óptimo, vamos lá
[otimoo vamooJ la]
cool, let's go

não, vou-me encontrar com a Maria
[nowng vohmi aynkohntrar kong a maree-a]
no, I'm meeting Maria

see you at Manoel's place tonight
▶ até mais logo em casa do Manoel hoje à noite
[ateh mīJ logoo na kaza doo manoo-ehl ohJ a-noh-it]

até logo ◀
[ateh logoo]
see you

download these scenarios as MP3s from:

9. Health

I'm not feeling very well
▶ não me sinto muito bem
[nowng mi **see**ntoo m**wee**ngtoo bayng]

can you get a doctor?
▶ pode chamar um médico?
[pod shamar oong **meh**dikoo]

▶ onde dói?
[ohnd doy]
where does it hurt?

it hurts here
▶ dói aqui
[doy ak**ee**]

▶ é uma dor constante?
[eh **oo**ma dohr konsht**ant**]
is the pain constant?

it's not a constant pain
▶ não é uma dor constante
[nowng eh **oo**ma dohr konsht**ant**]

can I make an appointment?
▶ posso marcar uma consulta?
[**p**oso markar **oo**ma kons**oo**lta]

can you give me something for ...?
▶ pode dar-me qualquer coisa para ...?
[pod **d**armi kwalk**eh**r k**oh**-iza para ...]

yes, I have insurance
▶ sim, tenho seguro
[seeng **tayn**-yoo sig**oo**roo]

antibiotics	os antibióticos	[antib-y**o**tikoosh]
antiseptic ointment	uma pomada anti-séptica	[poom**a**da antis**eh**ptika]
cystitis	cistite	[sisht**eet**]
dentist	o dentista	[dent**ee**shta]
diarrhoea	a diarreia	[d-yarr**ay**-a]
doctor	o médico	[**meh**dikoo]
hospital	o hospital	[oshpit**al**]
ill	doente	[dw**ay**nt]
medicine	o remédio	[rim**eh**d-yoo]
painkillers	os analgésicos	[analj**eh**zikoosh]
pharmacy	a farmácia	[farm**a**s-ya]
to prescribe	receitar	[risayt**ar**]
thrush	cândida	[**k**andida]

10. Language difficulties

a few words	poucas palavras	[**poh**kash pala**v**rash]
interpreter	o intérprete	[in**teh**rprit]
to translate	traduzir	[tradoo**zeer**]

o seu cartão de crédito foi recusado ◀
[oo **zay**-oo kar**tow**ng di kr**eh**ditoo **foh**-i rikooza̱doo]
your credit card has been refused

what, I don't understand; do you speak English?
▶ o quê, não percebo; fala inglês?
[oo kay nowng pirs**ay**boo; f**a**la ingl**ay**sh]

este cartão não é válido ◀
[aysht kar**tow**ng nowng eh v**a**lidoo]
this isn't valid

could you say that again?   slowly
▶ pode repetir, por favor?   ▶ devagar
[pod ripit**eer** poor fav**ohr**]   [div**a**gar]

I understand very little Portuguese
▶ percebo muito pouco português
[pirs**ay**boo m**wee**ngtoo p**oh**koo poortoog**ay**sh]

I speak Portuguese very badly
▶ falo muito mal o português
[f**a**loo m**wee**ngtoo mal oo poortoog**ay**sh]

não pode utilizar este cartão para pagar ◀
[nowng pod ootiliza̱r aysht kar**tow**ng para pagar]
you can't use this card to pay

▶ compreende?   sorry, no
[kompr-**yay**nd]   ▶ desculpe, não compreendo
do you understand?   [dishk**oo**lp nowng kompr-**yay**ndoo]

is there someone who speaks English?
▶ há alguém que fale inglês?
[a alg**ay**ng ki fal ingl**ay**sh]

oh, now I understand   is that ok now?
▶ ah, agora percebo   ▶ está tudo bem agora?
[ah ag**o**ra pirs**ay**boo]   [shta **too**doo bayng ag**o**ra]

11. Meeting people

hello
▸ olá
[oo**la**]

olá, o meu nome é Joana ◂
[oo**la** oo **may**-oo nohm eh Joo-**ana**]
hello, my name's Joana

Graham, from England, Thirsk
▸ chamo-me Graham; moro em Thirsk na Inglaterra
[**sha**moomi graham **mo**roo ayng thirsk na inglate**hr**ra]

não conheço, onde fica? ◂
[nowng kon-**yay**soo ohnd **fee**ka]
don't know that, where is it?

---

not far from York, in the North; and you?
▸ perto de York, no Norte, e você?
[**peh**rtoo di York noo Nort ee vos**ay**]

sou de Coimbra, está sozinho aqui? ◂
[soh di kw**ee**mbra, shta soz**ee**n-yoo ak**ee**]
I'm from Coimbra; here by yourself?

---

no, I'm with my wife and two kids
▸ não, estou com a minha mulher e dois filhos
[nowng stoh kong a m**ee**n-ya mool-**yeh**r ee d**oh**-ish f**ee**l-yoosh]

---

what do you do?   trabalho com computadores ◂
▸ qual é o seu emprego?   [trabal-yoo kong kompootad**oh**rish]
[kwal eh oo **say**-oo aympr**ay**goo]   **I'm in computers**

me too
▸ eu também
[**ay**-oo tamb**ay**ng]

here's my wife now
▸ aqui está a minha mulher
[ak**ee** shta a m**ee**n-ya mool-**yeh**r]

---

muito prazer ◂
[m**wee**ngtoo praz**ay**r]
nice to meet you

12. Post offices

airmail	correio aéreo	[koorray-oo a-ehr-yoo]
post card	o postal	[pooshtal]
post office	os correios	[koorray-oosh]
stamp	o selo	[sayloo]

what time does the post office close?
▶ a que horas fecham os correios?
[a k-yorash fayshowng oosh koorray-oosh]

▶ às cinco horas nos dias de semana
[ash seenkoo orash nooj dee-aj di simana]
five o'clock weekdays

is the post office open on Saturdays? até ao meio-dia ◀
▶ os correios abrem aos sábados? [ateh ow may-oo dee-a]
[oosh koorray-oosh abrayng owsh sabadoosh] **until midday**

I'd like to send this registered to England
▶ queria enviar isto registado para Inglaterra
[kiree-a aynv-yar eeshtoo rijishtadoo para inglatehrra]

com certeza, são 10 euros ◀
[kong sirtayza sowng dehz ay-ooroosh]
certainly, that will cost 10 euros

and also two stamps for England, please
▶ e mais dois selos para Inglaterra, por favor
[ee mīj doh-ish sayloosh para inglatehrra poor favohr]

do you have some airmail stickers?
▶ tem autocolantes para via aérea?
[tayng owtookoolantsh para vee-a a-ehr-ya]

do you have any mail for me?
▶ há algum correio para mim?
[a algoom koorray-oo para meeng]

| cartas | letters |
| encomendas | parcels |

13. Restaurants

bill	a conta	[**koh**nta]
menu	a ementa	[e**mayn**ta]
table	a mesa	[**may**za]

can we have a non-smoking table?
▶ queremos uma mesa para não fumadores
[ki**ray**mooz **oo**ma **may**za para nowng foomad**oh**rish]

there are two of us
▶ é para duas pessoas
[eh para **doo**-ash pis**oh**-ash]

there are four of us
▶ é para quatro pessoas
eh para **kwa**troo pis**oh**-ash]

what's this?
▶ o que é isto?
[oo k-yeh **eesh**too]

é um tipo de peixe ◀
[eh oong **tee**poo di paysh]
it's a type of fish

é uma especialidade local ◀
it's a local speciality
[eh **oo**ma shpis-yalidad look**al**]

venha cá que eu mostro-lhe ◀
[**vayn**-ya ka ki **ay**-oo m**osh**trool yi]
come inside and I'll show you

we would like two of these, one of these, and one of those
▶ queremos dois destes, um destes e um desses
[ki**ray**mooJ d**oh**-ish **day**shtish, oong **day**stish ee oong **day**sish]

▶ e para beber?
[ee para bi**bayr**]
and to drink?

red wine
▶ vinho tinto
[**veen**-yoo **teen**too]

white wine
▶ vinho branco
[**veen**-yoo **bran**koo]

a beer and two orange juices
▶ uma cerveja e dois sumos de laranja
[**oo**ma sir**vay**Ja ee d**oh**-ish **soo**mooJ di laran**J**a]

some more bread please
▶ mais pão, por favor
[mish powng poor fav**ohr**]

▶ estava tudo bem?
[sh**ta**va **too**doo bayng]
how was your meal?

excellent, very nice!
▶ excelente, muito bom!
[ish-sel**ay**nt m**ween**gtoo bong]

▶ mais alguma coisa?
[miz alg**oo**ma k**oh**-iza]
anything else?

just the bill thanks
▶ apenas a conta, por favor
[ap**ay**naz a **koh**nta poor fav**ohr**]

14. Shopping

posso ajudá-la? ◀
[**po**soo aɹoo**da**la]
can I help you?

can I just have a look around?
▶ posso só dar uma olhada?
[**po**soo saw dar **oo**ma ol-y**a**da]

yes, I'm looking for ...
sim, queria ...
[seeng kir**ee**-a …]

how much is this?
▶ quanto custa isto?
[kwantoo **koo**shta **ee**shtoo]

trinta e dois euros ◀
[**tree**ntĩ **doh**-iz **ay**-ooroosh]
thirty-two euros

OK, I think I'll have to leave it; it's a little too expensive for me
▶ tudo bem, acho que vou ter de desistir, é caro demais para mim
[**too**doo bayng, **a**shoo ki voh tayr di dizisht**eer** eh **ka**roo dim**ee**sh para meeng]

e que tal este? ◀
[ee ki tal aysht]
how about this?

can I pay by credit card?
▶ posso pagar com cartão de crédito?
[**po**soo pag**a**r kong kart**ow**ng di kr**eh**ditoo]

it's too big
▶ é demasiado grande
[eh dimaz-y**a**doo grand]

it's too small
▶ é demasiado pequeno
[eh dimaz-y**a**doo pik**ay**noo]

it's for my son – he's about this high
▶ é para o meu filho – ele é mais ou menos deste tamanho
[eh p**a**roo **may**-oo f**ee**l-yoo ayl eh mīz oh **may**noosh daysht tam**a**n-yoo]

▶ mais alguma coisa?
[mīz alg**oo**ma **koh**-iza]
will there be anything else?

that's all thanks
▶ isso é tudo obrigada
[**ee**soo eh **too**doo obrig**a**da]

make it twenty euros and I'll take it
▶ reduza para vinte euros e eu compro
[rid**oo**za para veent **ay**-ooroosh ee **ay**-oo k**oh**mproo]

fine, I'll take it
▶ está bem, fico com ele
[shta bayng f**ee**koo kong ayl]

aberto	open	saldos	sale
caixa	cash desk	trocar	to exchange
fechado	closed		

15. Sightseeing

art gallery	a galeria de arte	[galiree-a dart]
bus tour	uma excursão de autocarro	[shkoorsowng di owtookarroo]
city centre	o centro da cidade	[sayntroo da sidad]
closed	fechado	[fishadoo]
guide	o guia	[gee-a]
museum	o museu	[moozay-oo]
open	aberto	[abehrtoo]

I'm interested in seeing the old town
▶ estou interessado em conhecer a cidade antiga
[shtoh intrisadoo ayng kon-yisayr a sidad anteega]

are there guided tours?
▶ ha excursões com guia?
[a shkoorsowngsh kong gee-a]

▶ lamento, mas acabaram-se os lugares
[lamayntoo maz akabarowngsi ooz loogarish]
I'm sorry, it's fully booked

how much would you charge to drive us around for four hours?
▶ quanto cobraria para nos levar a passear por quatro horas?
[kwantoo koobraree-a para nooJ livar a pas-yar poor kwatroo orash]

can we book tickets for the concert here?
▶ podemos reservar bilhetes para o concerto aqui?
[poodaymoosh rizirvar bil-yaytsh paroo konsayrtoo akee]

▶ sim, em que nome?
[seeng ayng ki nohm]
yes, in what name?

▶ qual é o cartão de crédito?
[kwaleh oo kartowng di krehditoo]
which credit card?

where do we get the tickets?
▶ onde levantamos os bilhetes?
[ohnd livantamooz ooJ bil-yaytsh]

levante-os na entrada
[livant-yoosh na ayntrada]
just pick them up at the entrance

is it open on Sundays?
▶ abrem aos domingos?
[abrayng owJ doomeengoosh]

how much is it to get in?
▶ quanto é a entrada?
[kwantweh a ayntrada]

are there reductions for groups of 6?
▶ dão desconto para grupos de seis pessoas?
[downg dishkohntoo para groopooJ di saysh pisoh-ash]

that was really impressive!
▶ foi sensacional!
[foh-i saynsas-yoonal]

16. Trains

to change trains	mudar de comboio	[moodar di komboy-oo]
platform	a plataforma	[plataforma]
return	um bilhete de ida e volta	[bil-yayt deedi volta]
single	um bilhete de ida	[bil-yayt deeda]
station	a estação	[shtasowng]
stop	a paragem	[paraJayng]
ticket	o bilhete	[bil-yayt]

how much is ...?
▶ quanto é ...?
[kwantweh ...]

a single, second class to ...
▶ um bilhete de ida, segunda classe para ...
[oong bil-yayt deeda sigoonda klass para ...]

two returns, second class to ...
▶ dois bilhetes de ida e volta, segunda classe para...
[doh-ish bil-yaytsh deedi volta sigoonda klass para ...]

for today	**for tomorrow**	**for next Tuesday**
▶ para hoje	▶ para amanhã	▶ para a próxima terça-feira
[para ohJ]	[para aman-yang]	[para prosima tayrsa fayra]

há um suplemento para o Intercidades ◀
[a oong sooplimayntoo paroo intersidadsh]
there's a supplement for the Intercity

deseja reservar o seu assento? ◀
[disayJa rizirvar oo say-oo asayntoo]
do you want to make a seat reservation?

tem de mudar de comboio em Entroncamento ◀
[tayng di moodar di komboy-oo ayng ayntronkamayntoo]
you have to change at Entroncamento

is this seat free?
▶ este lugar está livre?
[aysht loogar shta leevr]

excuse me, which station are we at?
▶ se faz favor, que estação é esta?
[si fash favohr ki shtasowng eh ehshta]

is this where I change for Oporto?
▶ é aqui que faço a mudança para o Porto?
[eh akee ki faswa moodansa paroo pohrtoo]

English

→

Portuguese

A

a, an* um, uma [oong, **oo**ma]

about: about 20 mais ou
menos vinte [mīz oh **may**noosh
veent]

it's about 5 o'clock por volta
das cinco [poor – **seen**koo]

a film about Portugal um
filme sobre Portugal [oong
feelm sohbr poortoogal]

above acima [a**see**ma]

abroad no estrangeiro [noo
shtranj**av**rron]

absolutely! (I agree) com
certeza! [kong sirt**ay**za]

absorbent cotton o algodão
em rama [algood**ow**ng ayng]

accelerator o acelerador
[asilirad**ohr**]

accept aceitar [a**say**tar]

accident o acidente [aseed**aynt**]

there's been an accident
houve um acidente [ohv oong]

accommodation o alojamento
[aloojam**aynt**oo]

accurate exacto [ez**a**tuu]

ache a dor [dohr]

my back aches tenho dor nas
costas [**tayn**-yoo – nash k**osh**tash]

across: across the road do
outro lado da rua [doo **oh**troo
ladoo da r**oo**-a]

adapter o adaptador
[adaptad**ohr**]

address a morada [m**oo**rada]

what's your address? qual é a
sua morada? [kwal eh a s**oo**-a]

address book o livro de
moradas [**leev**roo di m**oo**radash],
o livro de endereços
[ayndir**ay**soosh]

admission charge a entrada
[ayntr**a**da]

adult (man/woman) o adulto
[ad**oo**ltoo], a adulta

advance: in advance
adiantado [ad-yant**a**doo]

aeroplane o avião [av-y**ow**ng]

Africa a África

African (adj) africano [afrik**a**noo]

after depois [dip**oh**-ish]

after you você primeiro [vos**ay**
prim**ay**roo]

after lunch depois do almoço
[dwalm**oh**son]

afternoon a tarde [tard]

in the afternoon à tarde

this afternoon esta tarde
[**ehsh**ta]

aftershave o aftershave

aftersun cream a loção para
depois do sol [loos**ow**ng
– dip**oh**-ish doo]

afterwards depois

again outra vez [**oh**tra vaysh]

against contra

age a idade [eed**a**d]

ago: a week ago há uma
semana [a **oo**ma simana]

an hour ago há uma hora
[**o**ra]

agree: I agree concordo
[konk**or**doo]

AIDS a SIDA [**see**da]

air o ar

by air de avião [dav-y**ow**ng]

air-conditioning o ar condicionado [kondis-yoonadoo]

airmail: by airmail por via aérea [poor vee-a-ehr-ya]

airmail envelope o envelope de avião [aynvilop dav-yowng]

airport o aeroporto [a-ayroopohrtoo]

to the airport, please para o aeroporto, se faz favor [paroo – si fash favohr]

airport bus o autocarro do aeroporto [owtookarroo doo]

aisle seat o lugar de corredor [loogar di koorridohr]

alarm clock o despertador [dishpirtadohr]

alcohol o álcool [alko-ol]

alcoholic alcoólico [alko-olikoo]

all: all the boys todos os meninos [tohdooz ooJ mineenoosh]

all the girls todas as meninas [tohdaz aJ mineenash]

all of it todo [tohdoo]

all of them todos [tohdoosh]

that's all, thanks (said by man/woman) é tudo, obrigado/obrigada [eh toodoo obrigadoo]

allergic: I'm allergic to ... (said by man/woman) sou alérgico/alérgica a ... [soh alehrJikoo]

allowed: is it allowed? é permitido? [eh pirmiteedoo]

all right está bem [shta bayng]

I'm all right estou bem [shtoh]

are you all right? (fam) estás bem? [shtash]

(pol) está bem? [shta]

almond a amêndoa [amayndoo-a]

almost quase [kwaz]

alone só [saw]

alphabet o alfabeto [alfabetoo]

a	a	j	Jota	s	ehs
b	bay	k	kapa	t	tay
c	say	l	el	u	oo
d	day	m	em	v	vay
e	eh	n	en	w	vay dooploo
f	ehf	o	o	x	sheesh
g	Jay	p	pay	y	eepsilon
h	aga	q	kay	z	zay
i	ee	r	err		

already já [Ja]

also também [tambayng]

although embora [aymbora]

altogether totalmente [tootalmaynt]

always sempre [saympr]

am*: I am sou [soh]; estou [shtoh]

a.m.: at seven a.m. às sete da manhã [ash – man-yang]

amazing (surprising) espantoso [shpantohzoo]

(very good) estupendo [shtoopayndoo]

ambulance a ambulância [amboolans-ya]

call an ambulance! chame uma ambulância! [sham ooma]

America a América

American americano [amirikanoo]

I'm American (man/woman) sou americano/americana

among entre [ayngtr]

amount a quantia [kwantee-ya]

amp: a 13-amp fuse um fusível de treze amperes [oong foozeevel di – ampehrish]

and e [ee]

angry zangado

animal o animal

ankle o tornozelo [toornoozayloo]

anniversary (wedding) o aniversário (de casamento) [anivirsar-yoo (di kazamayntoo)]

annoy: this man's annoying me este homem está a aborrecer-me [aysht ohmayng shta aboorrisayrmi]

annoying aborrecido [aboorriseedoo], importuno [importoonoo]

another outro [ohtroo]
can we have another room? pode dar-nos outro quarto? [pod dar-nooz – kwartoo]
another beer, please outra cerveja, por favor [sirvayJa poor favohr]

antibiotics os antibióticos [antib-yotikoosh]

antifreeze o anticongelante [–konJilant]

antihistamines os anti-histamínicos [–ishtameenikoosh]

antique: is it an antique? é uma antiguidade? [eh ooma antigweedad]

antique shop a casa de antiguidades [kaza dantigweedadsh]

antiseptic o anti-séptico

any: have you got any bread/ tomatoes? tem pão/tomates [tayng]
do you have any? tem?
sorry, I don't have any desculpe, não tenho [dishkoolp nowng tayn-yoo]

anybody* alguém [algayng]
does anybody speak English? alguém fala inglês? [inglaysh]
there wasn't anybody there não estava lá ninguém [nowng shtava la ningayng]

anything* qualquer coisa [kwalkehr koh-iza]

dialogues

anything else? mais alguma coisa? [mīz algooma koh-iza]
nothing else, thanks (said by man/woman) mais nada, obrigado/obrigada [obrigadoo]

would you like anything to drink? gostaria de beber alguma coisa? [goostaree-a di bibayr]
I don't want anything, thanks (said by man/woman) não quero nada, obrigado/ obrigada [nowng kehroo]

apart from além de [alayng di]

apartment o apartamento [apartamayntoo]

33

apartment block o bloco de apartamentos [blokoo dapartamayntoonsh]

aperitif o aperitivo [apiriteevoo]

apology as desculpas [diskoolpash]

appendicitis a apendicite [apendi-seet]

appetizer a entrada [ayntrada]

apple a maçã [masang]

appointment a marcação [markasowng]

dialogue

good morning, how can I help you? bom dia, que deseja? [bong dee-a ki disayja]

I'd like to make an appointment queria fazer uma marcação [kiree-a fazayr]

what time would you like? que hora prefere? [k-yora prefehri]

three o'clock três horas [trayz orash]

I'm afraid that's not possible, is four o'clock all right? infelizmente, não é possível, quatro horas está bem? [infilizmayngt nowng eh pooseevil kwatroo orash shta bayng]

yes, that will be fine sim, está bem [seeng]

the name was ...? o nome é ...? [oo nohm]

apricot o damasco [damashkoo]

April Abril [abreel]

Arab (adj) árabe [arabi]

are*: we are somos [sohmoosh]; estamos [shtamoosh]

you are (você) é [(vosay-)eh]; (você) está [shta]

they are são [sowng]; estão [shtowng]

area a região [riJ-yowng]

area code o código

arm o braço [brasoo]

arrange: will you arrange it for us? pode organizar isto para nós? [podi – eeshtoo – nosh]

arrival a chegada [shigada]

arrive chegar

when do we arrive? a que horas chegamos? [k-yorash shigamoosh]

has my fax arrived yet? meu fax já chegou? [may-oo – Ja shigoh]

we arrived today chegámos hoje [shigamoosh ohJ]

art a arte [art]

art gallery a galeria de arte [galiree-a dart]

artist (man/woman) o/a artista [arteeshta]

as: as big as tão grande quanto [towng grand kwantoo]

as soon as possible logo que possível [logoo ki pooseevil]

ashtray o cinzeiro [sinzayroo]

ask perguntar [pirgoontar], pedir [pideer]

I didn't ask for this não pedi isto [nowng pidee eeshtoo]

could you ask him to ...?
importa-se de lhe pedir
que ...? [importasi di l-yi – ki]
asleep: she's asleep ela está a
dormir [ehla shta a doormeer]
aspirin a aspirina [ashpireena]
asthma a asma [aJma]
astonishing espantoso
[shpantohzoo]
at: at the hotel no hotel [noo]
at the station na estação
[nashtasowng]
at six o'clock às seis horas [ash
sayz orash]
at Américo's na casa do
Américo [dwamehrikoo]
athletics o atletismo
[atleteeJmoo]
Atlantic Ocean o Oceano
Atlântico [ohs-yanoo atlantikoo]
attractive atraente [atra-aynt]
aubergine a beringela
[bireenJehla]
August Agosto [agohshtoo]
aunt a tia [tee-a]
Australia a Austrália
[owshtral-ya]
Australian (adj) australiano
[owshtral-yanoo]
I'm Australian (man/woman) sou
australiano/australiana [soh]
automatic automático
[owtoomatikoo]
automatic teller o caixa
automático [kīsha
owtoomatikoo]
autumn o Outono [ohtohnoo]
in the autumn no Outono
[noo]

avenue a avenida [avineeda]
average (not good) mais ou
menos [mīz oh maynoosh]
on average em média [ayng
mehd-ya]
awake; is he awake? ele já
acordou? [ayl Ja akoordoh]
away: go away! vá-se embora!
[vasi aymbora]
is it far away? fica longe?
[feeka lohnJ]
awful horrível [ohrreevil]
axle o eixo [ayshoo]

B

baby o bebé [bebeh]
baby food a comida de bebé
[koomeeda di]
baby's bottle o biberão
[bibirowng]
baby-sitter a baby-sitter
back (of body) as costas [koshtash]
(back part) a parte posterior
[part pooshteriohr]
at the back atrás [atrash]
can I have my money back?
posso reaver o meu dinheiro?
[posoo r-yavayr oo may-oo deen-
yayroo]
to come/go back voltar
backache a dor nas costas
[dohr nash koshtash]
bacon o bacon
bad mau [mow], (f) má
a bad headache uma dor
de cabeça forte [ooma dohr di
kabaysa fort]

badly mal

bag o saco [sakoo]
(handbag) a mala de mão [di mowng]
(suitcase) a mala

baggage a bagagem [bagaJayng]

baggage check o depósito de bagagem [dipozitoo di baga-Jayng]

baggage claim a reclamação de bagagens [riklamasowng di baga-Jayngsh]

bakery a padaria [padaree-a]

balcony a varanda
a room with a balcony um quarto com varanda [oong kwartoo kong]

bald careca [karehka]

ball a bola
(small) a bolinha [boleen-ya]

ballet o ballet

ballpoint pen a caneta esferográfica [shfiroo-grafika]

banana a banana

band (musical) a banda

bandage a ligadura [ligadoora]

Bandaid® o adesivo [adezeevoo]

bank (money) o banco [bankoo]

bank account a conta bancária [bankar-ya]

bar o bar
a bar of chocolate uma tablete de chocolate [tableht di shookoolat]

barber's o barbeiro [barbayroo]

basket o cesto [sayshtoo]
(in shop) o cesto de compras [di kohmprash]

bath o banho [ban-yoo]
can I have a bath? posso tomar banho? [posoo toomar]

bathroom a casa de banho [kaza di]
with a private bathroom com casa de banho [kong]

bath towel a toalha de banho [twal-ya]

bathtub a banheira [ban-yayra]

battery a pilha [peel-ya]
(for car) a bateria [batiree-a]

bay a baía [ba-ee-a]

be* ser [sayr]; estar [shtar]

beach a praia [prī-a]
on the beach na praia

beach mat o colchão de praia [kolshowng di prī-a]

beach umbrella o chapéu de sol [shapeh-oo]

beans os feijões [faiJoyngsh]
French beans os feijões-verdes [–vayrdsh]
broad beans as favas [favash]

beard a barba

beautiful bonito [booneetoo]

because porque [poorkay]
because of ... por causa do ... [poor kowza doo]

bed a cama
I'm going to bed now vou para a cama agora [voh]

bed and breakfast alojamento e pequeno almoço [alooJamayntwee pikaynoo almohsoo] bedroom o quarto [kwarton]

beef a carne de vaca [karn di]

beer a cerveja [sirvayJa]

two beers, please duas cervejas, por favor [doo-ash sirvayJash poor favolur]

before antes [antsh]

begin começar [koomesar]

when does it begin? quando é que começa? [kwandoo eh ki koomehsa]

beginner (man/woman) o/a principiante [prinsip-yant]

beginning: at the beginning no início [noo inees-yoo]

behind atrás [atrash]

behind me atrás de mim [ul meeng]

beige bege

Belgian (adj) belga

Belgium a Bélgica [behlJika]

believe acreditar

below abaixo [abīshoo]

belt o cinto [seentoo]

bend (in road) a curva [koorva]

berth (on ship) o beliche [bileesh]

beside: beside the ... junto da ... [Joonton]

best o melhor [mil-yor]

better melhor

are you feeling better? está melhor? [shta]

between entre [ayntr]

beyond para além de [paralayng di]

bicycle a bicicleta [bisiklehta]

big grande [grand]

too big grande demais [dimīsh]

it's not big enough não é suficientemente grande [nowng eh soofis-yayntimaynt]

bike a bicicleta [bisiklehta] (motorbike) a motocicleta [mootoosiklehta]

bikini o bikini

bill a conta (US) a nota

could I have the bill, please? pode-me dar a conta, por favor? [pod-mi – poor favohr]

bin o caixote de lixo [kishot di leeshoo]

bin liners os sacos de lixo [sakoosh]

bird o pássaro [pasaroo]

birthday o dia de anos [dee-a danoosh]

happy birthday! feliz aniversário! [fileez anivirsar-yoo]

biscuit a bolacha [boolasha]

bit: a little bit um pouco [oong pohkoo]

a big bit um pedaço grande [pidasoo grand]

a bit of ... um pedaço de ...

a bit expensive um pouco caro [pohkoo karoo]

bite (by insect) a picada [pikada] (by dog) a mordedura [moordedoora]

bitter (taste etc) amargo [amargoo]

black preto [praytoo]

blanket o cobertor [koobirtohr]

bleach (for toilet) a lixívia [lisheev-ya]

bless you! santinho! [santeen-yoo]

blind cego [**seh**goo]
blinds as persianas [pirs-y**a**nash]
blister a bolha [**bol**-ya]
blocked (road) cortado
  [koort**a**doo]
  (pipe, sink) entupido
  [aynt**oo**peedoo]
blond (adj) louro [**loh**roo]
blood o sangue [sang]
  high blood pressure a tensão
  arterial alta [tayns**ow**ng artir-y**a**l]
blouse a blusa [bl**oo**za]
blow-dry secar com secador
  [kong sikad**ohr**]
  I'd like a cut and blow-dry
  queria cortar e fazer brushing
  [kir**ee**-a – ee faz**ay**r]
blue azul [az**oo**l]
  blue eyes os olhos azuis [ol-
  yoosh az**oo**-ish]
blusher o blusher
boarding house a pensão
  [payns**ow**ng]
boarding pass o cartão de
  embarque [kart**ow**ng daymb**ark**]
boat o barco [b**ark**oo]
  (for passengers) o ferry-boat
body o corpo [k**ohr**poo]
boiled egg o ovo cozido [**oh**voo
  kooz**ee**doo]
boiler a caldeira [kald**ay**ra]
bone o osso [**oh**soo]
  (in fish) a espinha [shp**ee**n-ya]
bonnet (of car) o capot [kap**oh**]
book o livro [**lee**vroo]
  (verb) reservar [rizirv**ar**]
  can I book a seat? posso
  reservar um lugar? [p**o**soo
  – oong loog**ar**]

dialogue

I'd like to book a table for
two queria reservar uma
mesa para dois [kir**ee**-a
– **oo**ma m**ay**za para d**oh**-ish]
what time would you like
it booked for? para que
horas? [k-y**o**rash]
half past seven sete e meia
[**seh**-tee-m**ay**-a]
that's fine está bem [shta
bayng]
and your name? e o seu
nome? [yoo s**ay**-oo nohm]

bookshop a livraria [livrar**ee**-a]
bookstore a livraria [livrar**ee**-a]
boot (footwear) a bota
  (of car) o porta-bagagens
  [p**o**rta-baga**J**ayngsh]
border (of country) a fronteira
  [front**ay**ra]
bored: I'm bored (said by
man/woman) estou chateado/
chateada [shtoh shat-y**a**doo]
boring maçador [masad**ohr**]
born: I was born in
Manchester nasci em
Manchester [nash-**see** ayng]
I was born in 1960 nasci em
mil novecentos e sessenta
borrow pedir emprestado
  [pid**ee**r aymprisht**a**doo]
  may I borrow ...? posso
  pedir ... emprestado? [p**o**soo]
both ambos [**a**mboosh]
bother: sorry to bother you
  desculpe incomodá-lo

[dishkoolp eenkoo-moodaloo]

bottle a garrafa

a bottle of house red uma
garrafa de vinho da casa tinto
[ooma – di veen-yoo da kaza
teentoo]

bottle-opener o abre-garrafas
[abrigarrafash]

bottom (of person) o traseiro
[trazayroo]

at the bottom of ... (hill) no
sopé do ... [noo soopeh doo]

box a caixa [kīsha]

box office a bilheteira [bil-
yitayra]

boy o rapaz [rapash]

boyfriend o namorado
[namonradoo]

bra o soutien [soot-yang]

bracelet a pulseira [poolsayra]

brake o travão [travowng]

brandy o brandy

Brazil Brasil [brazeel]

Brazilian (adj) brasileiro
[brazilayroo]

bread o pão [powng]

white bread o pão branco
[brankoo]

brown bread o pão escuro
[shkooroo]

wholemeal bread o pão
integral [eentigral]

break partir

I've broken the ... quebrei o/a
... [kibray oo]

I think I've broken my wrist
acho que parti o pulso [ashoo
ki – oo poolsoo]

break down avariar

I've broken down meu carro
avariou [may-oo karroo avari-oh]

breakdown (mechanical) a avaria
[avarec-a]

breakdown service o pronto-
socorro [prohntoo suokohrroo]

breakfast o pequeno almoço
[pikaynoo almohsoo]

break-in: I've had a break-
in minha casa foi roubada
[meen-ya kaza foh-i rohbada]

breast o peito [paytoo]

breathe respirar [rishpirar]

breeze a brisa [brecza]

bridge (over river) a ponte [pohnt]

brief breve [brehv]

briefcase a pasta [pashta]

bright (light etc) brilhante [bril-
yant]

bright red vermelho vivo
[veevoo]

brilliant (idea, person) brilhante
[bril-yant]

bring trazer [trazayr]

I'll bring it back later trago
isto de volta mais tarde [tragoo
eeshtoo di – mīch tard]

Britain a Grã-Bretanha [grang
britan-ya]

British britânico [britanikoo]

brochure o folheto [fool-yaytoo]

broken partido [parteedoo]

bronchitis bronquite [bronkeet]

brooch o alfinete [alfinayt]

broom a vassoura [vasohra]

brother o irmão [eermowng]

brother-in-law o cunhado
[koon-yadoo]

brown castanho [kashtan-yoo]

bruise a contusão [kontoozowng]

brush (for hair, cleaning) a escova [shkova]

(artist's) o pincel [peensehl]

bucket o balde [bowld]

buffet car a carruagem restaurante [karrwa-Jayng rishtowrant]

buggy (for child) a cadeirinha de bebé [kadayreen-ya di bebeh]

building o edifício [idifees-yoo]

bulb (light bulb) a lâmpada

bullfight a tourada [tohrada]

bullfighter o toureiro [tohrayroo]

bullring a praça de touros [prasa di tohroosh]

bull-running as garraiadas [garri-adash]

bumper o pára-choques [para-shoksh]

bunk o beliche [bileesh]

bureau de change o câmbio [kamb-yoo]

burglary o roubo [rohboo]

burn a queimadura [kaymadoora]

(verb) queimar

burnt: this is burnt isto está queimado [eeshtoo shta kaymadoo]

burst: a burst pipe um cano rebentado [oong kanoo ribayntadoo]

bus o autocarro [owtokarroo]

what number bus is it to ...? qual é o número do autocarro para ...? [kwal-eh oo noomiroo doo

when is the next bus to ...? a que horas é o próximo autocarro para ...? [k-yoraz eh oo prosimoo]

what time is the last bus? a que horas é o último autocarro? [ooltimoo]

dialogue

does this bus go to ...?
este autocarro vai para ...?
[aysht – vī]
no, you need a number ...
não, tem que apanhar o número ... [nowng tayng k-yapang-yar oo noomiroo]

business o negócios [nigos-yoosh]

bus station a estação dos autocarros [shtasowng dooz owtookarroosh]

bus stop a paragem do autocarro [paraJayng doo owtookarroo]

bust o peito [paytoo]

busy (restaurant etc) frequentado [frikwayntadoo]

I'm busy tomorrow (said by man/woman) estou ocupado/ocupada amanhã [shtoh okoopadoo – aman-yang]

but mas [mash]

butcher's o talho [tal-yoo]

butter a manteiga [mantayga]

button o botão [bootowng]

buy comprar

where can I buy ...? onde

posso comprar ...? [ohnd posoo]

by*: by bus de autocarro [dowtookarroo]

by car de carro [di karroo]

written by ... escrito por ... [shkreetoo poor]

by the window à janela

by the sea à beira-mar

by Thursday na quinta-feira

bye adeus [aday-oosh]

C

cabbage a couve [kohv]

cabin (on ship) o camarote [kamarot]

cable car o teleférico [telefehrikoo]

café o café [kafeh]

cagoule o impermeável de nylon [impirmia-vil di]

cake o bolo [bohloo]

cake shop a pastelaria [pashtila-ree-a]

call chamar [shamar]
(to phone) telefonar [telefoonar]

what's it called? como se chama isto? [kohmoo si shama eeshtoo]

he/she is called ... ele/ela chama-se ... [ayl/ehla shamasi]

please call the doctor por favor, chame o médico [poor favohr sham-yoo mehdikoo]

please give me a call at ...

a.m. tomorrow chame-me, por favor, às ... horas amanhã [shami-mi – ash ... orash aman-yang]

please ask him to call me por favor, peça a ele que me telefone [pesa-a ayl ki-mi telefohn]

call back: I'll call back later volto mais tarde [voltoo mīsh tard]
(phone back) volto a telefonar mais tarde [voltwa telefoonar]

call round: I'll call round tomorrow vou aí amanhã [voh a-ee aman-yang]

camcorder a câmara de vídeo [di veed-yoo]

camera a máquina fotográfica [makina footoografika]

camera shop a loja de artigos fotográficos [loja darteegoosh fotografiknosh]

camp acampar

can we camp here? podemos acampar aqui? [poodaymoosh – akee]

camping gas o gás para campismo [gash par kampeeʒmoo]

campsite o parque de campismo [park di kampeeʒmoo]

can a lata

a can of beer uma lata de cerveja [di sirvayʒa]

can*: can you ...? você pode ...? [vosay pod]

can I have ...? posso ter ...?

[posoo tayr]
I can't ... não posso ... [nowng]
Canada o Canadá
Canadian canadiano [kanad-yanoo]
I'm Canadian (man/woman) sou canadiano/canadiana [soh]
canal o canal
cancel cancelar [kansilar]
candle a vela
candies os rebuçados [riboosadoosh]
canoe a canoa [kanoh-a]
canoeing a canoagem [kanwa-Jayng]
can-opener o abre-latas [abrilatash]
cap (hat) o boné [booneh]
(of bottle) a tampa
car o carro [karroo]
by car de carro
caravan a roulotte [roolot]
caravan site o parque de campismo [park di kampeeJmoo]
carburettor o carburador [karbooradohr]
card (birthday etc) o cartão [kartowng]
here's my (business) card aqui está o meu cartão (de visitas) [akee shta oo may-oo kartowng (di vizeetash)]
cardigan o casaco de malha [kazakoo di mal-ya]
cardphone o telefone de cartão [telefohn di kartowng]
careful cuidadoso [kwidadohzoo]
be careful! cuidado! [kwidadoo]

caretaker (man/woman) o/a guarda [gwarda]
car ferry o ferry-boat
car hire o aluguer de automóveis [aloogehr dowtoomovaysh]
carnival o carnaval
car park o parque de estacionamento [park di shtas-yonamayntoo]
carpet a carpete [karpeht]
carriage (of train) a carruagem [karrwa-Jayng]
carrier bag o saco plástico [sakoo plashtikoo]
carrot a cenoura [sinohra]
carry levar [livar]
carry-cot o porta-bebés [porta-behsh]
carton o pacote [pakot]
carwash a lavagem automática [lavaJayng owtoomatika]
case (suitcase) a mala
cash o dinheiro [deen-yayroo]
(verb) descontar [dishkongtar]
will you cash this for me? pode descontar isto para mim? [pod – eeshtoo – meeng]
cash desk a caixa [kīsha]
cash dispenser o caixa automático [owtoomatikoo]
cassette a cassete
cassette recorder o gravador de cassetes [gravadohr di]
castle o castelo [kashtehloo]
casualty department o serviço de urgências [sirveesoo doorJayns-yash]
cat o gato [gatoo]

catch pegar, apanhar [apan-yar]
where do we catch the
bus to ...? onde podemos
apanhar o autocarro para ...?
[ohnd poodaymooz apan-yar oo
owtookarroo]
cathedral a catedral [katidral]
Catholic (adj) católico
[katolikoo]
cauliflower a couve-flor [kohv-
flor]
cave a caverna
ceiling o tecto [tehtoo]
celery o alho francês [al-yoo
fransaysh]
cellar (for wine) a cave [kav]
cellular phone o telefone
celular [telefohn siloolar]
cemetery o cemitério [simitehr-
yoo]
centigrade* centígrado
[senteegradoo]
centimetre* o centímetro
[senteemitroo]
central central [sen-tral]
central heating o aquecimento
central [akesimayntoo]
centre o centro [sayntroo]
how do we get to the city
centre? como é que vamos
para o centro da cidade?
[kohmoo eh ki vamoosh – oo
sayntroo da sidad]
cereal os cereais [siri-īsh]
certainly certamente
[sirtamaynt]
certainly not certamente que
não [ki nowng]
chair a cadeira [kadayra]

champagne o champanhe
[shampan-yi]
change (money) o troco
[trohkoo]
(verb: money) trocar [trookar]
can I change this for ...?
posso trocar isto por ...?
[posoo – eeshtoo]
I don't have any change não
tenho troco [nowng tayn-yoo]
can you give me change for
a 20 euro note? pode trocar-
me uma nota de vinte euros?
[pod trookarmi oma – di voont ay-
ooroosh]

dialogue

do we have to change
(trains)? temos de mudar?
[taymoosh di moodar]
yes, change at Coimbra/
no, it's a direct train sim,
troque em Coimbra/não, é
um comboio directo [seeng
tro-keeng kweembra/nowng eh
oong komboh-yo dirchtoo]

changed: to get changed
mudar de roupa [moodar di
rohpa]
chapel a capela [kapehla]
charge o preço [praysoo]
(verb) custar [kooshtar]
charge card o cartão de débito
[kartowng di
dehbeetoo]
cheap barato [baratoo]
do you have anything

cheaper? tem alguma coisa mais barata? [tayng algooma koh-iza mish]

check (US) o cheque [shehk] (US: bill) a conta
see bill

check verificar
could you check the ..., please? pode verificar o ..., se faz favor? [pod – oo ... si fash favohr]

checkbook o livro de cheques [leevroo di shehksh]

check card o cartão de garantia [kartowng di garantee-a]

check-in o check-in

check in fazer o check-in [fazayr oo]
where do we have to check in? onde temos que fazer o check-in? [ohnd taymooshk]

cheek (on face) a bochecha [booshaysha]

cheerio! adeuzinho! [aday-oozeen-yoo]

cheers! (toast) saúde! [sa-ood]

cheese o queijo [kayJoo]

chemist's a farmácia [farmas-ya]

cheque o cheque [shehk]
do you take cheques? aceitam cheques? [asaytowng shehksh]

cheque book o livro de cheques [leevroo di shehksh]

cheque card o cartão de garantia [kartowng di garantee-a]

cherry a cereja [sirayJa]

chess o xadrez [shadraysh]

chest o peito [paytoo]

chewing gum a pastilha elástica [pashteel-ya ilashtika]

chicken o frango [frangoo]

chickenpox a varicela [varisehla]

child a criança [kry-ansa]
children as crianças [kry-ansash]

child minder a ama

children's pool a piscina infantil [pish-seena infanteel]

children's portion a dose para crianças [doz – kry-ansash]

chin o queixo [kayshoo]

china a porcelana [poorsilana]

Chinese (adj) chinês [shinaysh]

chips as batatas fritas [batatash freetash]

chocolate o chocolate [shookoolat]
milk chocolate o chocolate com leite [kong layt]
plain chocolate o chocolate puro [pooroo]
a hot chocolate um chocolate quente [oong – kaynt]

choose escolher [shkool-yayr]

Christian name o nome próprio [nohm propr-yoo]

Christmas o Natal
Christmas Eve a Véspera de Natal [vehshpira di]
merry Christmas! feliz Natal! [fileeJ]

church a igreja [igrayJa]

cider a cidra [seedra]

cigar o charuto [sharootoo]

cigarette o cigarro [sigarroo]
cigarette lighter o isqueiro [ishkayroo]
cinema o cinema [sinayma]
circle o círculo [seerkooloo]
 (in theatre) a plateia [platay-a]
city a cidade [sIdad]
city centre o centro da cidade [sayntroo]
clean (adj) limpo [leempoo]
 can you clean this for me?
 pode limpar isto para mim?
 [pod leempar eeshtoo – meeng]
cleaning solution (for contact lenses) a solução de limpeza [sooloosowng di leempayza]
cleansing lotion o creme de limpeza [kraym di]
clear claro [klaroo]
clever inteligente [intiliJaynt]
cliff o rochedo [rooshaydoo]
climb escalar [shkalar]
cling film a película aderente [pileekoola adiraynt]
clinic a clínica [kleenika]
cloakroom o vestiário [vishtyar-yoo]
clock o relógio [riloJ-yoo]
close (verb) fechar [fishar]

dialogue

what time do you close? a que horas fecham?
[k-yorash fayshowng]
we close at 8 p.m. on weekdays and 6 p.m. on Saturdays fechamos às oito da noite durante a
semana e às seis da tarde aos sábados [fisha-mooz az-oh itoo da noh-it dooranta simana yash saysh da tard owsh sabadoosh]
do you close for lunch?
fecham para almoço? [almohsoo]
yes, between 1 and 3.30 p.m. sim, entre a uma e as três e meia da tarde [seeng ayntri-a-ooma ee-ash traysh ee may-a da tard]
closed fechado [fishadoo]
cloth (fabric) o tecido [tiseedoo]
 (for cleaning etc) pano [panoo]
clothes a roupa [rohpa]

clothes line o estendal [shtendal]
clothes peg a mola de roupa [di rohpa]
cloud a nuvem [noovayng]
cloudy enevoado [inivwadoo]
clutch a embraiagem [aymbrī-aJayng]
coach (bus) o autocarro [owtookarroo]
 (on train) a carruagem [karrwa-Jayng]
coach station a estação dos autocarros [shtasowng dooz owtookarroosh]
coach trip a excursão [shkoorsowng]
coast a costa [koshta]
 on the coast na costa
coat (long coat) o sobretudo [soobritoodoo]

(jacket) o casaco [kazakoo]
coathanger a cruzeta
[kroozayta]
cockroach a barata
cocoa o cacau [kakow]
coconut o coco [kohkoo]
cod o bacalhau fresco [bakal-
yow frayshkoo]
  dried cod o bacalhau
code (for phoning) o indicativo
[indikateevoo]
  what's the (dialling) code for
  Oporto? qual é o indicativo
  do Porto? [kwal eh oo – doo
  pohrtoo]
coffee o café [kafeh]
  two coffees, please dois
  cafés, por favor [doh-ish
  kafehsh poor favohr]
coin a moeda [mwehda]
Coke® a coca-cola
cold frio [free-oo]
  I'm cold tenho frio [tayn-yoo]
  I have a cold estou
  constipado [shtoh konshtipadoo]
collapse: he's collapsed ele
  desmaiou [ayl diJmī-oh]
collar o colarinho [koolareen-
  yoo]
collect buscar [booshkar]
  I've come to collect ... vim
  buscar ... [veeng booshkar]
collect call a chamada paga no
  destinatário [shamada paga noo
  dishtinatar-yoo]
college o colégio [koolehJ-yoo]
colour a cor [kohr]
  do you have this in other
  colours? tem isto de outras

cores? [tayng eeshto-di ohtrash
kohrish]
colour film o filme colorido
[feelm koolooreedoo]
comb o pente [paynt]
come* vir [veer]

dialogue

where do you come from?
donde é? [dohndeh]
I come from Edinburgh
sou de Edimburgo [soh
dedeenboorgoo]

come back voltar
  I'll come back tomorrow
  volto amanhã [voltoo aman-
  yang]
come in entrar [ayntrar]
comfortable confortável
[konfoortavil]
compact disc o CD [say day]
company (business) a
  companhia [kompan-yee-a]
compartment (on train) o compartimento [kompartimayntoo]
compass a bússola [boosoola]
complain reclamar [riklamar]
complaint a reclamação
[riklamasowng]
  I have a complaint tenho uma
  reclamação [tayn-yoo]
completely completamente
[komplitamaynt]
computer o computador
[kompootadohr]
concert o concerto [konsayrtoo]
concussion o traumatismo

[trowmat**ee**Jmoo]

conditioner (for hair) o creme
amaciador [kraym amas-yad**ohr**]

condom o preservativo
[prizirvat**ee**voo]

conference a conferência
[konfir**ayns**-ya]

confirm confirmar [konfir**mar**]

congratulations! parabéns!
[parab**ayngsh**]

connecting flight o voo de
ligação [**voh**-oo di ligas**owng**]

connection a ligação

conscious consciente [konsh-
s**yaynt**]

constipation a prisão de ventre
[priz**owng** di vayntr]

consulate o consulado
[konsool**adoo**]

contact contactar

contact lenses as lentes de
contacto [layntsh di kont**atoo**]

contraceptive o contraceptivo
[kontrasipt**ee**voo]

convenient conveniente
[konvin-y**aynt**]

  that's not convenient não é
  conveniente [nowng eh]

cook cozinhar [kozeen-**yar**]

  not cooked mal cozido
  [kooz**ee**doo]

cooker o fogão [foog**owng**]

cookie a bolacha [bool**asha**]

cooking utensils os utensílios
de cozinha [ootaynseel-yoosh di
kooz**een**-ya]

cool fresco [**fray**shkoo]

cork a rolha [**rohl**-ya]

  (material) a cortiça [koort**eesa**]

corkscrew o saca-rolhas [saka-
rohl-yash]

corner o canto [**kan**too]

  in the corner no canto [noo]

cornflakes os cornflakes

correct (right) certo [**sehr**too]

corridor o corredor [koorrid**ohr**]

cosmetics os cosméticos
[kooJm**eh**tikoosh]

cost custar [koosh**tar**]

  how much does it cost?
  quanto custa? [**kwantoo
  koo**shta]

cot a cama de bebé [kama di
beb**eh**]

cotton a algodão [algood**owng**]

cotton wool o algodão em
rama [**ayng**]

couch (sofa) o sofá [soof**a**]

couchette o beliche [bil**ee**sh]

cough a tosse [tos]

cough medicine o xarope
[shar**op**]

could: could you ...? podia ...?
[pood**ee**-a]

  could I have ...? queria ...?
  [kir**ee**-a]

  I couldn't ... (wasn't able to) não
  pude ... [nowng pood]

country (nation) o país [pa-**eesh**]

  (countryside) o campo [**kam**poo]

countryside o campo

couple (two people) o casal
[ka**zal**]

  a couple of ... um par de ...
  [oong par di]

courgette a courgette

courier (man/woman) o/a guia
[gee-a]

course (main course etc) o prato [pratoo]

of course é claro [eh klaroo]

of course not claro que não [ki nowng]

cousin (male/female) o primo [preemoo], a prima

cow a vaca

crab o caranguejo [karang-gayJoo]

cracker a bolacha de água e sal [boolasha dagwa ee]

craft shop a loja de artesanato [loJa dartizanatoo]

crash a colisão [kolisowng]

I've had a crash tive uma colisão [teev ooma]

crazy doido [doh-idoo]

cream as natas [natash]

(lotion) o creme [kraym]

(colour) creme

creche a creche

credit card o cartão de crédito [kartowng di krehdeetoo]

do you take credit cards? aceitam cartões de crédito? [asaytowng kartoyngsh]

dialogue

can I pay by credit card? posso pagar com cartão de crédito? [posoo – kong]

which card do you want to use? que cartão deseja utilizar? [ki kartowng disayJa ootilizar]

Access/Visa

yes, sir sim, senhor [seeng sin-yor]

what's the number? qual é o número? [kwaleh oo noomiroo]

and the expiry date? e a data de validade? [ya data de validad]

crisps as batatas fritas [batatash freetash]

crockery a loiça [loh-isa]

crossing (by sea) a travessia [travisee-a]

crossroads o cruzamento [kroozamayntoo]

crowd a multidão [mooltidowng]

crowded apinhado [apeen-yadoo]

crown (on tooth) a ponte [pohnt]

cruise o cruzeiro [kroozayroo]

crutches as muletas [moolaytash]

cry chorar [shoorar]

cucumber o pepino [pipeenoo]

cup a chávena [shavena]

a cup of ..., please uma chávena de ..., se faz favor [si fash favohr]

cupboard o armário [armar-yoo]

cure curar [koorar]

curly encaracolado [ayn-karakooladoo]

current a corrente [koorraynt]

curtains as cortinas [koorteenash]

cushion a almofada [almoofada]

custom o hábito [abeetoo]

customs a alfândega [alfandiga]

cut o corte [kort]

(verb) cortar
I've cut myself cortei-me
[koortaymi]
cutlery os talheres [tal-yehrish]
cycling o ciclismo [sikleeJmoo]
cyclist (man/woman) o/a ciclista
[sikleeshta]

D

dad o papá
daily diariamente [d-yar-yamaynt]
(adj) diário [d-yar-yo]
damage avariar [avari-ar]
damaged avariado [avari-ado]
I'm sorry, I've damaged
this desculpe, avariei isto
[dishkoolp avari-ay eeshtoo]
damn! raios me partam!
[ra-yoosh mi partowng]
damp (adj) húmido
[oomeedoo]
dance a dança [dansa]
(verb) dançar
would you like to dance?
queres dançar? [kehrish]
dangerous perigoso [pirigohzoo]
Danish (adj, language)
dinamarquês [dinamarkaysh]
dark (adj) escuro [shkooroo]
it's getting dark está a
escurecer [shta-a-shkooresayr]
date*: what's the date today?
qual é a data hoje? [kwal eh
– ohJ]
let's make a date for next
Monday vamos marcar para

a próxima segunda-feira
[vamoosh – prosima sigoonda
fayra]
dates (fruit) as tâmaras
[tamarash]
daughter a filha [feel-ya]
daughter-in-law a nora
dawn a madrugada
[madroogada]
at dawn de madrugada [di]
day o dia [dee-a]
the day after o dia seguinte
[sigeent]
the day after tomorrow
depois de amanhã [dipoh-ish
daman-yang]
the day before o dia anterior
[antir-yohr]
the day before yesterday
anteontem [ant-yohntayng]
every day todos os dias
[tohdooz-ooJ dee-ash]
all day o dia todo [tohdoo]
in two days' time dentro de
dois dias [dayntroo di doh-iJ]
have a nice day bom dia
[bong]
day trip a excursão de um
dia [shkoorsowng doong dee-a]
dead morto [mohrtoo]
deaf surdo [soordoo]
deal (business) o negócio [nigos-yoo]
it's a deal é negócio fechado
[eh – fishadoo]
death a morte [mort]
decaffeinated coffee o café
descafeinado [kafeh dishkafay-eenadoo]

December Dezembro
[dezaymbroo]
decide decidir [disideer]
we haven't decided yet ainda
não decidimos [a-eenda nowng
disidee-moosh]
decision a decisão [disizowng]
deck (on ship) o convés
[konvehsh]
deckchair a cadeira de lona
[kadayra di lohna]
deep fundo [foondoo]
definitely de certeza [di sirtayza]
definitely not de certeza que
não [ki nowng]
degree (qualification) a
licenciatura [lisayns-yatoora]
delay o atraso [atrazoo]
deliberately de propósito [di
proopozitoo]
delicatessen a charcutaria
[sharkootaree-a]
delicious delicioso [dilis-
yohzo]
deliver entregar [ayntrigar]
delivery (of mail) a distribuição
[dishtribweesowng]
Denmark a Dinamarca
[dinamarka]
dental floss o fio dentário
[fee-oo dentar-yoo]
dentist (man/woman) o/a
dentista [denteeshta]

dialogue

it's this one here é este
aqui [eh ayshtakee]
this one? este?

no, that one não, aquele
[nowng akayl]
here aqui
yes sim [seeng]

dentures a dentadura postiça
[dentadoora pooshteesa]
deodorant o desodorizante
[dizoodoorizant]
department o departamento
[dipartamayntoo]
department store os grandes
armazéns [grandz armazayngsh]
departure a saída [sa-eeda]
departure lounge a sala de
embarque [daymbark]
depend: it depends depende
[dipaynd]
it depends on ... depende
de ... [di]
deposit (payment) o depósito
[dipozitoo]
description a descrição [dishkri-
sowng]
dessert a sobremesa
[sobrimayza]
destination o destino
[dishteenoo]
develop desenvolver
[disaynvolvayr]

dialogue

could you develop these
films? pode revelar estas
películas? [pod rivilar ehshtash
pileekoolash]
yes, certainly sim, com
certeza [seeng kong sirtayza]

when will they be ready?
quando ficam prontas?
[kwandoo **fee**kowng pro**h**ntash]
tomorrow afternoon
amanhã à tarde [aman-yang
a tard]
how much is the four-hour
service? quanto custa o
serviço de quatro horas?
[kwantoo **koo**shtoo sir**vee**soo di
kwatroo-**wo**rash]

diabetic (man/woman) o
diabético [d-yab**eh**tikoo], a
diabética
diabetic foods os alimentos
para diabéticos [alimayntoosh
d-yab**eh**tikoosh]
dial marcar
dialling code o indicativo
[indikat**ee**voo]
diamond o diamante
[d-yamant]
diaper a fralda
diarrhoea a diarreia
[dy-array-a]
do you have something
for diarrhoea? tem algum
antilaxante? [tayng al**goo**ng anti-
lashant]
diary (for business) a agenda
[a**j**aynda]
(for personal experiences) o diário
[oo diar-yoo]
dictionary o dicionário [dis-
yoo**nar**-yoo]
didn't* see not
die morrer [moor**rayr**]
diesel o gasóleo [gaz**ol**-yoo]

diet a dieta [d-y**eh**ta]
I'm on a diet estou de dieta
[shtoh di]
I have to follow a special diet
tenho que seguir uma dieta
especial [tayn-yoo ki sig**eer oo**ma
– shpis-yal]
difference a diferença
[difir**ayn**sa]
what's the difference? qual é
a diferença? [kwal eh]
different diferente [difirayn**t**]
this one is different este é
diferente [aysht eh]
a different table outra mesa
[**oh**tra may**za**]
difficult difícil [dif**ee**sil]
difficulty a dificuldade
[difikool**dad**]
dinghy o bote de borracha [bot
di boor**rasha**]
dining room a sala de jantar
[di **j**antar]
dinner (evening meal) o jantar
to have dinner jantar
direct (adj) directo [dir**eh**too]
is there a direct train? há
um comboio directo? [a oong
komb**oh**-yo]
direction a direcção
[direhs**owng**]
which direction is it? em que
direcção fica? [ayng ki – **fee**ka]
is it in this direction? fica
nesta direcção? [**neh**shta]
directory enquiries as
informações [infoormas**oy**ngsh]
dirt a sujidade [sooji**dad**]
dirty sujo [**soo**joo]

disabled deficiente [difis-yaynt]
is there access for the disabled? há acesso para deficientes? [a asehsoo – difis-yayntsh]
disappear desaparecer [dizaparisayr]
it's disappeared desapareceu [dizaparisay-oo]
disappointed decepcionado [disips-yoonadoo]
disappointing decepcionante [disips-yonant]
disaster a tragédia [traJehd-ya]
disco o disco [deeshkoo]
discount o desconto [dishkohntoo]
is there a discount? pode fazer-me um desconto? [pod fazayrm-oong]
disease a doença [dwaynsa]
disgusting nojento [nooJayntoo]
dish (meal) o prato [pratoo]
(bowl) a tigela [tiJehla]
dishcloth o pano de loiça [panoo di loh-isa]
disinfectant o desinfectante [dizinfitant]
disk (for computer) a disquete [dishkeht]
disposable diapers/nappies as fraldas descartáveis [fraldaJ dishkartavaysh]
distance a distância [dishtans-ya]
in the distance ao longe [ow lohnJ]
distilled water a água destilada [agwa dishtilada]

district o bairro [bīrroo]
disturb perturbar [pirtoobar]
diversion (detour) o desvio [diJvee-oo]
diving board a prancha de saltos [pransha di saltoosh]
divorced divorciado [divoors-yadoo]
dizzy: I feel dizzy sinto tonturas [seentoo tontoorash]
do* fazer [fazayr]
what shall we do? que vamos fazer? [ki-vamoosh]
how do you do it? como se faz? [kohmoo si fash]
will you do it for me? importa-se de mo fazer? [importasi di moo]

dialogues

how do you do? muito prazer [mweengtoo prazayr]
nice to meet you muito prazer
what do you do? (work) o que é que faz? [oo ki eh-ki faJ]
I'm a teacher, and you? (said by man/woman) sou professor/professora, e você? [soh – ee vosay]
I'm a student sou estudante

what are you doing this evening? que vai fazer hoje à noite? [ki vī – ohJ-ya noh-it] we're going out for a drink, do you want to join us? vamos tomar uma bebida, quer vir conosco? [**va**moosh too**mar oo**ma bib**ee**da kehr veer kon**oh**shkoo]

do you want cream? quer natas? [natash]

I do, but she doesn't quero, mas ela não [**keh**roo maz-**eh**la nowng]

doctor (man/woman) o médico [**meh**dikoo], a médica

we need a doctor precisamos de um médico [prisiz**a**moosh doong]

please call a doctor por favor, chame um médico [poor fav**ohr** sham oong]

dialogue

where does it hurt? onde dói? [ohnd doy]

right here bem aqui [bayng akee]

does that hurt now? dói agora?

yes sim [seeng]

take this to the pharmacy leve isto à farmácia [lehv **ee**sht-wa farmas-ya]

document o documento [dookoom**ay**ntoo]

dog o cão [kowng]

doll a boneca [boon**eh**ka]

domestic flight voo doméstico [**voh**oo doom**eh**shtikoo]

donkey o burro [**boor**roo]

don't!* não! [nowng]

don't do that! não faça isto! [fasa **ee**shtoo]

door a porta

doorman o porteiro [poort**ay**roo]

double duplo [**doo**ploo]

double bed a cama de casal [di kaz**al**]

double room o quarto de casal [**kwar**too]

doughnut a fartura [fart**oo**ra]

down embaixo [aymb**ee**shoo]

down here aqui embaixo [ak**ee**]

put it down over there deite-o lá [d**ay**t-yoo la]

it's down there on the right é lá embaixo, à direita [eh – a dir**ay**ta]

it's further down the road é nesta rua mais abaixo [n**e**shta **roo**-a mīz ab**ee**shoo]

downmarket (restaurant etc) barato [bar**a**too]

downstairs embaixo [aymb**ee**shoo]

dozen a dúzia [**dooz**-ya]

half a dozen a meia dúzia [**may**-a]

drain (in sink, in road) o cano de esgoto [**ka**noo diJg**oh**too]

draught beer imperial [eempir-**yal**]

draughty: it's draughty faz corrente de ar [fash koor**raynt** dar] drawer a gaveta [gav**ay**ta]

drawing o desenho [dis**ayn**-yoo]

dreadful horrível [ohrr**ee**vil]

dream o sonho [**soh**n-yoo]

dress o vestido
[visht**ee**doo]

dressed: to get dressed vestir-
se [visht**eer**si]

dressing (for cut) o penso
[**payn**soo]

salad dressing o tempero
[taymp**ay**roo]

dressing gown o roupão
[rohp**owng**]

drink a bebida [bib**ee**da]
(verb) beber [bib**ayr**]

a cold drink uma bebida
fresca [**oo**ma – fr**aysh**ka]

fancy a quick drink? vamos
tomar uma bebida?
[v**a**moosh toom**ar oo**ma
bib**ee**da]

can I get you a drink? o que
bebe? [oo ki behb]

what would you like (to
drink)? o que gostaria de
beber? [gooshtar**ee**-ya di]

I don't drink não bebo [nowng
b**ay**boo]

I'll just have a drink of water
só um copo de água [saw oong
k**o**poo d**a**gwa]

drinking water a água potável
[**a**gwa poot**a**vil]

is this drinking water? esta
água é potável? [**sh**ta – eh]

drive conduzir [kondooz**eer**]

we drove here viemos de
carro [v-y**ay**moosh di k**a**rroo]

I'll drive you home levo-o a
casa de carro [**l**ehvoo a k**a**za di
k**a**rroo]

driver (of car: man/woman) o
condutor [kondoot**ohr**], a
condut**o**ra
(of bus: man/woman) o/a
motorista [mootoor**ee**shta]

driving licence a carta de
condução [di kondoos**owng**]

drop: just a drop, please (of
drink) só um pouco, se faz
favor [saw oong **poh**koo si fash
fav**ohr**]

drug o medicamento
[medikam**ayn**too]

drugs (narcotics) a dr**o**ga

drunk (adj) bêbado
[**bay**badoo]

drunken driving a condução
enquanto embriagado
[kondoos**owng** aynkw**ant**oo aymbr-
yag**a**doo]

dry (adj) seco [**say**koo]

dry-cleaner a tinturaria
[teentoorar**ee**-a]

duck o pato [**pa**too]

due: he was due to arrive
yesterday ele devia chegar
ontem [ayl div**ee**-a shigar
ohntayng]

when is the train due? a que
horas é o comboio? [k-y**o**raz eh
oo komb**oh**-yo]

dull (pain) moinho [moo-**een**-yoo]

dummy (baby's) a chupeta
[shoop**ay**ta]

during durante [door**ant**]

dust o pó [paw]

dustbin o caixote de lixo [kīsh**ot** di lee**shoo**]
dusty empoeirado [aympoo-ayra**doo**]
Dutch holandês [oland**aysh**]
duty-free (goods) duty-free
duty-free shop a free-shop
duvet o edredão [idridowng]

E

each (every) cada
  how much are they each?
  quanto é cada um? [kwantw**eh** – oong]
ear a orelha [or**ay**l-ya]
earache: I have earache tenho
  dor de ouvidos [t**ayn**-yoo dohr
  dohveedoosh]
early cedo [s**ay**doo]
  early in the morning de
  manhã cedo [di man-yang]
  I called by earlier passei
  aqui mais cedo [pas**ay** akee
  mīsh]
earrings os brincos [br**ee**nkoosh]
east o leste [l**eh**sht]
  in the east no leste
Easter Semana Santa [simana],
  Páscoa [pashkwa]
easy fácil [fasil]
eat comer [koom**ay**r]
  we've already eaten,
  thanks (said by man/woman) já
  comemos, obrigado/
  obrigada [Ja koom**ay**moosh
  obriga**doo**]
eau de toilette a eau de toilette

EC CE [say eh]
economy class classe económica [klas-ekoon**oh**mika]
Edinburgh Edimburgo
  [edeenb**oor**goo]
eels as enguias [ing**ee**-ash]
egg o ovo [**oh**voo]
eggplant a beringela
  [bireenJ**eh**la]
either: either ... or ... ou ...
  ou ... [oh]
  either of them qualquer um
  deles [kwalkayr**oom** daylish]
elastic o elástico [ilashtikoo]
elastic band o elástico
elbow o cotovelo [kootoov**ay**loo]
electric eléctrico [el**eh**trikoo]
electrical appliances os
  aparelhos eléctricos [apar**ay**l-
  yoosh]
electric fire o aquecedor
  eléctrico [akesid**ohr**]
electrician o electricista
  [eletris**ee**shta]
electricity a electricidade
  [eletrisidad]
elevator (in building) o elevador
  [elevad**ohr**]
else: something else outra
  coisa [**oh**tra koh-iza]
  somewhere else noutro sítio
  [**noh**troo seet-yoo]

dialogue

> **would you like anything**
> **else?** deseja mais alguma
> coisa? [disayJa mīz alg**oo**ma
> koh-iza]

no, nothing else, thanks (said by man/woman) não, mais nada, obrigado/obrigada [nowng mīsh – obrigadoo]

e-mail o correio eletrônico [koorray-oo elehtronikoo]
embassy a embaixada [aymbīshada]
emergency a emergência [emirJaynss-ya]
this is an emergency! isto é uma emergência! [eeshtoo eh ooma]
emergency exit a saída de emergência [sa-eeda di emayrJaynss-ya]
empty vazio [vazee-oo]
end o fim [feeng]
at the end of the street no fim da rua [noo feeng da roo-a]
when does it end? quando acaba? [kwandoo]
engaged (toilet, telephone) ocupado [okoopadoo]
(to be married) noivo [noh-ivoo]
engine (car) o motor [mootohr]
England a Inglaterra [inglatehrra]
English (adj, language) inglês [inglaysh]
I'm English (man/woman) sou inglês/inglesa [soh]
do you speak English? fala inglês?
enjoy: to enjoy oneself divertir-se [divirteersi]

dialogue

how did you like the film? gostou do filme? [goostoh doo feelm]
I enjoyed it very much; did you enjoy it? gostei imenso, você gostou? [gooshtay imaynsoo vosay gooshtoh]

enjoyable divertido [divirteedoo]
enlargement (of photo) a ampliação [ampl-yasowng]
enormous enorme [enorm]
enough suficiente [soofis-yaynt]
there's not enough ... não há suficiente ... [nowng a]
it's not big enough não é suficientemente grande [eh soofis-yayntimaynt]
that's enough, thanks (said by man/woman) está bem, obrigado/obrigada [shta bayng obrigadoo]
entrance a entrada [ayntrada]
envelope o envelope [aynvilop]
epileptic (man/woman) o epiléptico [epilehptikoo], a epiléptica
equipment o equipamento [ekipamayntoo]
error un erro [ayrroo]
especially especialmente [shpis-yalmaynt]
essential essencial [esayns-yal]
it is essential that ... é essencial que ... [eh – ki]
EU UE [oo eh]

Euro o euro [**ay**-ooroo]
Eurocheque o Eurocheque [ay-oorooshe**hk**]
Eurocheque card o cartão Eurocheque [kart**ow**ng]
Europe a Europa [ay-oor**o**pa]
European (adj) europeu [ay-ooroop**ay**-oo], (f) europeia [ay-ooroop**ay**-a]
even: even the British até os britânicos [at**eh**-oosh britanik**oo**sh]
even men até mesmo os homens [at**eh** may**J**mo osh **oh**mayngsh]
even if ... mesmo se ... [si]
evening a noite [**noh**-it]
this evening esta noite [**eh**shta]
in the evening à noite
evening meal o jantar [oo **J**antar]
eventually no fim [noo feeng]
ever já [**J**a]

dialogue

have you ever been to Lamego? já esteve alguma vez em Lamego? [**J**a sht**ay**v alg**oo**ma vaysh ayng lam**ay**goo]
yes, I was there two years ago sim, estive lá há dois anos [seeng sht**ee**v la a d**oh**-iz **a**noosh]

every cada
every day todos os dias [**toh**dooz-ooz d**ee**-ash]

everyone toda a gente [**toh**da a **J**aynt]
everything tudo [**too**doo]
everywhere em toda a parte [ayng **toh**da part]
exactly! exactamente! [ezatam**ay**nt]
exam o exame [ez**a**m]
example o exemplo [ez**ay**mploo]
for example por exemplo [poor]
excellent excelente [ish-sil**ay**nt]
excellent! excelente!
except excepto [ish-s**eh**too]
excess baggage o excesso de bagagem [ish-s**eh**soo di bag**aJ**ayng]
exchange rate a cotação cambial [kootas**ow**ng kamby**al**]
exciting emocionante [emoos-yoonant]
excuse me (to get past) com licença [kong lis**ay**nsa]
(to get attention) se faz favor [si fash fav**ohr**]
(to say sorry) desculpe [dishk**oo**lp]
exhaust (pipe) o tubo de escape [**too**boo dishk**a**p]
exhausted (tired) exausto [ez**ow**shtoo]
exhibition a exposição [shpoozis**ow**ng]
exit a saída [sa-**ee**da]
where's the nearest exit? onde é a saída mais próxima? [ohnd**eh** – mish pr**o**sima]
expect esperar [shpir**ar**]

expensive caro [karoo]
experienced experiente [shpir-yaynt]
explain explicar [shplikar]
can you explain that? pode explicar-me isso? [pod shplikarm eesoo]
express (mail) o correio expresso [koorray-oo shprehsoo]
(train) o Rápido [rapidoo]
extension (telephone) a extensão [shtensowng]
extension 221, please extensão duzentos e vinte e um, por favor [doozayntooz ee veenti-oong poor favohr]
extension lead a extensão [shtensowng]
extra: can we have an extra one? pode dar-nos mais um/uma? [pod dar-noosh mīsh oong/ooma]
do you charge extra for that? paga-se extra por isto? [pagasi ayshtra poor eeshtoo]
extraordinary extraordinário [shtra-ohrdinar-yoo]
extremely extremamente [shtremamaynt]
eye o olho [ohl-yoo]
will you keep an eye on my suitcase for me? pode dar uma olhada na minha mala, por favor? [pod dar-oomool-yada na meen-ya mala poor avohr]
eyebrow pencil o lápis para as sobrancelhas [lapsh parash sobransayl-yash]

eye drops as gotas para os olhos [gohtash parooz ol-yoosh]
eyeglasses (US) os óculos [okooloosh]
eyeliner o lápis para os olhos [lapsh parooz ol-yoosh]
eye make-up remover o desmaquilhador de olhos [dishmakil-yadohr dol-yoosh]
eye shadow a sombra para os olhos

F

face a cara [kara]
factory a fábrica [fabrika]
Fahrenheit* Fahrenheit
faint (verb) desmaiar [dijmī-ar]
she's fainted ela desmaiou [ehla dijmī-oh]
I feel faint sinto que vou desmaiar [seentoo ki voh dijmī-ar]
fair (funfair, tradefair) a feira [fayra]
(adj) justo [Jooshtoo]
fairly bastante [bashtant]
fake falso [falsoo]
fall cair [ka-eer]
she's had a fall ela deu uma queda [ehla day-oo ooma kehda]
fall (US) o Outono [ohtohnoo]
in the fall no Outono [noo ohtohnoo]
false falso [falsoo]
family a família [fameel-ya]
famous famoso [famohzoo]
fan (electrical) a ventoinha [vayntween-ya]

(handheld) o leque [lehk]
(sports: man/woman) o adepto [adehptoo], a adepta
fan belt a correia da ventoinha [koorray-a da vayntween-ya]
fantastic fantástico [fantashtikoo]
far longe [lohnJ]

dialogue

is it far from here? é longe daqui? [eh – dakee]
no, not very far não, não é muito longe [nowng – mweenytoo]
well how far? bem, qual é a distância? [bayng kwal eh a dishtans-ya]
it's about 20 kilometres são mais ou menos vinte quilómetros [sowng mīz oh maynoosh veengt kilomitroosh]

fare o bilhete [bil-yayt]
farm a quinta [keenta]
fashionable na moda
fast rápido [rapidoo]
fat (person) gordo [gohrdoo]
(on meat) a gordura [goordoora]
father o pai [pī]
father-in-law o sogro [sohgroo]
faucet a torneira [toornayra]
fault o defeito [difaytoo]
sorry, it was my fault desculpe, foi culpa minha [foh-i koolpa meen-ya]
it's not my fault a culpa não é minha [nowng eh meen-ya]

faulty avariado [avariadoo]
favourite favorito [favooreetoo]
fax o fax
to send a fax mandar um fax
February Fevereiro [fivrayroo]
feel sentir [saynteer]
I feel hot estou com calor [shtoh kong kalohr]
I feel unwell não me sinto bem [nowng mi seentoo bayng]
I feel like going for a walk estou com vontade de dar um passeio [shtoh kong vontad di dar oong pasav-oo]
how are you feeling? como se sente? [kohmoo si saynt]
I'm feeling better sinto-me melhor [seentoomi mil-yor]
felt-tip (pen) a caneta de feltro [kanayta di fayltroo]
fence a vedação [vidasowng]
fender o pára-choques [para-shoksh]
ferry o ferry-boat
festival o festival [fishtival]
fetch buscar [booshkar]
I'll fetch him vou buscá-lo [voh booshka-loo]
will you come and fetch me later? pode vir buscar-me mais tarde? [pod veer booshkarmi mīsh tard]
feverish febril [febreel]
few: a few alguns [algoonsh]
I'll give you a few dou-lhe alguns [dohl-yalgoonsh]
a few days poucos dias [pohkoosh dee-ash]
fiancé o noivo [noh-ivoo]

fiancée a noiva

field o campo [kampoo]

fight a briga [breega]

figs os figos [feegoosh]

fill in preencher [pri-aynshayr]
do I have to fill this in? tenho de preencher isto? [tayn-yoo di – eeshtoo]

fill up encher [aynshayr]
fill it up, please encha o depósito, por favor [aynsha oo depozitoo por favohr]

filling (in cake, sandwich) recheio [rishay-oo]
(in tooth) o chumbo [shoomboo]

film o filme [feelm]

dialogue

do you have this kind of film? tem este tipo de filme? [tayng aysht teepo]
yes, how many exposures? sim, quantas fotografias? [seeng kwantash footoografee-ash]
36 trinta-e-seis [treenti-saysh]

film processing a revelação de filmes [rivilasowng di feelmsh]

filter coffee o café de filtro [kafeh di feeltroo]

filter papers os filtros de café [feeltroosh]

filthy nojento [noojayntoo]

find encontrar [aynkontrar]
I can't find it não consigo encontrar [nowng konseegoo

I've found it encontrei-o [aynkongtray-oo]

find out descobrir [dishkoobreer]
could you find out for me? pode descobrir para mim? [pod — meeng]

fine (weather) bom [bong]
(punishment) a multa [moolta]

dialogues

how are you? como está? [kohmoo shta]
I'm fine, thanks (said by man/woman) bem, obrigado/obrigada [bayng obrigadoo]

is that OK? assim está bem? [aseeng shta bayng]
that's fine, thanks está bem, obrigado/obrigada [shta]

finger o dedo [daydoo]

finish terminar
I haven't finished yet ainda não terminei [a-eenda nowng terminay]
when does it finish? quando é que termina? [kwandoo eh ki termeena]

fire o fogo [fohgoo]
(blaze) o incêndio [insaynd-yoo]
fire! fogo!
can we light a fire here? podemos fazer uma fogueira aqui? [poodaymoosh fazayr ooma foogayra akee]

it's on fire está a arder [shta a ardayr]

fire alarm o alarme de incêndios [alarm dinsaynd-yoosh]

fire brigade os bombeiros [bombayroosh]

fire escape a saída de emergência [sa-eeda demirJayns-ya]

fire extinguisher o extintor [shtintohr]

first primeiro [primayroo]

I was first (said by man/woman) eu era o primeiro/a primeira [ay-oo ehra]

at first ao princípio [ow prinseep-yoo]

the first time a primeira vez [vaysh]

first on the left primeira à esquerda [a-shkayrda]

first aid os primeiros socorros [primayroosh sookorroosh]

first aid kit a caixa de primeiros socorros [kisha di]

first class (travel etc) primeira classe [klas]

first floor o primeiro andar (US) o rés de chão [rehJ doo]

first name o nome próprio [nohm propr-yoo]

fish o peixe [paysh] (verb) pescar [pishkar]

fishing village a aldeia de pescadores [alday-a di pishkadohrish]

fishmonger's a peixaria [paysharee-a]

fit (attack) ataque [atak]

fit: it doesn't fit me não me serve [nowng mi sehrv]

fitting room a cabina de provas [kabeena di provash]

fix (repair) reparar can you fix this? (repair) pode reparar isto? [pod – eeshtoo]

fizzy gasoso [gazohzoo]

flag a bandeira [bandayra]

flannel a toalha de cara [twal-ya di]

flash (for camera) o flash

flat (apartment) o apartamento [apartamayntoo] (adj) plano [planno]

I've got a flat tyre tenho um pneu furado [tayn-yoo oong pnay-oo fooradoo]

flavour o sabor [sabohr]

flea a pulga [poolga]

flight o voo [voh-oo]

flight number o número de voo [noomiroo di]

flippers as barbatanas [barbata-nash]

flood a inundação [inoondasowng]

floor (of room) o chão [showng] (storey) o andar on the floor no chão

florist a florista [flooreeshta]

flour a farinha [fareen-ya]

flower a flor [flohr]

flu a gripe [greep]

fluent: he speaks fluent Portuguese ele fala português fluentemente [el – poortoogaysh flwentimaynt]

Fl

fly a mosca [**mo**shka]
(verb: person) ir de avião [eer dav-**yow**ng]
fog o nevoeiro [nivw**a**yroo]
foggy: it's foggy está enevoado [shta inivw**a**doo]
folk dancing a dança folclórica [dansa foolkl**o**rika]
folk music a música folclórica [m**oo**zika]
follow seguir [sig**ee**r]
follow me siga-me [s**ee**gami]
food a comida [koom**ee**da]
food poisoning a intoxicação alimentar [intoksikas**ow**ng]
food shop/store a mercearia [mirs-yar**ee**-a]
foot* (of person, measurement) o pé [peh]
on foot a pé
football (game) o futebol [f**oo**tbol]
(ball) a bola de futebol
football match o desafio de futebol [dizaf**ee**-oo di]
for: do you have something for ...? (headache/diarrhoea etc) tem alguma coisa para ...? [tayng alg**oo**ma k**o**h-iza]

dialogues

who's the bacalhau for?
para quem é o bacalhau?
[kayng eh-oo bakal-y**ow**]
that's for me é para mim
[eh – m**ee**ng]
and this one? e este? [ee-**ay**sht]

that's for her é para ela
[**eh**la]

where do I get the bus for Castelo de São Jorge?
onde posso apanhar o autocarro para o Castelo de São Jorge? [ohnd p**o**soo apan-y**a**r oo owtook**a**rroo paroo kasht**eh**loo di sowng JorJ]
the bus for o Castelo de São Jorge leaves from Praça do Comércio o autocarro para o Castelo de São Jorge sai da Praça do Comércio [sī da pr**a**sa doo koom**eh**rsyo]

how long have you been here for? há quanto tempo está aqui? [a kw**a**ntoo t**a**ympoo shta ak**ee**]
I've been here for two days, how about you? estou aqui há dois dias, e você? [shtoh ak**ee** a d**o**h-iJ d**ee**-ash ee vos**ay**]
I've been here for a week estou aqui há uma semana [shtoh ak**ee** a **oo**ma simana]

forehead a testa [t**eh**shta]
foreign estrangeiro [shtranJ**ay**roo]
foreigner (man/woman) o estrangeiro [shtranJ**ay**roo], a estrang**ei**ra
forest a floresta [floor**eh**shta]

62

forget esquecer [shkisayr]
I forget, I've forgotten
esqueci-me [shkiseemi]
fork o garfo [garfoo]
(in road) a bifurcação
[bifoorkasowng]
form (document) o impresso
[imprehsou]
formal (dress) de cerimónia [di
sirimon-ya]
fortnight a quinzena
[keenzayna]
fortunately felizmente
[filiJmaynt]
forward: could you forward
my mail? pode passar a
enviar-me o correio? [pod
– aynv-yarmi oo koorray-oo]
forwarding address a nova
morada [moorada]
foundation cream o creme de
base [kraym di baz]
fountain a fonte [fohnt]
foyer (of hotel, theatre) o foyer
[fwI-ay]
fracture a fractura
[fratoora]
France a França [fransa]
free livre [leevr]
(no charge) gratuito [gratoo-
eetoo]
is it free (of charge)? é
gratuito? [eh]
freeway a autoestrada
[owtooshtrada]
freezer o congelador
[konJiladohr]
French (adj, language) francês
[fransaysh]

French fries as batatas fritas
[batatash freetash]
frequent frequente
[trikwaynt]
how frequent is the bus to
Évora? com que frequência
há autocarros para Évora?
[kong ki frikwaynsya a
owtookarroosh – ehvoora]
fresh fresco [frayshkoo]
fresh orange o sumo natural
de laranja [soomoo natooral di
laranJa]
Friday sexta-feira [sayshta fayra]
fridge o frigorífico [frigoo-
reefikoo]
fried frito [freetoo]
fried egg o ovo estrelado
[ohvoo shtriladoo]
friend (male/female) o amigo
[ameegoo], a amiga
friendly simpático [simpatikoo]
from de [di]
when does the next train from
Braga arrive? quando chega o
próximo comboio de Braga?
[kwandon shayg-oo prosimoo
komboh-yo di]
from Monday to Friday de
segunda a sexta-feira [di
sigoonda-a sayshta fayra]
from next Thursday a partir
da próxima quinta-feira [a
parteer da prosima keenta fayra]

dialogue

where are you from? de
onde é? [dohnd-eh]

I'm from Slough sou de Slough [soh di]

front a frente [fraynt]
in front em frente [ayng]
in front of the hotel em frente ao hotel [ow]
at the front na frente [na]
frost a geada [J-yada]
frozen gelado [Jiladoo]
frozen food a comida congelada [koomeeda konJilada]
fruit a fruta [froota]
fruit juice o sumo de fruta [soomoo di froota]
fry fritar
frying pan a frigideira [friJidayra]
full cheio [shay-oo]
it's full of ... está cheio de ... [shta – di]
I'm full (said by man/woman) estou satisfeito/satisfeita [shtoh satisfaytoo]
full board a pensão completa [paynsowng komplehta]
fun: it was fun foi divertido [foh-i diverteedoo]
funeral o funeral [fooneral]
funny (strange) estranho [shtran-yoo]
(amusing) engraçado [ayngrasadoo]
furniture a mobília [moobeel-ya]
further mais longe [mīJ lohnJ]
it's further down the road é mais abaixo na rua [abīshoo na roo-a]

dialogue

how much further is it to Santarém? quantos quilómetros faltam para Santarém? [kwantoosh kilomitroosh faltowng – santarayng]
about 5 kilometres mais ou menos cinco quilómetros [mīz oh maynoosh seenkoo]

fuse o fusível [foozeevil]
the lights have fused as luzes fundiram-se [aJ loozish foondeerowngsi]
fuse box a caixa de fusíveis [kīsha di foozeevaysh]
fuse wire o fio de fusível [fee-oo di foozeevil]
future o futuro [footooroo]
in future no futuro [noo]

G

gallon* o galão [galowng]
game (cards, match etc) o jogo [Johgoo]
(meat) a caça [kasa]
garage (for fuel) a bomba de gasolina [di gazooleena]
(for repairs, parking) a garagem [garaJayng]
garden o jardim [Jardeeng]
garlic o alho [al-yoo]
gas o gás [gash]
gas cylinder (camping gas) a bilha de gás [beel-ya di gash]

gasoline (US) a gasolina
[gazooleena]

gas permeable lenses as lentes
semi-rígidas [layntsh simi-reeJidash]

gas station a bomba de
gasolina [bohmba di gazooleena]

gate o portão [poortowng]
(at airport) o portão de
embarque [daymbark]

gay o homossexual
[ohmooseksway]

gay bar o gay bar

gearbox a caixa de velocidades
[kīsha di viloosidadsh]

gear lever a alavanca das
mudanças [dash moodansgah]

gears a mudança [moodansa]

general (adj) geral [Jeral]

gents (toilet) a casa de banho
dos homens [kaza di ban-yoo
dooz ohmayngsh]

genuine (antique etc) genuíno
[Jinweenoo]

German (adj, language) alemão
[alimowng]

German measles a rubéola
[roobeh-ola]

Germany a Alemanha [aliman-ya]

get (fetch) ir buscar [eer]
will you get me another
one, please? pode trazer-
me outro, por favor? [pod
trazayrmohtroo poor favohr]
how do I get to ...? como vou
para ...? [kohmoo voh]
do you know where I can

get this? sabe onde posso
comprar isto? [sahbohnd posoo
– eeshtoo]

dialogue

can I get you a drink?
posso oferecer-lhe uma
bebida? [posoo ofrisayrl-
yooma bibeeda]
no, I'll get this one, what
would you like? não, eu
ofereço esta, o que gostaria?
[nowng ay-oo ofrAysoo ehohta
oo ki
gooshtaree-a]
a glass of red wine um
copo de vinho tinto
[oong kopoo di veen-yoo
teento]

get back (return) voltar

get in (arrive) chegar [shigar]

get off sair [sa-eer]
where do I get off? onde é
que saio? [ohndeh ki sī-yoo]

get on (to train etc) apanhar
[apan-yar]

get out (of car etc) sair [sa-eer]

get up (in the morning) levantar-
se [livantarsi]

gift a lembrança [laymbransa]

gift shop a loja de
lembranças [loJa di
laymbransash]

gin o gin [Jeeng]
a gin and tonic, please um
gin-tónico por favor [oong
Jeeng tonikoo poor favohr]

girl a rapariga [rapareega]

girlfriend a namorada

give* dar

can you give me some change? pode dar-me troco? [pod darmi trohkoo]

I gave it to him dei-lhe [dayl-yi]

will you give this to ...? pode dar isto a ...? [eeshtoo]

dialogue

how much do you want for this? quanto quer por isto? [kwantoo kehr poor eeshtoo]

20 euros vinte euros [veent ay-ooroosh]

I'll give you 15 euros dou-lhe quinze euros [dohl-yi keenz]

give back devolver [divolvayr]

glad contente [kontaynt]

glass (material) o vidro [veedroo] (for drinking) o copo [kopoo]

a glass of wine um copo de vinho [oong – di veen-yoo]

glasses os óculos [okooloosh]

gloves as luvas [loovash]

glue a cola

go* ir [eer]

we'd like to go to the Museu de Arte Antiga queremos ir ao Museu de Arte Antiga [kiraymoosh eer ow moosay-oo dartanteega]

where are you going? onde vai? [ohnd vī]

where does this bus go? para onde vai este autocarro? [aysht owtookarroo]

let's go! vamos! [vamoosh]

she's gone (left) ele foi-se embora [ayl foh-isaymbora]

where has he gone? onde ele foi? [ohndayl foh-i]

I went there last week fui lá na semana passada [fwee la na simana]

hamburger to go o hamburger para levar

go away ir embora [eer aymbora]

go away! vá-se embora! [vas-aymbora]

go back (return) voltar

go down (the stairs etc) descer [dishsayr]

go in entrar [ayntrar]

go out* (in the evening) sair [sa-eer]

do you want to go out tonight? quer sair esta noite? [kehr – ehshta noh-it]

go through atravessar

go up (the stairs etc) subir [soobeer]

goat a cabra

goat's cheese o queijo de cabra [kayjoo di]

God Deus [day-oosh]

goggles os óculos protectores [okooloosh prootetohrish]

gold o ouro [ohroo]

golf o golfe [golf]

golf course o campo de golfe [kampoo di]

good bom [bong]
good! bem! [bayng]
it's no good não presta [nowng prehshta]
goodbye adeus [aday-oosh]
good evening boa noite [boh-a noh-it]
Good Friday Sexta-Feira Santa [sayshta fayra]
good morning bom dia [bong dee-a]
good night boa noite [boh-a noh-it]
goose o ganso [gansoo]
got: we've got to leave temos que ir [taymoosh ki-eer]
have you got any ...? tem ...? [tayng]
government o governo [goovayrnoo]
gradually gradualmente [gradwalmaynt]
grammar a gramática
gram(me) o grama
granddaughter a neta [nehta]
grandfather o avô [avoh]
grandmother a avó [avaw]
grandson o neto [nehtoo]
grapefruit a toranja [tooranJa]
grapefruit juice o sumo de toranja [soomoo di tooranJa]
grapes as uvas [oovash]
grass a relva [rehlva]
grateful agradecido [agradiseedoo]
gravy o molho [mohl-yo]
great (excellent) óptimo [otimoo]
that's great! isso é optimo! [eesoo eh]

a great success um grande sucesso [oong grand soosehsoo]
Great Britain a Grã-Bretanha [gran britan-ya]
Greece a Grécia [grehs-ya]
greedy (for food) glutão [glootowng]
Greek (adj, language) grego [graygoo]
green verde [vayrd]
green card (car insurance) a carta verde
greengrocer's o lugar [loogar]
grey cinzento [sinzayntoo]
grill o grelhador [gril-yadohr]
grilled grelhado [gril-yadou]
grocer's o merceeiro [mirs-yayroo]
ground o chão [showng]
on the ground no chão [noo]
ground floor o rés de chão [rehJ doo]
group o grupo [groopoo]
guarantee a garantia [garantee-a]
is it guaranteed? tem garantia? [tayng]
guest (man/woman) o convidado [konvidadoo], a convidada
guesthouse a pensão [paynsowng]
guide (person) a guia [gee-a]
guidebook o livro-guia [leevroo–]
guided tour a excursão com guia [shkoorsowng kong]
guitar a viola
gum (in mouth) a gengiva [JenJeeva]

gun a pistola [pisht**o**la]
gym o ginásio [Jin**a**z-yoo]

H

hair o cabelo [kab**ay**loo]
hairbrush a escova de cabelo [shk**oh**va di]
haircut o corte de cabelo [kort]
hairdresser's (unisex, women's) o cabeleireiro [kabilay**ray**roo]
(men's) o barbeiro [barb**ay**roo]
hairdryer o secador de cabelo [sikad**oh**r di kab**ay**loo]
hair gel o gel para o cabelo [Jehl p**a**roo]
hairgrips a mola para o cabelo
hair spray a laca
half* a metade [mit**a**d]
half an hour meia hora [**may**-a **o**ra]
half a litre meio litro [**may**-oo l**ee**troo]
about half that mais ou menos metade disto [m**ī**z oh m**ay**noosh mit**a**d-d**ee**shtoo]
half board a meia pensão [**may**-a payns**ow**ng]
half-bottle a meia garrafa
half fare o meio bilhete [**may**-oo bil-**yayt**]
half price metade do preço [mit**a**d doo pr**ay**soo]
ham o fiambre [f-y**a**mbr]
hamburger o hamburger [amb**oo**rger]
hammer o martelo [mart**eh**loo]
hand a mão [m**ow**ng]

handbag a mala de mão [di]
handbrake o travão de mão [trav**ow**ng]
handkerchief o lenço [**layn**soo]
handle (on door) o fecho [**fay**shoo]
(on suitcase etc) a pega [**peh**ga]
hand luggage a bagagem de mão [bag**a**Jayng]
hang-gliding a asa-delta [aza-**deh**lta]
hangover a ressaca [ris**a**ka]
I've got a hangover estou de ressaca [shtoh di]
happen acontecer [akontis**ayr**]
what's happening? o que se passa? [oo ki si]
what has happened? o que aconteceu? [oo ki-akoontis**ay**-oo]
happy contente [kont**ay**nt]
I'm not happy about this não estou contente com isso [n**ow**ng shtoh – kong **ee**soo]
harbour o porto [**poh**rtoo]
hard duro [**doo**roo]
(difficult) difícil [dif**ee**sil]
hard-boiled egg o ovo cozido [**oh**voo kooz**ee**doo]
hard lenses as lentes rígidas [**layn**tsh r**ee**Jidash]
hardly mal
hardly ever quase nunca [kw**a**z n**oo**nka]
hardware shop a loja de ferragens [**lo**Ja di firra**Jayng**sh]
hat o chapéu [shap**eh**-oo]
hate detestar [ditisht**ar**]
have* ter [t**ay**r]
can I have a ...? pode dar-

me ...? [pod darmi]
do you have ...? tem ...?
[tayng]
what'll you have? o que vai
tomar? [oo kI vī toomar]
I have to leave now tenho de
ir agora [tayn-yoo deer]
do I have to ...? tenho de ...?
[di]
can we have some ...? posso
ter ...? [posoo tayr]
hayfever a febre dos fenos
[fehbr doosh faynoosh]
hazelnuts as avelãs [avelangsh]
he* ele [el]
head a cabeça [kabaysa]
headache a dor de cabeça [di]
headlights o farol
headphones os auscultadores
[owshkooltadohrish]
health food shop a loja de
produtos naturais [loja di
proodootoosh natoorīsh]
healthy saudável [sowdavil]
hear ouvir [ohveer]

dialogue

can you hear me?
consegue ouvir-me?
[konsehg ohveer-mi]
I can't hear you, could you
repeat that? não o consigo
ouvir, podia repetir?
[nowng oo konseegoo – poodee-
a ripiteer]

hearing aid o aparelho para a
surdez [aparayl-yoo – soordaysh]

heart o coração [koorasowng]
heart attack o enfarte [aynfart]
heat o calor [kalohr]
heater o aquecedor [akesidohr]
heating o aquecimento
[akesimaynton]
heavy pesado [pizadoo]
heel (of foot) o calcanhar [kalkan-
yar]
(of shoe) o salto
could you put new heels on
these? podia pôr uns saltos
novos? [poodee-a pohr oongsh
saltoosh novoosh]
heelbar o sapateiro rápido
[sapatayroo rapidoo]
height (of person) a altura
[altoora]
(mountain) a altitude [altitood]
helicopter o helicóptero
[elikoptiroo]
hello olá
(answer on phone) está [shta]
helmet (for motorcycle) o
capacete [kapasayt]
help a ajuda [ajooda]
(verb) ajudar
help! socorro! [sookohrroo]
can you help me? pode
ajudar-me? [pod – mi]
thank you very much for
your help (said by man/woman)
obrigado/obrigada pela sua
ajuda [obrigadoo – pila soo-a]
helpful prestável [preshtavil]
hepatitis a hepatite [epateet]
her*: I haven't seen her não a
vi [nowng a vee]
to her para ela [ehla]

with her com ela [kong]
for her para ela
that's her é ela [eh]
that's her towel esta é a toalha dela [ehshta-eh – dehla]
herbal tea o chá de ervas [sha dehrvash]
herbs as ervas
here aqui [akee]
here is/are ... aqui está/estão ... [shta/shtowng]
here you are aqui tem [tayng]
hers* dela [dehla]
that's hers isso é dela [eesoo eh]
hey! eh!
hi! (hello) olá! [oola]
hide esconder [shkondayr]
high alto [altoo]
highchair a cadeira de bébé [kadayra di bebeh]
highway a autoestrada [owtooshtrada]
hill o monte [mohnt]
him*: I haven't seen him não o vi [nowng oo vee]
to him para ele [ayl]
with him com ele [kong]
for him para ele
that's him é ele [eh]
hip a anca
hire alugar [aloogar]
for hire para alugar
where can I hire a bike? onde posso alugar uma bicicleta? [ohnd posoo]
his*: it's his car é o carro dele [eh-oo karroo dayl]
that's his isto é dele [eeshtweh]

hit bater [batayr]
hitch-hike andar à boleia [boolay-a]
hobby o passatempo [–taympoo]
hold segurar [sigoorar]
hole o buraco [boorakoo]
holiday as férias [fehr-yash]
on holiday de férias [shtoh di]
Holland Holanda [olanda]
home a casa [kaza]
at home (in my house etc) em casa [ayng]
(in my country) no meu país [noo may-oo pa-eesh]
we go home tomorrow vamos embora amanhã [vamoosh aymbora aman-yang]
honest honesto [onehshtoo]
honey o mel [mehl]
honeymoon a lua-de-mel [loo-a di]
hood (US: of car) o capot [kapoh]
hope esperar [shpirar]
I hope so espero que sim [shpehroo ki seeng]
I hope not espero que não [nowng]
hopefully: hopefully ... espero que ...
horn (of car) a buzina [boozeena]
horrible horrível [ohrreevil]
horse o cavalo [kavaloo]
horse riding andar a cavalo
hospital o hospital [oshpital]
hospitality a hospitalidade [oshpitalidad]
thank you for your hospitality (said by man/woman)

obrigado/obrigada pela sua hospitalidade [obriga**doo** – pila **soo**-a]

hot quente [**kaynt**]

(spicy) picante [pi**kant**]

I'm hot tenho calor [**tayn**-yoo ka**lohr**]

it's hot today está imenso calor hoje [shta ima**ynsoo** – **ohJ**]

hotel o hotel [oh**tehl**]

hotel room o quarto de hotel [**kwar**too doh**tehl**]

hour a hora [**ora**]

house a casa [**kaza**]

house wine o vinho da casa [**veen**-yoo]

how como [**koh**moo]

how many? quantos? [**kwan**toosh]

how do you do? muito prazer [**mwee**ngtoo pra**zayr**]

dialogues

how are you? como está? [shta]

fine, thanks, and you? (said by man/woman) bem, obrigado/obrigada, e você? [bayng obriga**doo** – ee vos**ay**]

how much is it? quanto é? [kwant**weh**]

it's 20 euros são vinte euros [sowng veent **ay**-ooroosh]

I'll take it vou levar [voh]

humid húmido [**oo**meedoo]

hunger a fome [**fohm**]

hungry: are you hungry? tens fome? [taynsh]

hurry apressar-se [apri**sarsi**]

I'm in a hurry estou com pressa [shtoh kong pr**ehsa**]

there's no hurry não há pressa [nowng a]

hurry up! despacha-te! [dishp**ash**at]

hurt doer [d**wayr**]

it really hurts dói-me [**doyml**]

husband o meu marido [**may**-oo ma**reedoo**]

hydrofoil o hidroplano [idrooplanoo]

hypermarket hipermercado [eepermerk**adoo**]

I
■

I* eu [**ay**-oo]

ice gelo [**J**ay**loo**]

with ice com gelo [kong]

no ice, thanks (said by man/ woman) sem gelo, obrigado/ obrigada [sayng – obriga**doo**]

ice cream o gelado [Jila**doo**]

ice-cream cone o cone de gelado [kohn di]

iced coffee o café glacé [kaf**eh** glas**ay**]

ice lolly o gelado [Jila**doo**]

ice rink o rinque de patinagem [**reenk** di patina**Jayng**]

ice skates os patins de gelo [pa**teenJ** di **J**ay**loo**] idea a ideia [id**ay**-a]

idiot o idiota [id-y**o**ta]

if se [si]

ignition a ignição [ignis**ow**ng]

ill doente [dw**ay**nt]
  I feel ill sinto-me doente
  [s**ee**ntoomi]

illness a doença [dw**ay**nsa]

imitation (leather etc) a imitação
  [imitas**ow**ng]

immediately imediatamente
  [imed-yatam**ay**nt]

important importante
  [impo**or**tant]
  it's very important é muito
  importante [eh m**wee**ngtoo]
  it's not important não é
  importante [n**ow**ng]

impossible impossível
  [impoos**ee**vil]

impressive impressionante
  [impris-yoon**an**t]

improve melhorar [mil-yor**ar**]
  I want to improve my
  Portuguese quero melhorar
  o meu português [k**eh**roo – oo
  may-oo poortoog**ay**sh]

in*: it's in the centre fica no
  centro [f**ee**ka noo s**ay**ntroo]
  in my car no meu carro [noo
  may-oo k**a**rroo]
  in Beja em Beja [ayng b**eh**ʒa]
  in two days from now daqui a
  dois dias [dak**ee** a d**o**-iʒ d**ee**-ash]
  in five minutes em cinco
  minutos [ayng s**ee**nkoo
  min**oo**toosh]
  in May em Maio [m**ī**-oo]
  in English em inglês [ingl**ay**sh]

in Portuguese em português
  [poortoog**ay**sh]

is he in? ele está? [el shta]

inch* a polegada [pool**i**gada]

include incluir [inkl**wee**r]
  does that include meals?
  isso inclui as refeições? [**ee**soo
  inkl**oo**-i refays**oy**ngsh]
  is that included? isso está
  incluído no preço? [shta
  inkl**wee**doo noo pr**ay**soo]

inconvenient pouco
  conveniente [p**oh**koo konvin-
  y**ay**nt]

incredible incrível [inkr**ee**vil]

Indian (adj) indiano [ind-y**a**noo]

indicator o indicador
  [indikad**oh**r]

indigestion a indigestão
  [indiʒisht**ow**ng]

indoor pool a piscina coberta
  [pish-s**ee**na koob**eh**rta]

indoors dentro de casa
  [d**ay**ntroo di k**a**za], em recinto
  fechado [ayng ris**ee**ntoo fish**a**doo]

inexpensive barato [bar**a**too]

infection a infecção
  [infehs**ow**ng]

infectious infeccioso [infehs-
  y**oh**zoo]

inflammation a inflamação
  [inflamas**ow**ng]

informal informal [infoorm**a**l]

information a informação
  [infoormas**ow**ng]
  do you have any information
  about ...? tem alguma
  informação sobre ...? [tayng
  alg**oo**ma – s**oh**br]

information desk o balcão de informações [balk**ow**ng dInfoormas**oy**ngsh]

injection a injecção [inJeh**sow**ng]

injured ferido [f**ee**redoo]

she's been injured ela ficou ferida [**eh**la fik**oh** t**ee**reda]

in-laws os sogros [oosh s**o**groosh]

inner tube (for tyre) a câmara de ar [k**a**ma-ra dar]

innocent inocente [in**oo**saynt]

insect o insecto [ins**eh**too]

insect bite a picada de insecto [dins**eh**too]

do you have anything for insect bites? tem alguma coisa para picada de insectos? [layng alg**oo**ma k**oh**-iza – ins**eh**toosh]

insect repellent o repele-insectos [rip**eh**l ins**eh**toosh]

inside dentro [d**ay**ntroo]

inside the hotel dentro do hotel [dwoht**eh**l]

let's sit inside vamos sentar-nos lá dentro [v**a**moosh sentar-n**oo**sh]

insist insistir [insisht**ee**r]

I insist insisto [ins**ee**shtoo]

insomnia a insónia [ins**o**n-ya]

instant coffee o café instantâneo [kaf**eh** inshtantan-yoo]

instead em vez [ayng vaysh]

give me that one instead dê-me antes aquele [daym antsh ak**ay**l]

**instead of ... em vez de ... [di]

insulin a insulina [insool**ee**na]

insurance o seguro [sig**oo**roo]

intelligent inteligente [intili**J**aynt]

interested: I'm interested in ... (said by a man/woman) estou muito interessado/interessada em ... [shtoh mw**ee**ngtoo intris**a**doo – ayng]

interesting interessante [intris**a**nt]

that's very interesting isso é muito interessante [**ee**soo eh mw**ee**ngtoo]

international internacional [intaynas-yoon**a**l]

Internet Internet [intirn**eh**t]

interpret interpretar [interprit**a**r]

interpreter (man/woman) o/a intérprete [int**eh**rprit]

intersection o cruzamento [kroozam**ay**ntoo]

interval (at theatre) o intervalo [interval**oo**]

into para

I'm not into ... não me interesso por ... [nowng mintr**eh**soo poor]

introduce apresentar [aprizent**a**r]

may I introduce ...? posso apresentar ... [p**o**soo]

invitation o convite [konv**ee**t]

invite convidar [konvid**a**r]

Ireland a Irlanda [eerl**a**nda]

Irish irlandês [eerland**ay**sh]

I'm Irish (man/woman) sou

irlandês/sou irlandesa [soh – eerlandayza]

iron (for ironing) o ferro de engomar [fehrroo dayngoomar]

can you iron these for me? pode engomar-me isto? [pod ayngoomarm eeshtoo]

is* é [eh]; está [shta]

island a ilha [eel-ya]

it* o [oo], (f) a

it is ... é ... [eh]; está ... [shta]

is it ...? é ...?; está ...?

where is it? onde é? [ohndeh]; onde está?

it's him é ele [ayl]

it was ... era ... [ehra]; estava ... [shtava]

Italian (adj, language) italiano [ital-yanoo]

Italy Itália [ital-ya]

itch: it itches faz comichão [fash koomishowng]

J

jack (for car) o macaco [makakoo]

jacket o casaco [kazakoo]

jam a compota

jammed: it's jammed está encravado [shta aynkravadoo]

January Janeiro [Janayroo]

jar o jarro

jaw a maxila [makseela]

jazz o jazz

jealous ciumento [s-yoomayntoo]

jeans os jeans

jellyfish a alforreca [alfoorrehka]

jersey a camisola [kamizola]

jetty o pontão [pontowng]

jeweller's a ourivesaria [ohrivezaree-a]

jewellery a joalharia [Jwal-yaree-a]

Jewish judaico [Joodīkoo]

job o emprego [aympraygoo]

jogging o jogging

to go jogging praticar jogging

joke a piada [p-yada]

journey a viagem [v-yaJayng]

have a good journey! boa viagem! [boh-a]

jug o jarro [Jarroo]

a jug of water um jarro de água [oong – dagwa]

juice o sumo [soomoo]

July Julho [Jool-yoo]

jump pular [poolar]

jumper a camisola [kamizola]

jump leads os cabos para ligar a bateria [kaboosh – batiree-a]

junction o cruzamento [kroozamayntoo]

June Junho [Joon-yoo]

just (only) só [saw]

just two só dois/duas

just for me só para mim [meeng]

just here aqui mesmo [akee mayJmoo]

not just now agora não [nowng]

we've just arrived acabámos de chegar [akabamooJ di shigar]

K

keep guardar [gwardar]
keep the change guarde o
troco [gward oo trohkoo]
can I keep it? posso ficar
com ele/ela? [posoo fikar kong
ayl/**eh**la]
you can keep it pode ficar
com ele/ela [pod]
ketchup o ketchup
kettle a chaleira [shalayra]
key a chave [shav]
the key for room 201, please
a chave do quarto duzentos
e um, faz favor [doo kwartoo
doozayntoosh young tash favohr]
keyring o chaveiro
[shavayroo]
kidneys (in body, food) os rins
[reengsh]
kill matar
kilo* o quilo [keeloo]
kilometre* o quilómetro
[kilomitroo]
how many kilometres is it
to ...? quantos quilómetros
são até ...? [kwantoosh
kilomitroosh sowng ateh]
kind (generous) amável
that's very kind é muito
amável [eh mweengtoo]

dialogue

which kind do you want?
que tipo deseja? [ki **tee**poo
disay**J**a]

I want this/that kind desejo
este/aquele tipo [aysht/
akayl]

king o rei [ray]
kiosk o quiosque [k-yoshk]
kiss o beijo [bay**J**oo]
(verb) beijar [bay**J**ar]
kitchen a cozinha
[koozeen-ya]
kitchenette a cozinha pequena
[pikayna]
Kleenex® os lenços de papel
[laynsoosh di papohl]
knee o joelho [**J**wayl-yoo]
knickers as cuecas de mulher
[ash kwehka**J** di mool-**yehr**]
knife a faca [faka]
knock bater [batayr]
knock down atropelar
[atropilar]
he's been knocked down
ele foi atropelado [el **foh**-i
atropilado]
knock over (object) derrubar
[dirroobar]
(pedestrian) atropelar
[atropilar]
know* (somebody, a place)
conhecer [koon-yisair]
(something) saber
I don't know não sei [nowng
say]
I didn't know that não sabia
isso [nowng sabee-a **ee**soo]
do you know where I can
find ...? sabe onde posso
encontrar ...? [sabohnd
poswaynkontrar]

L

label (on clothes) a etiqueta [etik**ay**ta]
(on bottles etc) o rótulo [r**o**tooloo]

ladies' room, ladies' (toilets) o quarto de banho das senhoras [kw**a**rtoo di b**a**n-yoo dash sin-y**o**rash]

ladies' wear a roupa de senhoras [r**oh**pa di]

lady a senhora [sin-y**o**ra]

lager a cerveja [sirv**ay**-Ja]

lake o lago [l**a**goo]

lamb (meat) o borrego [boorr**ay**goo]

lamp o candeeiro [kand-y**ay**roo]

lane (motorway) a faixa [f**i**sha]
(small road) a viela [v-y**eh**la]

language a língua [l**ee**ngwa]

language course o curso de línguas [k**oo**rsoo di l**ee**ngwash]

large grande [grand]

last o último [**oo**ltimoo]

last week semana passada [sim**a**na]

last Friday sexta-feira passada [s**ay**shta-f**ay**ra]

last night ontem à noite [**oh**ntayng a n**oh**-it]

what time is the last train to Fátima? a que horas parte o último comboio para Fátima? [kyorash part-yoo-**oo**ltimoo komb**oh**-yo]

late tarde [tard]

sorry I'm late desculpe o atraso [dishk**oo**lp oo atr**a**zoo]

the train was late o comboio estava atrasado [oo komb**oh**-yo sht**a**va atraz**a**doo]

we must go – we'll be late temos que ir – vamos atrasar-nos [t**ay**moosh ki-**ee**r – v**a**mooz-atraz**a**r noosh]

it's getting late está a ficar tarde [sht**a**-a fik**a**r]

later, later on mais tarde [m**i**sh]

I'll come back later volto mais tarde [v**o**ltoo]

see you later até logo [a-t**eh**]

latest o último [**oo**ltimoo]

by Wednesday at the latest quarta-feira o mais tard**a**r [kw**a**rta-f**ay**ra oo m**i**sh]

laugh rir [reer]

launderette a lavandaria automática [lavandar**ee**-a owtoom**a**tika]

laundromat a lavandaria automática [lavandar**ee**-a owtoom**a**tika]

laundry (clothes) a roupa para lavar [r**oh**pa]
(place) a lavandaria [lavandar**ee**-a]

lavatory os lavabos [lav**a**boosh]

law a lei [lay]

lawn o relvado [relv**a**doo]

lawyer (man/woman) o advogado [advoog**a**doo], a advog**a**da

laxative o laxativo [lashat**ee**voo]

lazy preguiçoso [prigis**oh**zoo]

lead (electrical) o fio [f**ee**-oo]
(verb) conduzir [kondooz**ee**r]

where does this lead to? onde vai ter esta estrada? [ohnd v**i** tayr **eh**shta shtr**a**da] leaf a folha [**foh**l-ya]

leaflet o panfleto [panfl**ay**too]

leak a fuga [**foo**ga]

(verb) ter uma fuga [tayr **oo**ma]

the roof leaks há uma fuga de
água no telhado [a – d**ag**wa noo
til-**y**adoo]

learn aprender [apraynd**ayr**]

least: not in the least de
nenhum modo [di nin-**yoo**ng
modoo]

at least pelo menos [**pi**loo
may**noo**sh]

leather o cabedal [kabi**dal**]

leave (depart) partir [part**ee**r]
(behind) deixar [**day**shar]

I am leaving tomorrow parto
amanhã [**par**too aman-**yang**]

he left yesterday ele partiu
ontem [ayl part**ee**-oo **oh**ntayng]

may I leave this here? posso
deixar isto aqui? [**po**soo
– **ee**shtwak**ee**]

I left my coat in the bar deixei
meu casaco no bar [day**shay**
may-oo ka**za**koo noo]

when does the bus for
Lagos leave? quando parte
o autocarro para Lagos?
[**kwa**ndoo **par**too owtook**a**rroo
– **la**goosh]

leeks o alho francês [**al**-yoo
frans**ay**sh]

left esquerdo [sh**kay**rdoo]

on the left, to the left à
esquerda [a sh**kay**rda]

turn left vire à esquerda [**vee**ra]

there's none left não há mais
[nowng a m**ī**sh]

left-handed canhoto [kan-
yohtoo]

left luggage (office) o depósito
de bagagem [di**po**zitoo di
bag**a**ɹayng]

leg a perna [**peh**rna]

lemon o limão [li**mow**ng]

lemonade a limonada
[limoo**na**da]

lemon tea o chá de limão [sha
di li**mow**ng]

lend emprestar [aympr**ish**tar]

will you lend me your ...?
empresta-me o seu ...?
[aympr**oh**shtam**oo** **say**-oo]

lens (of camera) a objectiva
[ob**je**t**ee**va]

lesbian a lésbica [**leh**ɹbika]

less* menos [**may**noosh]

less than menos do que [doo
kɪ]

less expensive mais barato
[m**ī**ɹ bar**a**too]

lesson a lição [li**sow**ng]

let (allow) deixar [**day**shar]

will you let me know? diz-me
depois? [**dee**ɹmi dip**oh**-ish]

I'll let you know depois digo-
lhe [**dee**gool-yɪ]

let's go for something to
eat vamos sair para comer
alguma coisa [**va**moosh sa-**eer**
– koo**mayr** alg**oo**ma k**oh**-iza]

let off: will you let me off at ...?
é capaz de parar em ...? [eh
kap**a**ɹ di – ayng]

letter a carta

do you have any letters for
me? tem alguma carta para

mim? [tayng alg**oo**ma – meeng]
letterbox o marco de correio
[m**a**rkoo di koor**ay**-oo]
lettuce a alface [**a**lfas]
lever a alav**a**nca
library a biblioteca [bibl-
yoot**eh**ka]
licence a licença [lis**ay**nsa]
lid a t**a**mpa
lie (verb: tell untruth) mentir
[maynt**ee**r]
lie down deitar-se [d**ay**tarsi]
life a vida [**vee**da]
lifebelt o cinto de salvação
[**s**eentoo di salvas**ow**ng]
lifeguard o banheiro [ban-
yayroo]
life jacket o colete de salvação
[kool**ay**t di salvas**ow**ng]
lift (in building) o elevador
[elevad**oh**r]
could you give me a lift?
pode dar-me uma boleia? [pod
darm**oo**ma bool**ay**-a]
would you like a lift? quer
uma boleia? [kehr]
light a luz [l**oo**sh]
(not heavy) leve [l**eh**v]
do you have a light? (for
cigarette) tem lume? [tayng
loom]
light green verde claro [v**ay**rd
kl**a**roo]
light bulb a l**â**mpada
I need a new light bulb
preciso duma lâmpada
[pris**ee**zoo d**oo**ma]
lighter (cigarette) o isqueiro
[shk**ay**roo]

lightning a trovoada [troovw**a**da]
like gostar [g**oo**shtar]
I like it gosto [g**o**shtoo]
I like going for walks gosto de
passear a pé [di pas-y**a**r a peh]
I like you gosto de si [di see]
I don't like it não gosto
[nowng]
do you like ...? você gosta
de ...? [vos**ay** g**o**shta di]
I'd like a beer queria uma
cerveja [kir**ee**-a **oo**ma sirvay**J**a]
I'd like to go swimming
queria ir nadar [eer]
would you like a drink?
gostaria duma bebida?
[gooshtar**ee**-a d**oo**ma bib**ee**da]
would you like to go for a
walk? quer ir dar uma volta?
[kehr]
what's it like? como é?
[k**oh**moo eh]
I want one like this quero
um como este [k**eh**roo oong
kohmw**ay**sht]
lime a lima [**lee**ma]
lime cordial o sumo de lima
[**s**oomoo di]
line a linha [**lee**n-ya]
could you give me an outside
line? dá-me uma linha?
[dam**oo**ma]
lips os lábios [l**a**b-yoosh]
lip salve o baton para o cieiro
[bat**o**ng – oo s-y**ay**roo]
lipstick o baton [bat**o**ng]
liqueur o licor [lik**oh**r]
Lisbon Lisboa [liJb**oh**-a]
listen escutar [shk**oo**tar]

litre* o litro [**lee**troo]
a litre of white wine um litro de vinho branco [di **vee**n-yoo **bran**koo]
little pequeno [pik**ay**noo]
just a little, thanks só um pouco, por favor [saw oong **poh**koo poor fa**vohr**]
a little milk pouco leite [layt]
a little bit more um pouquinho mais [oong poh**keen**-yoo mïsh]
live (verb) viver [vi**vayr**]
we live together vivemos juntos [vi**vay**moosh **joon**toosh]

dialogue

where do you live? onde é que vive? [ohnd**eh** ki veev]
I live in London vivo em Londres [**vee**vwayng **lohn**drish]

lively animado [ani**ma**doo]
liver (in body, food) o fígado [**fee**gadoo]
loaf o pão [powng]
lobby (in hotel) o hall
lobster a lagosta [la**gohsh**ta]
local local [loo**kal**]
can you recommend a local wine? pode recomendar um vinho da região? [pod rikoo**mayn**dar oong **veen**-yoo da riJ-**yowng**]
can you recommend a local restaurant? pode recomendar um restaurante local?

[rish**tawrant**]
lock a fechadura [fisha**doo**ra]
(verb) fechar à chave [fi**shar** a shav]
it's locked está fechado à chave [shta fi**sha**doo shav]
lock out: I've locked myself out (of room) fechei o quarto com a chave lá dentro [fi**shay** oo **kwart**oo kong – **dayn**troo]
locker (for luggage etc) o cacifo [ka**see**foo]
lollipop o chupa-chupa [**shoo**pa–]
London Londres [**lohn**drish]
long comprido [kom**pree**doo]
how long will it take to fix it? quanto tempo vai demorar para consertar? [**kwant**oo **taym**poo vï dimoo**rar** – konsir**tar**]
how long does it take? quanto tempo demora? [di**mora**]
a long time muito tempo [**mween**gtoo]
one day/two days longer mais um dia/dois dias [mïz oong dee-a/do-ï dee-ash]
long-distance call a chamada de longa distância [sha**ma**da di – dish**tans**-ya]
look: I'm just looking, thanks (said by man/woman) estou só a ver, obrigado/obrigada [shtoh saw a vayr obri**ga**doo]
you don't look well parece não estar bem [pa**rehs** nowng shtar bayng]
look out! cuidado! [kwi**da**doo]

can I have a look? posso ver?
[**po**soo vayr]
look after tomar conta (de)
[too**mar ko**hnta]
look at olhar (para) [ol-**yar**]
look for procurar [prookoo**rar**]
I'm looking for ... procuro ...
[prook**oo**roo]
loose (handle etc) solto [**soh**ltoo]
lorry o camião [kam-**yow**ng]
lose perder [pir**dayr**]
I've lost my way perdi-me
[pir**deem**]
I'm lost, I want to get to ...
(said by man/woman) estou
perdido/perdida, quero ir
para ... [shtoh pir**dee**doo – **keh**roo
eer]
I've lost my bag perdi o meu
saco [pir**dee** oo **may**-oo **sa**koo]
lost property (office) a secção
de perdidos e achados
[sehk**sow**ng di pir**dee**dooz ee-
a**sha**doosh]
lot: a lot, lots muito
[**mwee**ngtoo]
not a lot não muito [nowng]
a lot of people muita gente
[**mwee**ngta **Jay**ngt]
a lot bigger muito maior [mī-
or]
I like it a lot gosto imenso
[**gosh**too i**mayn**soo]
lotion a loção [loo**sow**ng]
loud alto [**al**too]
lounge (in house, hotel) a sala
(in airport) a sala de espera
[dish**peh**ra]
love o amor [a**mohr**]

(verb) amar
I love Portugal adoro
Portugal [a**do**roo poor**too**gal]
lovely (meal, food) delicioso
[dilis-**yoh**zoo]
(view) encantador
[aynkanta**dohr**]
(weather) excelente [ish-si**laynt**]
(present) adorável
low baixo [**bī**shoo]
luck a sorte [**sort**]
good luck! boa sorte! [**boh**-a]
luggage a bagagem [ba**ga**Jayng]
luggage trolley o carrinho de
bagagem [ka**rreen**-yoo di]
lump (on body) o inchaço
[in**sha**soo]
lunch o almoço [al**moh**soo]
lungs os pulmões [pool**moy**ngsh]
luxurious (hotel, furnishings)
luxuoso [loosh-**woh**zoo]
luxury o luxo [**loo**shoo]

M

machine a máquina [**ma**kina]
mad (insane) doido [**doh**-idoo]
(angry) zangado [zan**ga**doo]
Madeira (place) a Madeira
[ma**day**ra]
(wine) o (vinho da) Madeira
[**veen**-yoo]
magazine a revista [ri**vees**hta]
maid (in hotel) a criada [kr-**ya**da]
maiden name o nome de
solteira [nohm di sool**tay**ra]
mail o correio [koo**rray**-oo]
(verb) pôr no correio [pohr noo]

is there any mail for me? há algum correio para mim? [a algoom – meeng]

mailbox o marco de correio [markoo di kooray-oo], a caixa do correio [kīsha doo]

main principal [prinsipal]

main course o prato principal [pratoo prinsipal]

main post office a central de correios [sentral di kooray-oosh]

main road (in town) a rua principal [roo-a prinsipal] (in country) a estrada principal [shtrada]

mains switch o disjuntor principal [dijoontohr]

make* (brand name) a marca (verb) fazer [fazayr]

I make it 50 euros calculo que sejam cinquenta euros [kalkooloo ki sayjowng sinkwaynta ay-ooroosh]

what is it made of? de que é feito? [di k-yeh faytoo]

make-up a maquilhagem [makil-yaJayng]

man o homem [ohmayng]

manager o gerente [Jeraynt]

can I see the manager? pode chamar o gerente? [pod shamar]

manageress a gerente

manual manual [manwal]

many muitos [mweengtoosh]

not many não muitos [nowng]

map o mapa

March Março [marsoo]

margarine a margarina

[margareena]

market o mercado [mirkadoo]

marmalade a compota de laranja [di laranJa]

married: I'm married (said by a man/woman) sou casado/casada [soh kazadoo]

are you married? você é casado/casada? [vosay eh]

mascara o rímel [reemil]

match (football etc) o jogo [Johgoo]

matches os fósforos [foshfooroosh]

material (fabric) o tecido [tiseedoo]

matter: it doesn't matter não faz mal [nowng faJ mal]

what's the matter? o que se passa? [oo ki si]

mattress o colchão [koolshowng]

May Maio [mī-oo]

may: may I have another one? (different one) pode dar-me outro/outra? [pod darmi ohtroo]

may I come in? posso entrar? [poswayntrar]

may I see it? posso vê-lo/vê-la? [posoo vayloo/vayla]

may I sit here? posso sentar-me aqui? [posoo sayntarm akee]

maybe talvez [talvaysh]

mayonnaise a maionese [mī-onehz]

me* mim [meeng]

that's for me isto é para mim [eeshtweh para meeng]

send it to me envie-o/a para

mim [aynvee-yoo]
me too eu também [ay-oo tambayng]
meal a refeição [rifaysowng]

dialogue

did you enjoy your meal?
gostou da comida?
[gooshtoh da koomeeda]
it was excellent, thank you
(said by man/woman) estava
excelente, obrigado/
obrigada [shtava ish-selaynt
obrigadoo]

mean: what do you mean?
o que quer dizer? [oo ki kehr dizayr]

dialogue

what does this word
mean? o que significa esta
palavra? [oo ki signifeeka ehshta]
it means ... in English
significa ... em inglês [ayng inglaysh]

measles o sarampo [sarampoo]
meat a carne [karn]
mechanic o mecânico [mekanikoo]
medicine o remédio [rimehd-yoo]
Mediterranean o
Mediterrâneo [miditirran-yoo]
medium médio [mehd-yoo]

medium-dry meio seco [may-oo saykoo]
medium-rare médio [mehd-yoo]
medium-sized de tamanho médio [di taman-yoo]
meet encontrar [aynkontrar]
nice to meet you muito prazer [mweengtoo prazayr]
where shall I meet you?
onde nos encontramos? [ohnd noozaynkontramoosh]
meeting a reunião [r-yoon-yowng]
meeting place o local de encontro [lookal daynkohntroo]
melon o melão [milowng]
men os homens [ohmayngsh]
mend consertar [konsirtar]
could you mend this for me?
pode consertar-me isto? [pod konsirtarm eeshtoo]
menswear a roupa de homens [rohpa dohmayngsh]
mention mencionar [maynsyoonar]
don't mention it não tem de quê [nowng tayng di kay]
menu a ementa [emaynta]
may I see the menu, please?
posso ver a ementa, faz favor [posoo vayr īmaynta fash favohr]
see menu reader page 214
message o recado [rikadoo]
are there any messages for me? há algum recado para mim? [a algoong – meeng]
I want to leave a message for ... gostava de deixar um

Me

recado para ... [gooshtava di dayshar oong]
metal o metal [mital]
metre* o metro [mehtroo]
microwave (oven) microondas [mikroo-**oh**ndash]
midday o meio-dia [**may**-oo **dee**-a]
at midday ao meio-dia [ow]
middle: in the middle no meio [noo **may**-oo]
in the middle of the night no meio da noite [**noh**-it]
the middle one o/a do meio [**oo**/a doo]
midnight a meia-noite [**may**-a **noh**-it]
at midnight à meia-noite
might: I might go pode ser que eu vá [pod sayr ki-**ay**-oo]
I might not go pode ser que eu não vá [nowng]
I might want to stay another day sou capaz de querer ficar mais um dia [soh kapaʒ di kirayr fikar mish oong **dee**-a]
migraine a enxaqueca [aynshak**ay**ka]
mild (taste) suave [swav] (weather) ameno [am**ay**noo]
mile* a milha [**meel**-ya]
milk o leite [layt]
milkshake o batido [bat**ee**doo]
millimetre* o milímetro [mil**ee**mitroo]
minced meat a carne picada [karn pikada]
mind: never mind não faz mal [nowng faʒ mal]

I've changed my mind mudei de ideias [mood**ay** did**ay**-yash]

dialogue

do you mind if I open the window? importa-se se abrir a janela? [imp**o**rtasi s-yabr**ee**r a ʒan**eh**la]
no, I don't mind não, não me importo [nowng nowng mimp**o**rtoo]

mine*: it's mine é meu [eh m**ay**-oo]
mineral water a água mineral [**a**gwa]
mints as pastilhas de mentol [pasht**ee**l-yaʒ di]
minute o minuto [min**oo**too]
in a minute dentro de um momento [**day**ntroo doong moom**ay**ntoo]
just a minute um momento [oong]
mirror o espelho [shp**ay**l-yoo]
Miss a Senhora [sin-**yo**ra]
Miss! se faz favor! [si fash fav**oh**r]
miss: I missed the bus perdi o autocarro [pird**ee** oo-owtook**a**rro]
missing falta
there's a suitcase missing falta uma mala [**oo**ma]
mist a névoa [**neh**vwa]
mistake o erro [**ay**rroo]
I think there's a mistake julgo que há um erro [ʒ**oo**lgoo k-ya oong]

sorry, I've made a mistake desculpe, enganei-me [dishkoolp aynganaym]

misunderstanding o mal-entendido [malayntayndeedoo]

mix-up: sorry, there's been a mix-up desculpe, houve uma confusão [ohvooma konfoozowng]

mobile phone o telemóvel [telemovil]

modern moderno [moodehrnoo]

modern art gallery a galeria de arte moderna [galiree-a dart moodehrna]

moisturizer o creme hidratante [kraymeedratant]

moment: I won't be a moment não demoro nada [nowng dimoroo]

monastery o mosteiro [mooshtayroo]

Monday segunda-feira [segoonda fayra]

money o dinheiro [deen-yayroo]

month o mês [maysh]

monument o monumento [moonoomayntoo]

moon a lua [loo-a]

Moor o mouro [moh-ooroo]

Moorish mourisco [moreeshkoo]

moped a motorizada [mootoorizada]

more* mais [mīsh]

can I have some more water, please? mais água, por favor [mīz agwa poor favohr]

more expensive mais caro [maīsh karoo]

more interesting mais interessante [mīzintrisant]

more than 50 mais de cinquenta [mīz di sinkwaynta]

more than that mais do que isso [mīz doo ki eesoo]

a lot more muito mais [mweengtoo mīsh]

dialogue

would you like some more? deseja um pouco mais? [disayJa oong pohkoo mīsh]

no, no more for me, thanks (said by man/woman) não, não mais para mim, obrigado/obrigada [nowng – meeng obrigadoo]

how about you? e você? [ee vosay]

I don't want any more, thanks (said by man/woman) não quero mais, obrigado/obrigada [nowng kehroo mīsh]

morning a manhã [man-yang]

this morning esta manhã [ehshta]

in the morning de manhã [di]

Morocco o Marrocos [marrokoosh]

mosquito o mosquito [mooshkeetoo]

mosquito repellent o repele-mosquitos [ripehl mooshkeetoosh] most: I like this one most of all gosto mais deste [goshtoo mīj daysht]

most of the time a maior parte do tempo [a mī-or part doo taympoo]

most tourists a maioria dos turistas [mī-ooree-a doosh tooreeshtash]

mostly principalmente [prinsipalmaynt]

mother a mãe [mayng]

motorbike a motocicleta [mootoosiklehta]

motorboat o barco a motor [barkwa mootohr]

motorway a autoestrada [owtooshtrada]

mountain a montanha [montan-ya]

in the mountains nas montanhas [naj montan-yash]

mountaineering o alpinismo [alpineejmoo]

mouse o rato [ratoo]

moustache o bigode [bigod]

mouth a boca [bohka]

mouth ulcer a afta

move (one's car, house etc) mudar [moodar]

he's moved to another room mudou-se para outra sala [moodohsi para ohtra]

could you move your car? podia mudar o seu carro? [poodee-a]

could you move up a little? pode chegar um pouquinho para lá? [pod shigar oong pohkeen-yoo]

where has it moved to? para onde se mudou? [ohndsi moodoh]

movie o filme [feelm]

movie theater o cinema [sinayma]

Mr o Senhor [sin-yohr]

Mrs a Senhora [sin-yora]

much muito [mweengtoo]

much better/worse muito melhor/pior [mil-yor/pi-or]

much hotter muito mais quente [mīsh kaynt]

not (very) much não muito [nowng]

I don't want very much não quero muito [kehroo]

mud a lama

mug (for drinking) a caneca [kanehka]

I've been mugged (said by man/woman) fui assaltado/assaltada [fwee asaltadoo]

mum a mamã [mamang]

mumps a papeira [papayra]

museum o museu [moozay-oo]

mushrooms os cogumelos [kogoomehloosh]

music a música [moozika]

musician (man) o músico [moozikoo]

Muslim (adj) muçulmano [moosoolmanoo]

mussels os mexilhões [mishil-yoyngsh]

must: I must ... tenho de ... [tayn-yoo di]

I mustn't drink alcohol não

devo beber álcool [nowng dayvoo bibayr alko-ol]
mustard a mostarda [mooshtarda]
my* o meu [may-oo], a minha [meen-ya], os meus [may-oosh], as minhas [meen-yash]
myself: I'll do it myself (said by man/woman) eu mesmo/mesma faço isso [ay-oo mayɹmoo – fasoo eesoo]
by myself (said by man/woman) sozinho [sozeen-yoo]/sozinha

N

nail (finger) a unha [oon-ya]
(metal) o prego [prehgoo]
nailbrush a escova de unhas [shkohva doon-yash]
nail varnish o verniz de unhas [virneeɹ doon-yash]
name o nome [nohm]
my name's John o meu nome é John [oo may-oo nohm eh]
what's your name? como se chama? [kohmoo si shama]
what is the name of this street? qual é o nome desta rua? [kawleh oo nohm dehshta roo-a]
napkin o guardanapo [gwardanapoo]
nappy a fralda
narrow (street) estreito [shtraytoo]
nasty (person) mau [mow], (f) má (weather, accident) grave [grav]

national nacional [nas-yoonal]
nationality a nacionalidade [nas-yoonalidad]
natural natural [natooral]
nausea as náuseas [nowz-yash]
navy (blue) azul-marinho [azool mareen-yoo]
near perto [pehrtoo]
is it near the city centre? é perto do centro da cidade? [eh – doo sayntroo da sidad]
do you go near the Paço Real? passa perto do Passo Real? [pehrtoo doo pasoo ri-al]
where is the nearest ...? onde fica o/a ... mais próximo/próxima ...? [ohnd feeka oo/a ... mish prosimoo]
nearby perto daqui [pehrtoo dakee]
nearly quase [kwaz]
necessary necessário [nisisar-yoo]
neck o pescoço [pishkohsoo]
necklace o colar [koolar]
necktie a gravata
need: I need ... preciso de ... [priseezoo di]
do I need to pay? preciso de pagar?
needle a agulha [agool-ya]
negative (film) o negativo [nigateevoo]
neither: neither (one) of them nenhum deles [nin-yoong daylish]
neither ... nor ... nem ... nem ... [nayng]

nephew o sobrinho [soobreen-yoo]

net (in sport) a rede [rayd]

Netherlands a Holanda [olanda]

network map o mapa

never nunca [noonka]

dialogue

have you ever been to Fátima? já esteve em Fátima? [Jashtayvayng]

no, never, I've never been there não, nunca estive lá [nowng noonkshteev la]

new novo [nohvoo]

news (radio, TV etc) as notícias [nootees-yash]

newsagent's a tabacaria [tabakaree-a]

newspaper o jornal [Joornal]

newspaper kiosk o quiosque de jornais [k-yoshk di Joornish]

New Year Ano Novo [anoo nohvoo]

Happy New Year! Feliz Ano Novo! [fileez anoo nohvoo]

New Year's Eve a véspera do dia de Ano Novo [vehshpira doo dee-a danoo]

New Zealand Nova Zelândia [nova ziland-ya]

New Zealander: I'm a New Zealander (man/woman) sou neo-zelandês/neo-zelandesa [soh neh-o zilandaysh/neh-o zilandayza]

next próximo [prosimoo]

the next corner/street on the left a próxima esquina/rua à esquerda [shkeena/roo-a a shkayrda]

at the next stop na próxima paragem [paraJayng]

next week na próxima semana [simana]

next to próximo de [di]

nice (food, person) agradável (looks, view etc) bonito [booneetoo]

niece a sobrinha [soobreen-ya]

night a noite [noh-it]

at night à noite

good night boa noite [boh-a]

dialogue

do you have a single room for one night? tem um quarto individual para uma noite? [tayn-yoong kwartwindividwal para ooma]

yes, madam sim, senhora [seeng sin-yora]

how much is it per night? quanto é por noite? [kwantweh poor]

it's 35 euros for one night são trinta e cinco euros por uma noite [sowng treentī-seenkoo ay-ooroosh poor ooma]

thank you, I'll take it (said by man/woman) obrigado/obrigada, fico com ele [obrigadoo – feekoo kong ayl] nightclub a boite [bwat]

nightdress a camisa de dormir [kameeza di doormeer]

night porter o porteiro da noite [poortayroo da noh-it]

no* não [nowng]

I've no change não tenho troco [tayn-yoo trohkoo]

there's no ... left não há mais ... [a mīsh]

no way! de maneira nenhuma! [di manayra nin-yooma]

oh no! (upset) oh não! [nowng]

nobody* ninguém [ningayng]

there's nobody there não há ninguém lá [nowng a – la]

noise o barulho [barool-yoo]

noisy: it's too noisy é barulhento demais [eh barool-yayntoo dimīsh]

non-alcoholic não alcoólico [nowng alkwolikoo]

none* nenhum [nin-yoong]

nonsmoking carriage a carruagem para não fumadores [karrwaJayng – nowng foomadohrish]

noon o meio-dia [may-oo dee-a]

no-one* ninguém [ningayng]

nor: nor do I nem eu [nayng ay-oo]

normal normal

north o norte [nort]

in the north no norte [noo]

to the north ao norte [ow]

north of Braga ao norte de Braga [di]

northeast o nordeste [noordehsht]

northern setentrional [setayntr-yoonal]

Northern Ireland a Irlanda do Norte [eerlanda doo nort]

northwest o noroeste [norwehsht]

Norway a Noruega [noorwehga]

Norwegian (adj) norueguês [noorwegaysh]

nose o nariz [nareesh]

nosebleed a hemorragia nasal [emoorraJee-ya nazal]

not* não [nowng]

no, I'm not hungry não, não tenho fome [tayn-yoo fohm]

I don't want anything, thank you (said by man/woman) não quero nada, obrigado/obrigada [kehr oo – obrigadoo]

it's not necessary não é necessário [eh nesesar-yoo]

I didn't know that não sabia [sabee-a]

not that one – this one esse não – este [ays – aysht]

note (banknote) a nota

notebook o bloco de apontamentos [blokoo dapontamayntoosh]

notepaper (for letters) o papel de carta [papehl di]

nothing* nada

nothing for me, thanks (said by man/woman) nada para mim, obrigado/obrigada [meeng obrigadoo]

nothing else mais nada [mīJ]

novel o romance [roomans]

November Novembro
[noovaymbroo]

now agora

number o número [noomiroo]

I've got the wrong number
enganei-me no número
[aynganaym noo]

what is your phone number?
qual é o número do seu
telefone? [kwaleh oo – doo say-
oo telefohn]

number plate a chapa
da matrícula [shapa da
matreekoola]

nurse (man/woman) o
enfermeiro [aynfermayroo], a
enfermeira

nut (for bolt) a porca

nuts a noz [nosh]

O

occupied (toilet, telephone)
ocupado [okoopadoo]

o'clock* horas [orash]

October Outubro [ohtoobroo]

odd (strange) estranho [shtran-
yoo]

of* de [di]

off (lights) desligado [diJligadoo]

it's just off Praça do
Comércio mesmo ao lado da
Praça do Comércio [meJmoo
ow ladoo da prasa doo koomehrs-
yoo]

we're off tomorrow partimos
amanhã [parteemoozaman-yang]

offensive (language, behaviour)
ofensivo [ofaynseevoo]

office (place of work) o escritório
[shkritor-yoo]

officer (said to policeman) Senhor
Guarda [sin-yohr gwarda]

often muitas vezes [mweengtaJ
vayzish]

not often não muitas vezes
[nowng]

how often are the buses?
com que frequência há
autocarros? [kong ki frikwaynsya
a owtookarroosh]

oil (for car, for cooking) o óleo
[ol-yoo]

ointment a pomada
[poomada]

OK está bem [shta bayng]

are you OK? você está bem?
[vosay shta bayng]

is that OK with you? está bem
para si? [see]

is it OK to ...? pode-se ...?
[podsi]

that's OK thanks (said by man/
woman) está bem obrigado/
obrigada [obrigadoo]

I'm OK, thanks (I've got enough)
não quero, obrigado/
obrigada [nowng kehro]

(I feel OK) sinto-me bem
[seentoom]

is this train OK for ...? este
comboio vai para ... [aysht
kombohyoo vi]

I'm sorry, OK? desculpe-me,
está bem? [dishkoolpimi]

old velho [vehl-yoo]

dialogue

how old are you? que idade tem? [keedad tayng]
I'm 25 tenho vinte-e-cinco anos [tayn-yoo veentiseenkoo]
and you? e você? [ee vosay]

old-fashioned antiquado [antikwadoo]
old town (old part of town) a cidade antiga [sidad anteega]
  in the old town na cidade antiga
olive oil o azeite [azayt]
olives a azeitona [azaytohna]
  black/green olives as azeitonas pretas/verdes [azaytohnash praytash/vayrdsh]
omelette a omeleta [omilayta]
on* sobre [sohbr]
  on the street/beach na praia/rua
  is it on this road? é nesta rua? [eh nehshta]
  on the plane no avião [nwav-yowng]
  on Saturday no sábado [noo]
  on television na televisão
  I haven't got it on me não o tenho comigo [nowng oo tayn-yoo koomeegoo]
  this one's on me (drink) esta bebida sou eu que pago [ehshta bibeeda soh ay-oo kih pagoo]
  the light wasn't on a luz não estava acesa [looj nowng shtava asayza]

what's on tonight? qual é o programa para esta noite? [kwaleh oo proograma parehshta noh-it]
once (one time) uma vez [ooma vaysh]
  at once (immediately) imediatamente [imid-yatamaynt]
one* um [oong], uma [ooma]
  the white one o/a branco/branca [oo/a brankoo]
one-way ticket o bilhete simples [bil-yayt seemplish]
onion a cebola [sibohla]
only só [saw], somente [somaynt]
  only one só um/uma [oong/ooma]
  it's only 6 o'clock ainda são só seis horas [a-eenda sowng saw sayz orash]
  I've only just got here acabei de chegar [akabay di shigar]
on/off switch o interruptor de ligar/desligar [intirrooptohr di ligar/diJligar]
open* (adj) aberto [abehrtoo] (verb) abrir [abreer]
  when do you open? quando abre? [kwandwabr]
  I can't get it open não consigo abrir [nowng konseegwabreer]
  in the open air ao ar livre [ow ar leevr]
opening times as horas de abertura [orash dabirtoora]
open ticket o bilhete em

aberto [bil-**yay**tayng a**beh**rtoo]

opera a ópera [**o**pira]

operation (medical) a operação [opira**sowng**]

operator (telephone: man/woman) o/a telefonista [telefoo**nee**shta]

opposite: the opposite direction na direcção oposta [direh**sow**ng o**posh**ta]

the bar opposite o bar do outro lado [doo **oh**troo la**doo**]

opposite my hotel em frente ao meu hotel [ayng fraynt ow]

optician o oculista [okoo**lee**shta]

or ou [oh]

orange (fruit) a laranja [la**ran**ja]

(colour) cor de laranja [kohr di]

orange juice (fresh) o sumo de laranja [**soo**moo]

(fizzy) a laranjada com gás [laran**ja**da kong**ash**]

(diluted) o refresco de laranja [rifr**ay**shkoo di]

orchestra a orquestra [or**keh**shtra]

order: can we order now? (in restaurant) podemos pedir agora? [poo**day**moosh pi**deer**]

I've already ordered, thanks (said by man/woman) já pedi, obrigado/obrigada [ja pi**dee** obri**ga**doo]

I didn't order this não pedi isto [nowng – **ee**shtoo]

out of order avariado [avar-**ya**doo]

ordinary vulgar [vool**gar**]

other outro [**oh**troo]

the other one o outro [oo]

the other day outro dia [**dee**-a]

I'm waiting for the others estou a esperar outras pessoas [stoh a shpi**rar oh**trash pi**soh**-ash]

do you have any others? tem mais algum/alguma? [tayng mīsh al**goo**ng/al**goo**ma]

otherwise doutro modo [**doh**troo **mo**doo]

our* nosso [**no**soo], nossa [**no**sa], nossos [**no**soosh], nossas [**no**sash]

ours* nosso, nossa, nossos, nossas

out: he's out saiu [sa **oo**-oo]

three kilometres out of town a três quilómetros da cidade [traysh ki**lo**mitrooj da si**dad**]

outdoors fora de casa [di **ka**za]

outside do lado de fora [doo la**doo** di]

can we sit outside? podemos sentar-nos lá fora? [poo**day**moosh sayn**tar**noosh]

oven o forno [**foh**rnoo]

over: over here aqui [a**kee**]

over there ali [a**lee**]

over five hundred mais de quinhentos/quinhentas [mīsh di]

it's over terminado [tirmi**na**doo]

overcharge: you've overcharged me você vendeu-me mais caro [vo**say** ven**day**-oomi mīsh ka**roo**]

overcoat o sobretudo [soobri**too**doo]

overlooking: I'd like a room

overlooking the courtyard
queria um quarto que dê para
o pátio [kiree-a oong kwartoo ki
day paroo pat-yoo]

overnight (travel) de noite [di
noh-it]

overtake ultrapassar
[ooltrapasar]

owe: how much do I owe you?
quanto lhe devo? [kwantoo l-yi
dayvoo]

own: my own ... o meu
próprio ... [oo may-oo propr-yoo]
are you on your own? (to man/
woman) está sozinho/sozinha?
[shta sawzeen-yoo]
I'm on my own (said by man/
woman) estou sozinho/sozinha
[shtoh]

owner (man/woman) o dono
[dohnoo], a dona

oysters as ostras [ohshtrash]

P

pack fazer as malas [fazayr aJ
malash]
a pack of ... um pacote de ...
[oong pakot di]

package (parcel) a encomenda
[aynkoomaynda]

package holiday a excursão
organizada [shkoorsowng
organizada]

packed lunch o almoço
embalado [almohsw-
aymbaladoo]

packet: a packet of cigarettes
o maço de cigarros [masoo di
sigarroosh]

padlock o cadeado [kad-yadoo]

page (of book) a página [paJina]
could you page Mr ...? pode
chamar o Sr ...? [pod shamar oo
sin-yohr]

pain a dor [dohr]
I have a pain here tenho uma
dor aqui [tayn-yoo ooma dohr
akee]

painful doloroso [dooloorohzoo]

painkillers os analgésicos
[analJehzikoosh]

paint a tinta [teenta]

painting a pintura [pintoora]

pair: a pair of ... um par de ...
[oong di]

Pakistani (adj) paquistanês
[pakishtanaysh]

palace o palácio [palas-yoo]

pale pálido [palidoo]
pale blue azul claro [azool
klaroo]

pan a panela [panehla]

panties as cuecas [kwehkash]

pants (underwear) as cuecas
[kwehkash]
(US) as calças [kalsash]

pantyhose os collants
[koolansh]

paper o papel [papehl]
(newspaper) o jornal [Joornal]
a sheet of paper uma folha
de papel [ooma fohlya di]

paper handkerchiefs os lenços
de papel [laynsoosh]

paragliding o parapentismo
[parapaynteeJmoo]

parcel a encomenda [aynkoomaynda]

pardon (me)? (didn't understand/hear) desculpe? [dishkoolp], como? [kohmoo]

parents os pais [pīsh]

parents-in-law os sogros [sohgroosh]

park o jardim público [Jardeeng pooblikoo]

(verb) estacionar [shtas-yoonar]

can I park here? posso estacionar aqui? [posoo – akee]

parking lot o parque de estacionamento [park di shtas-yoonamayntoo]

part a parte [part]

partner (boyfriend/girlfriend) o companheiro [kompan-yayroo], a companheira

party (group) o grupo [groopoo] (celebration) a festa [fehshta]

pass (in mountains) o desfiladeiro [dishfiladayroo]

passenger (man/woman) o passageiro [pasaJayroo], a passageira

passport o passaporte [pasaport]

past*: in the past no passado [noo pasadoo]

just past the information office logo a seguir ao escritório de informações [logoo a sigeer owshkritor-yoo dinfoormasoyngsh]

path o caminho [kameen-yoo]

pattern o desenho [dizayn-yoo]

pavement o passeio [pasay-oo]

on the pavement no passeio [noo]

pavement café o café de esplanada [kafeh dishplanada]

pay pagar

can I pay, please? por favor, queria pagar [poor favohr kiree-a]

it's already paid for já está pago [Ja shta pagoo]

dialogue

who's paying? quem vai pagar? [kayng vī]
I'll pay eu pago [ay-oo pagoo]
no, you paid last time, I'll pay não, você pagou da última vez, eu pago [nowng vosay pagoh da-ooltima vaysh]

pay phone o telefone público [telefohn pooblikoo]

peaceful tranquilo [trankweeloo]

peach o pêssego [paysigoo]

peanuts os amendoins [amayndweensh]

pear a pêra [payra]

peas as ervilhas [irveel-yash]

peculiar (taste, custom) estranho [shtran-yoo]

pedestrian crossing o passagem de peões [pasaJayng di p-yoyngsh], a pasadeira de peões [pasadayra]

pedestrian precinct a zona para peões [zohna para p-yoyngsh]

peg (for washing) a mola
(for tent) a cavilha [kaveel-ya]
pen a caneta [kanayta]
pencil o lápis [lapsh]
penfriend (man/woman)
o/a correspondente
[koorrishpondaynt]
penicillin a penicilina
[penisileena]
penknife o canivete [kaniveht]
pensioner (man/woman) o
reformado [rifoormadoo], a
reformada
people a gente [Jaynt]
the other people in the hotel
as outras pessoas no hotel
[azohtrash pisoh-ash nwohtehl]
too many people gente
demais [dimish]
pepper (spice) a pimenta
[pimaynta]
(vegetable) o pimento
[pimayntoo]
peppermint (sweet) a hortelã-
pimenta [ortilang pimaynta]
per: per night por noite [poor
noh-it]
how much per day? quanto é
por dia? [kwantweh poor dee-a]
per cent por cento [sayntoo]
perfect perfeito [pirfaytoo]
perfume o perfume [pirfoom]
perhaps talvez [talvaysh]
perhaps not talvez não
[nowng]
period (of time, menstruation) o
período [piree-oodoo]
perm a permanente
[pirmanaynt]

permit a licença [lisaynsa]
person a pessoa [pisoh-a]
personal stereo o Walkman®
petrol a gasolina [gazooleena]
petrol can a lata de gasolina [di
gazooleena]
petrol station a bomba de
gasolina [bohmba di]
pharmacy a farmácia [farmas-
ya]
phone o telefone [telefohn]
(verb) telefonar [telefoonar]
phone book a lista telefónica
[leeshta telefohnika]
phone box a cabina telefónica
[kabeena]
phonecard o cartão de
telefone [kartowng di telefohn]
phone number o número de
telefone [noomiroo]
photo a fotografia [footoografee-
a]
excuse me, could you take a
photo of us? faz favor, pode
tirar-nos uma fotografia?
[fash favohr pod tirarnooz ooma]
phrasebook o livro
de expressões [leevroo
dishprisoyngsh]
piano o piano [p-yanoo]
pickpocket (man/woman) o/a
carteirista [kartayreeshta]
pick up: will you be there to
pick me up? estarás lá para
apanhar-me? [shtaraJ – apan-
yarmi]
picnic o piquenique [pikineek]
picture (drawing, painting) a
pintura [peentoora]

(photograph) a fotografia [footoografee a]

pie a tarte [tart]

piece o pedaço [pidasoo]
a piece of ... um bocado de ... [oong bookadoo di]

pilchards as sardinhas [sardeen-yash]

pill a pílula [peeloola]
I'm on the pill estou a tomar a pílula [shtoh a toomar]

pillow a almofada [almoofada]

pillow case a fronha da almofada [frohn-ya]

pin o alfinete [alfinayt]

pineapple o ananás [ananash]

pineapple juice o sumo de ananás [soomoo dananash]

pink cor de rosa [kohr di roza]

pipe (for smoking) o cachimbo [kasheemboo]
(for water) o cano [kanoo]

pipe cleaner o desentupidor de cachimbo [dizayntoopidohr di kasheemboo]

pity: it's a pity é uma pena [eh ooma payna]

pizza a pizza

place o lugar [loogar]
at your place na sua casa [soo-a kaza]
at his place na casa dele [dayl]

plain (not patterned) liso [leezoo]

plane o avião [av-yowng]
by plane de avião [dav-yowng]

plant a planta

plaster cast o gesso [Jaysoo]

plasters o adesivo [adizeevoo]

plastic o plástico [plashtikoo]

plastic bag o saco de plástico [sakoo di]

plate o prato [pratoo]

platform o cais [kish]
which platform is it for Fátima? qual é o cais para Fátima? [kwaleh oo]

play (verb) jogar [Joogar]
(in theatre) a peça de teatro [pehsa di t-yatroo]

playground o pátio de recreio [pat-yoo di rikray-oo]

pleasant agradável

please se faz favor [si fash favohr], por favor [poor]
yes please sim, por favor [seeng]
could you please ...? por favor, pode ...? [pod]
please don't por favor, não faça isto [nowng fasa eeshtoo]

pleased: pleased to meet you (said to man/woman) muito prazer em conhecê-lo/ conhecê-la [mweengtoo prazayr ayng koon-yisayloo]

pleasure: my pleasure de nada [di]

plenty: plenty of ... muito ... [mweengtoo]
there's plenty of time temos muito tempo [taymooJ – taympoo]
that's plenty, thanks (said by man/woman) chega, obrigado/ obrigada [shayga obrigadoo]

pliers o alicate [alikat]

plug (electrical) a tomada [toomada]

(for car) a vela [**veh**la]

(in sink) a tampa do ralo [doo **ra**loo]

plumber o canalizador [kanaliza**dohr**]

p.m.* da tarde [tard]

poached egg o ovo escalfado [**oh**voo shkal**fa**doo]

pocket o bolso [oo **boh**lsoo]

point: two point five dois virgula cinco [**doh**-ij **veer**goola **seen**koo]

there's no point não vale a pena [nowng **val**-ya **payn**a]

points (in car) os platinados [platin**a**doosh]

poisonous venenoso [vinin**oh**zoo]

police a polícia [pool**ees**-ya]

call the police! chamem a polícia! [**sha**mayng]

policeman o polícia [oo pool**ees**-ya]

police station o Posto da Polícia [**poh**shtoo]

policewoman a mulher-polícia [mool-**yehr**]

polish (for shoes) a pomada para calçados [poo**ma**da para kal**sa**doosh]

polite bem-educado [bayng idooka**do**]

polluted contaminado [kontamin**a**doo]

pony o pónei [**po**nay]

pool (for swimming) a piscina [pish-**see**na]

poor (not rich) pobre [**pobr**]

(quality) mau [mow], (f) má

pop music a música pop [**moo**zika]

pop singer (man/woman) o cantor pop [kan**tohr**], a cant**o**ra pop

popular popular [poopoo**lar**]

population a população [poopoolas**owng**]

pork a carne de porco [karn di **pohr**koo]

port (for boats) o porto [**pohr**too]

(drink) o vinho do Porto [veen-yoo doo]

porter (in hotel) o porteiro [poor**tay**roo]

portrait o retrato [ri**tra**too]

Portugal Portugal [poor**to**gal]

Portuguese (adj) português [poortoo**gaysh**]

(language) português

(man) o português

(woman) a portuguesa

the Portuguese os portugueses [poortoo**gay**zish]

posh (restaurant, people) chique [sheek]

possible possível [poo**see**vil]

is it possible to ...? é possível ...? [eh]

as ... as possible tão ... quanto possível [**towng** ... **kwan**too]

post (mail) o correio [koor**ray**-oo]

(verb) pôr no correio [pohr noo]

could you post this for me? podia-me pôr isto no correio? [poo**dee**-ami – **ee**shtoo noo] postbox a caixa do correio [kīsha doo]

postcard o postal [pooshtal]

postcode o código postal [kudigoo pooshtal]

poster (for room) o poster (in street) o cartaz [kartash]

poste restante a posta-restante [poshta rishtant]

post office os correios [koorray-oosh]

potato a batata

potato chips as batatas fritas [batatash freetash]

pots and pans as panelas e tachos [panehlazee tashoosh]

pottery (objects) a loiça de barro [loh-isa di barroo]

pound* (money, weight) a libra [leebra]

power cut o corte de energia [kort denirJee-a]

power point a tomada [toomada]

practise: I want to practise my Portuguese quero praticar o meu português [kehroo pratikaroo may-oo poortoogaysh]

prawn a gamba

prefer: I prefer ... prefiro ... [prifeeroo]

pregnant grávida

prescription (for medicine) a receita [risayta]

present (gift) o presente [prizaynt]

president (of country: man/woman) o/a presidente [prizidaynt]

pretty bonito [booneetoo]

it's pretty expensive é muito caro [mweengtoo karoo]

price o preço [praysoo]

priest o padre [padr]

prime minister (man/woman) o primeiro ministro [primayroo mineeshtroo], a primeira ministra

printed matter os impressos [imprehsoosh]

priority (in driving) a prioridade [pr-vooridad]

prison a cadeia [kaday-a]

private privado [privadoo]

private bathroom a casa de banho privativa [kaza di ban-yoo privateeva]

probably provavelmente [proovavilmaynt]

problem o problema [prooblayma]

no problem! tudo bem! [toodoo bayng]

program(me) o programa [proograma]

promise: I promise prometo [proomaytoo]

pronounce: how is this pronounced? como se pronuncia? [kohmoo si proonoonsee-a]

properly (repaired, locked etc) bem [bayng]

protection factor (of suntan lotion) o factor de protecção [fatohr di prootehsowng]

Protestant protestante [prootishtant]

public convenience a casa de banho pública [kaza di ban-yoo pooblika]

public holiday o feriado [fir-yadoo]

pudding (dessert) a sobremesa [sobrimayza]

pull puxar [pooshar]

pullover o pullover

puncture o furo [fooroo]

purple roxo [rohshoo]

purse (for money) a carteira [kartayra]
(US) a mala de mão [di]

push empurrar [aympoorrar]

pushchair o carrinho de bebé [karreen-yoo di bebeh]

put* pôr [pohr]
where can I put ...? onde posso pôr ...? [ohnd posoo]
could you put us up for the night? pode dar-nos acomodação para uma noite? [pod darnooz akoomoodasowng para ooma]

pyjamas o pijama [piJama]

Q

quality a qualidade [kwalidad]

quarantine a quarentena [kwarayntayna]

quarter a quarta parte [kwarta part]

quayside: on the quayside no cais [noo kish]

question a pergunta [pirgoonta]

queue a bicha [beesha]

quick rápido [rapidoo]
that was quick! que rápido que foi! [ki – foh-i]
what's the quickest way there? qual é o caminho mais rápido para lá? [kwaleh oo kameen-yoo mish rapidoo]

quickly depressa [diprehsa]

quiet (place, hotel) silencioso [silayns-yohzoo]
quiet! cale-se! [kalsi]

quite (fairly) bastante [bashtant]
(very) muito [mweengtoo]
that's quite right está certo [shta sehrtoo]
quite a lot bastante

R

rabbit o coelho [kwayl-yoo]

race (for runners, cars) a corrida [koorreeda]

racket (tennis, squash) a raqueta [rakehta]

radiator (of car, in room) o radiador [rad-yadohr]

radio o rádio [rad-yoo]
on the radio no rádio [noo]

rail: by rail por caminho de ferro [poor kameen-yoo di fehrroo]

railway o caminho de ferro

rain a chuva [shoova]
in the rain à chuva
it's raining está a chover [shta-a shoovayr]

raincoat o impermeável [impirm-yavil]

rape a violação [v-yoolas**owng**]

rare (uncommon) raro [**rar**oo]
(steak) mal passado [pasadoo]

rash (on skin) a erupção [eroopsowng]

raspberry a framboesa [framb**way**za]

rat a ratazana

rate (for changing money) o câmbio [**kamb**-yoo]

rather: it's rather good é bastante bom/boa [eh bash**tant** **bong**/**boh**-a]
I'd rather ... prefiro ... [prif**ee**roo]

razor (electric) a máquina de barbear [**mak**ina di barb-**yar**]

razor blades as lâminas para barbear [**lam**inash]

read ler [layr]

ready pronto [pr**oh**ntoo]
are you ready? (said to man/woman) estás pronto/pronta? [shtash pr**oh**ntoo]
I'm not ready yet (said by man/woman) ainda não estou pronto/pronta [a-**ee**nda nowng shtoh]

dialogue

when will it be ready?
quando estará pronto?
[kwandoo sht**ara**]
it should be ready in a couple of days deve ficar pronto em dois dias [dehv fikar – ayng d**oh**-iJ d**ee**-ash]

real verdadeiro [virdad**ay**roo]

really realmente [r-yalm**aynt**]
I'm really sorry lamento imenso [lam**aynt**oo im**ay**nsoo]
that's really great isso é fantástico [**ee**sweh fanta**sh**tikoo]
really? (doubt) de verdade? [di virdad]
(polite interest) sim? [seeng]

rear lights as luzes de trás [**loo**zish di trash]

rearview mirror o espelho retrovisor [shp**ay**l-yoo ritroovi**zohr**]

reasonable (prices etc) razoável [razw**av**il]

receipt o recibo [ris**ee**boo]

recently há pouco [a p**oh**koo]

reception (in hotel, for guests) a recepção [risehs**owng**]
at reception na recepção

reception desk o balcão da recepção [balk**owng**]

receptionist (man/woman) o/a recepcionista [risehs-yoon**ee**shta]

recognize reconhecer [rikoon-yis**ayr**]

recommend: could you recommend ...? podia recomendar ...? [pood**ee**-a rikoomaynd**ar**]

record (music) o disco [**dee**shkoo]

red vermelho [virm**ay**l-yoo]

red wine o vinho tinto [**veen**-yoo t**ee**ntoo]

refund o reembolso [ri-aymb**oh**lsoo]
can I have a refund? pode

dar-me o reembolso? [pod darmoo]

region a região [riJ-**yow**ng]

registered: by registered mail por correio registado [poor koor**ray**-oo riJishtadoo]

registration number a matrícula [matr**eek**oola]

relative (noun: male/female) o/a parente [par**aynt**]

religion a religião [riliJ-**yow**ng]

remember: I remember lembro-me [**lay**mbroomi] I don't remember não me lembro [**now**ng mi **lay**mbroo] do you remember? lembra-se? [**lay**mbrasi]

rent (noun: for apartment etc) o aluguer [aloog**ehr**] (verb: car etc) alugar to rent para alugar

rented car o carro de aluguer [**karr**oo daloog**ehr**]

repair reparar can you repair this? pode reparar isto? [pod riparar **ee**shtoo]

repeat repetir [ripit**eer**] could you repeat that? podia repetir? [pood**ee**-a]

reservation a reserva [riz**ehr**va] I'd like to make a reservation queria fazer uma reserva [kir**ee**-a faz**ayr oo**ma]

dialogue

I have a reservation tenho uma reserva [**tayn**-yoo **oo**ma] yes sir, what name please?

sim senhor, que nome, por favor? [seeng sin-**yohr** ki nohm poor fav**ohr**]

reserve (verb) reservar [rizirvar]

dialogue

can I reserve a table for tonight? posso reservar uma mesa para esta noite? [**po**soo – **oo**ma m**ay**za para **eh**shta n**oh**-it] yes madam, for how many people? sim senhora, para quantas pessoas? [seeng sin-**yo**ra para kwantash pis**oh**-ash] for two para duas [**doo**-ash] and for what time? e para que hora? [i – ki-**o**ra] for eight o'clock para as oito horas [az**oh**-itorash] and could I have your name, please? pode dizer-me o seu nome, por favor? [pod diz**ayr**moo **say**-oo nohm poor fav**ohr**] see alphabet for spelling

rest: I need a rest preciso dum descanso [pris**ee**zoo doong dishk**an**soo] the rest of the group o resto do grupo [**reh**shtoo doo gr**oo**poo]

restaurant o restaurante [rishtowrant]

restaurant car a carruagem restaurante [karrwaJayng rishtowrant]

rest room a casa de banho
[kaza di ban-yoo]
see toilet
retired: I'm retired (said by man/
woman) estou reformado/
reformada [shtoh rifoormadoo]
return: a return to ... um
bilhete de ida e volta a ...
[oong bil-**yayt** deeda ee]
return ticket o bilhete de ida
e volta
see ticket
reverse charge call a chamada
paga no destinatário [shamada
– noo dishtinatar-yoo]
reverse gear a marcha atrás
[marshatrash]
revolting repugnante
[ripoognant]
rib a costela [kooshtehla]
rice o arroz [arrohsh]
rich (person) rico [reekoo]
(food) forte [fort]
ridiculous ridículo [rideekooloo]
right (correct) certo [sehrtoo]
(not left) direito [diraytoo]
you were right tinhas razão
[teen-yaJ razowng]
that's right está certo [shta]
this can't be right isto não
pode estar certo [eeshtoo nowng
pod shtar]
right! está bem! [bayng]
is this the right road for ...?
esta é a estrada certa para ...?
[ehshta eh a shtrada]
on the right à direita [dirayta]
turn right vire à direita [veer]
right-hand drive com volante à

direita [kong voolant]
ring (on finger) o anel [anehl]
I'll ring you eu telefono-lhe
[ay-oo telefohnool-yi]
ring back voltar a telefonar
[telefoonar]
ripe (fruit) maduro [madooroo]
rip-off: it's a rip-off isso é um
roubo [eesoo eh oong rohboo]
rip-off prices os preços
exorbitantes [praysooz
ezoorbitantsh]
risky arriscado [arrishkadoo]
river o rio [ree-oo]
road (in town) a rua [roo-a]
(in country) a estrada [shtrada]
is this the road for ...? é esta a
estrada para ...? [ehshta]
it's just down the road é aqui
perto [eh akee pehrtoo]
road accident o acidente de
viação [asidaynt di v-yasowng]
road map o mapa das estradas
[daz shtradash]
roadsign o sinal
rob: I've been robbed (said by
man/woman) fui roubado/
roubada [fwee rohbadoo]
rock a rocha [rosha]
(music) a música rock [moozika]
on the rocks (with ice) com
gelo [kong Jayloo]
roll (bread) o paposseco
[papoosaykoo]
roof (of house) o telhado [til-
yadoo]
(of car) o tejadilho [tiJadeel-yoo]
roof rack o porta-bagagens no
tejadilho [porta bagaJayngsh]

room o quarto [kwartoo]
 in my room no meu quarto [noo may-oo]
room service o serviço de quartos [sirveesoo di kwartoosh]
rope a corda
rosé (wine) rosé [roozay]
roughly (approximately) aproximadamente [aproosimadamaynt]
round: it's my round é a minha rodada [eh a meen-ya roodada]
roundabout (for traffic) a rotunda [rootoonda]
round trip ticket o bilhete de ida e volta [bil-yayt deeda ee volta] see ticket
route o trajecto [trajehtoo]
 what's the best route? qual é o melhor trajecto? [kwal eh-oo mil-yor]
rubber (material, eraser) a borracha [boorrasha]
rubber band o elástico [ilashtikoo]
rubbish (waste) o lixo [leeshoo] (poor quality goods) o refugo [rifoogoo]
rubbish! (nonsense) que disparate! [ki dishparat]
rucksack a mochila [moosheela]
rude grosseiro [groosayroo]
ruins as ruínas [rweenash]
rum o rum [roong]
 a rum and Coke® uma cuba livre [ooma kooba leevr]
run (verb: person) correr [koorrayr]
 how often do the buses run?

de quanto em quanto tempo há autocarros? [di kwantoo ayng kwantoo taympoo a owtookarroosh]
I've run out of money o meu dinheiro acabou [oo may-oo din-yayroo akaboh]
rush hour a hora de ponta [ora di pohnta]

S

sad triste [treesht]
saddle a sela [sehla]
safe (adj) seguro [sigooroo]
safety pin o alfinete de segurança [alfinayt di sigooransa]
sail a vela [vehla] (verb) velejar [viliJar]
sailboard a prancha de windsurf [pransha di]
sailboarding praticar windsurf [pratikar]
salad a salada
salad dressing o tempero da salada [taympayroo]
sale: for sale à venda [vaynda]
salmon o salmão [salmowng]
salt o sal
same: the same o mesmo [mayJmoo]
 the same as this igual a este [igwal a aysht]
 the same again, please o mesmo, por favor [poor favohr]
 it's all the same to me tanto faz [tantoo fash]
sand a areia [aray-a]

sandals as sandálias [sandal-yash]

sandwich a sandes [sandsh]

sanitary napkins/towels os pensos higiénicos [paynsoo7 ij-yehnikoosh]

sardine a sardinha [sardeen-ya]

Saturday sábado [sabadoo]

sauce o molho [mohl-yoo]

saucepan a panela [panehla]

saucer o pires [peersh]

sauna a sauna [sowna]

sausage a salsicha [salseesha]

say* dizer [dizayr]

how do you say ... in Portuguese? como se diz ... em português? [kohmoo si deez ... ayng poortoogaysh]

what did he say? o que é que ele disse? [oo k-yeh kayl dees]

he said ... ele disse ...

could you say that again? pode repetir? [pod ripiteer]

scarf (for neck) o lenço de pescoço [laynsoo di pishkohsoo] (for head) o lenço de cabeça [kabaysa]

scenery a paisagem [pizaJayng]

schedule (US) o horário [oo orar-yoo]

scheduled flight o voo regular [voh-oo rigoolar]

school a escola [shkola]

scissors: a pair of scissors a tesoura [tizohra]

scooter a motoreta [mootoorayta]

scotch o whisky [weeshkee]

Scotch tape® a fita gomada [feeta goomada]

Scotland a Escócia [shkos-ya]

Scottish escocês [shkoosaysh]

I'm Scottish (man/woman) sou escocês/escocesa [soh – shkoosayza]

scrambled eggs os ovos mexidos [ovoosh misheedoosh]

scratch o arranhão [arran-yowng]

screw o parafuso [parafoozoo]

screwdriver a chave de fendas [shav di fayndash]

sea o mar

by the sea à beira-mar [bayra]

seafood os mariscos [mareeshkoosh]

seafood restaurant a marisqueira [marishkayra]

seafront a praia [prī-a]

on the seafront junto à praia [Joontwa]

seagull a gaivota [givota]

search procurar [prookourar]

seashell a concha do mar [kohnsha doo]

seasick: I feel seasick (said by man/woman) estou enjoado/enjoada [shtoh aynJwadoo]

I get seasick enjoo sempre [aynJoh-oo saympr]

seaside: by the seaside à beira do mar [bayra doo]

seat o assento [asayntoo]

is this seat taken? este lugar está ocupado? [aysht loogar shta okoopadoo]

seat belt o cinto de segurança [seentoo di sigooransa]

English → Portuguese

sea urchin o ouriço-do-mar [ohreesoo doo]
seaweed a alga
secluded retirado [ritiradoo]
second (adj) segundo [sigoondoo]
(of time) o segundo
just a second! espere um momento! [shpayroong moomayntoo]
second class (travel) segunda classe [sigoonda klas]
second floor o segundo andar [sigoondoo]
(US) o primeiro andar [primayroo]
second-hand em segunda mão [ayng sigoonda mowng]
see* ver [vayr]
can I see? posso ver? [posoo]
have you seen the ...? viu o/a ...? [vee-oo]
I saw him this morning vi-o esta manhã [vee-oo ehshta man-yang]
see you! até logo! [ateh logoo]
I see (I understand) percebo [pirsayboo]
self-catering apartment o aparthotel [apartohtehl]
self-service o self-service
sell vender [vayndayr]
do you sell ...? vende ...? [vaynd]
Sellotape® a fita gomada [feeta goomada]
send mandar
I want to send this to England quero mandar isto para

Inglaterra [kehroo – eeshtoo paringlatehrra]
senior citizen (man/woman) o cidadão de terceira idade [sidadowng di tirsayra idad], a cidadã de terceira idade [sidadang]
separate separado [siparadoo]
separated: I'm separated (said by man/woman) estou separado/separada [shtoh]
separately (pay, travel) separadamente [siparadamaynt]
September Setembro [sitaymbroo]
septic séptico [sehptikoo]
serious sério [sehr-yoo]
service charge (in restaurant) a taxa de serviço [tasha di sirveesoo]
service station a estação de serviço [shtasowng]
serviette o guardanapo [gwardanapoo]
set menu a ementa fixa [emaynta feeksa]
several vários [var-yoosh]
sew coser [koozayr]
could you sew this back on? podia coser-me isto? [poodee-a koozayrm eeshtoo]
sex o sexo [sehxoo]
sexy sexy [sehxi]
shade: in the shade à sombra [sohmbra]
shallow (water) pouco profundo [pohkoo proofoondoo]
shame: what a shame! que pena! [ki payna]

104

shampoo o champô [shampoh]
shampoo and set lavagem e mise [lavaJayng i meezi]
share (room, table etc) partilhar [partil-yar]
sharp (knife) afiado [af-yadoo]
(taste) ácido [asidoo]
(pain) agudo [agoodoo]
shattered (very tired) estafado [shtafadoo]
shaver a máquina de barbear [makina di barb-yar]
shaving foam a espuma de barbear [shpooma]
shaving point a tomada para a máquina de barbear [toomada para makina]
she* ela [ehla]
is she here? ela está aqui? [shta akee]
sheet (for bed) o lençol [laynsol]
shelf a prateleira [pratilayra]
shellfish os mariscos [mareeshkoosh]
sherry o vinho de Xerêz [veen-yoo di shiraysh]
ship o navio [navee-o]
by ship de navio [di]
shirt a camisa [kameeza]
shit! merda! [mehrda]
shock o choque [shok]
I got an electric shock from the ... apanhei um choque eléctrico do ... [apan-yay oong – elehtrikoo doo]
shock-absorber o amortecedor [amoortisidohr]
shocking chocante [shookant]
shoe os sapatos [sapatoosh]

a pair of shoes um par de sapatos [oong par di]
shoelaces os atacadores [atakadohrish]
shoe polish a graxa para sapatos [grasha para sapatoosh]
shoe repairer o sapateiro [sapatayroo]
shop a loja [loJa]
shopping: I'm going shopping vou às compras [voh ash kohmprash]
shopping centro o centro comercial [sayntroo komayrs-yal]
shop window a montra [mohntra]
shore (of sea, lake) a margem [marJayng]
short (person) baixo [bīshoo]
(time, journey) curto [koortoo]
shortcut o atalho [atal-yoo]
shorts os calções [kalsoyngsh]
should: what should I do? que devo fazer? [ki dayvoo fazayr]
he should be back soon ele deve voltar logo [ayl dehv vooltar logoo]
you should ... devia [divee-a]
you shouldn't ... não devia ... [nowng]
shoulder o ombro [ohmbroo]
shout gritar
show (in theatre) o espetáculo [shpitakooloo]
could you show me? podia mostrar-me? [poodee-a mooshtrarmi]
shower (in bathroom) o duche [doosh]

(of rain) o aguaceiro
[agwas**ay**roo]

with shower com duche
[kong]

shower gel o gel de duche [Jehl
di doosh]

shrimp a gamba

shut (verb) fechar [fish**ar**]
  when do you shut? a que
  horas fecha? [k-y**or**ash f**eh**sha]
  when does it shut? a que
  horas fecha?
  it's shut está fechado/
  fechada [shta fish**a**doo]
  I've shut myself out fechei
  a porta e deixei a chave
  dentro [fish**ay** – i daysh**ay** a shav
  d**ayn**troo]
  shut up! cale-se! [**kalisi**]

shutter (on camera) o obturador
[obtoorad**ohr**]
  (on window) os postigos
  [pooshte**ee**goosh]

shy tímido [t**ee**midoo]

sick (unwell) doente [dwaynt]
  I'm going to be sick (vomit)
  vou vomitar [voh voomit**ar**]

side o lado [l**a**doo]
  the other side of the street o
  outro lado da rua [oo **oh**troo
  – **roo**-a]

sidelights as luzes de presença
[aJ **loo**ziJ di priz**aynsa**]

side salad a salada a
acompanhar [akompan-y**ar**]

side street a rua secundária
[**roo**-a sikoondar-ya]

sidewalk o passeio [pas**ay**-oo]

sight: the sights of ... os

centros de interesse de ...
[oosh s**ayn**troosh dintr**ays** di]

sightseeing: we're going
sightseeing vamos ver os
lugares de interesse [**va**moosh
vayr oosh loog**ar**ish]

sightseeing tour o circuito
turístico [sirk**oo**-eetoo
toor**ee**shtikoo]

sign (roadsign etc) o sinal

signal: he didn't give a signal
(driver, cyclist) ele não deu um
sinal [ayl nowng d**ay**-oo oong
sin**al**]

signature a assinatura
[asinat**oora**]

signpost o poste indicador
[posht indikad**ohr**]

silence o silêncio [sil**ayns**-yoo]

silk a seda [**say**da]

silly tolo [t**oh**loo]

silver a prata

silver foil o papel de alumínio
[pap**ehl** daloom**een**-yoo]

similar semelhante [simil-yant]

simple (easy) simples [**see**mplish]

since: since last week desde
a semana passada [**day**Jda
sim**ana**]
  since I got here desde que
  cheguei [**day**Jd ki shig**ay**]

sing cantar

singer (man/woman) o cantor
[kant**ohr**], a cantora

single: a single to ... uma
bilhete simples para ... [**oo**ng
bil-y**ayt** s**ee**mplish]
  I'm single (said by man/woman)
  sou solteiro/solteira [soh
  soolt**ay**roo]

single bed a cama individual [individwal]

single room o quarto individual [kwartoo]

single ticket o bilhete simples [bil-yayt seemplish]

sink (in kitchen) a lava-louça [lava lohsa]

sister a irmã [eermang]

sister-in-law a cunhada [koonyada]

sit: can I sit here? posso sentar-me aqui? [posoo sayntarmi akee]

is anyone sitting here? está alguém sentado aqui? [shta algayng sayntadoo akee]

sit down sentar-se [sayntarsi]

sit down sente-se [sayntsi]

size o tamanho [taman-yoo]

skin a pele [pehl]

skin-diving mergulhar [mirgoolyar]

skinny magricela [magrisehla]

skirt a saia [sī-ya]

sky o céu [seh-oo]

sleep dormir [doormeer]

did you sleep well? dormiu bem? [doormee-oo bayng]

sleeper (on train) a carruagem-cama [karrwaJayng kama]

sleeping bag o saco de dormir [sakoo di doormeer]

sleeping car (on train) a carruagem-cama [karrwaJayng kama]

sleeping pill o comprimido para dormir [komprimeedoo para doormeer]

sleepy: I'm feeling sleepy estou com sono [shtoh kong sohnoo]

sleeve a manga

slide (photographic) o diapositivo [d-yapooziteevoo]

slip (garment) a combinação [kombinasowng]

slippery escorregadio [shkoorrigadee-oo]

slow lento [layntoo]

slow down! (driving) mais devagar! [mīJ divagar]

slowly devagar

very slowly muito devagar [mweengtoo]

could you speak more slowly? pode falar mais devagar? [pod – mīJ]

small pequeno [pikaynoo]

smell: it smells (smells bad) cheira mal [shayra]

smile sorrir [soorreer]

smoke o fumo [foomoo]

do you mind if I smoke? importa-se que fume? [importasi ki foomi]

I don't smoke não fumo [nowng]

do you smoke? fuma? [fooma]

snack: just a snack só um snack [saw oong]

sneeze o espirro [shpeerroo]

snorkel o snorkel

snow a neve [nehv]

it's snowing está a nevar [shta]

so: it's so good! é tão bom! [eh towng bong]

it's so expensive! é tão caro!
[karoo]

not so much não tanto [nowng
tantoo]

it's not so bad não é tão mau/
má [eh towng mow]

so am I, so do I eu também
[ay-oo tambayng]

so-so mais ou menos
[mizohmaynoosh]

soaking solution (for contact
lenses) a solução para as lentes
de contacto [sooloosowng paraJ
layntsh di kontatoo]

soap o sabonete [saboonayt]

soap powder o detergente
[deterJaynt]

sober sóbrio [sobr-yoo]

sock a peúga [p-yooga]

socket (electrical) a tomada
[toomada]

soda (water) a soda

sofa o sofá [soofa]

soft (material etc) mole [mol]

soft-boiled egg o ovo quente
[ohvoo kaynt]

soft drink a bebida não
alcoólica [bibeeda nowng alko-
olika]

soft lenses as lentes
gelatinosas [layntsh Jilatinozash]

sole (of shoe, of foot) a sola

could you put new soles on
these? pode pôr-lhes solas
novas? [pod pohrl-yish solash
novash]

some: can I have some
water? pode trazer-me água?
[trazayrm]

can I have some of this?
pode dar-me um pouco
disto? [darmoong pohkoo
deeshtoo]

somebody, someone alguém
[algayng]

something alguma coisa
[algooma koh-iza]

something to eat alguma
coisa para comer [koomair]

sometimes às vezes [ash
vayzish]

somewhere nalguma parte
[nalgooma part]

son o filho [feel-yoo]

song a canção [kansowng]

son-in-law o genro [Jaynroo]

soon em breve [ayng brev]

I'll be back soon estarei de
volta em breve [shtaray di
vohltayng]

as soon as possible logo que
possível [logoo ki pooseevil]

sore: it's sore dói-me [doymi]

sore throat a dor de garganta
[dohr di]

sorry: (I'm) sorry tenho muita
pena [tayn-yoo mweengta payna]

sorry? (didn't understand) como?
[kohmoo]

sort: what sort of ...? que tipo
de ...? [ki teepoo di]

soup a sopa [sohpa]

sour (taste) azedo [azaydoo]

south o sul [sool]

in the south no sul [noo]

South Africa a África do Sul
[doo]

South African (adj) sul-africano

[soolafrikanoo]
I'm South African (man/woman)
sou sul-africano/sul-africana
[soh]
southeast o sudeste [soodehsht]
southwest o sudoeste
[soodwehsht]
souvenir a lembrança
[laymbransa]
Spain a Espanha [shpan-ya]
Spanish espanhol [shpan-yol]
spanner a chave de porcas
[shav di porkash]
spare part a peça sobresselente
[pehsa sobrisilaynt]
spare tyre o pneu
sobresselente [p-nay-oo]
spark plug a vela [vehla]
sparkling wine o vinho
espumante [veen-yooshpoomant]
speak: do you speak English?
fala inglês? [inglaysh]
I don't speak ... não falo ...
[nowng faloo]

dialogue

can I speak to Roberto?
posso falar com o
Roberto? [posoo – kong oo]
who's calling? quem fala?
[kayng]
it's Patricia é Patricia [eh]
**I'm sorry, he's not in, can I
take a message?** desculpe,
ele não está, quer deixar
um recado? [dishkoolp ayl
nowng shta kehr dayshar oong
rikadoo]

**no thanks, I'll call back
later** não, obrigada, ligarei
mais tarde [ligaray mish tard]
please tell him I called
por favor, diga-lhe que
telefonei [poor tavohr deegal-
yi ki telefoonay]

spectacles os óculos [okooloosh]
speed a velocidade [viloosidad]
speed limit o limite de
velocidade [limeet di]
speedometer o velocímetro
[vilooseemitroo]
spell: how do you spell it?
como é que se soletra?
[kohmoo eh ki si soolehtra]
see **alphabet**
spend gastar [gashtar]
spider a aranha [aran-ya]
spin-dryer o secador de roupa
[sikadohr di rohpa]
splinter a pua [poo-a]
spoke (in wheel) o raio [rī-oo]
spoon a colher [kool-yehr]
sport o desporto [dishpohrtoo]
sprain: I've sprained my ...
torci o ... [toorsee oo]
spring (season) a Primavera
[primavehra]
(of car, seat) a mola [mola]
square (in town) a praça [prasa]
squash o squash
stairs a escada [shkada]
stale (bread) duro [dooroo]
stall: the engine keeps stalling
o motor está sempre a falhar
[oo mootohr shta saympra fal-yar]
stamp o selo [sayloo]

109

dialogue

a stamp for England, please um selo para Inglaterra, faz favor [oong sayloo para inglatehrra fash favohr]
what are you sending? o que vai enviar? [oo ki vī aynv-yar]
this postcard este postal [aysht pooshtal]

standby standby
star a estrela [shtrayla]
(in film: man/woman) o actor principal [atohr prinsipal], a actriz principal [atreesh]
start o começo [koomaysoo] (verb) começar [koomisar]
when does it start? quando começa? [kwandoo koomehsa]
the car won't start o carro não pega [oo karroo nowng pehga]
starter (of car) o motor de arranque [mootohr darrank] (food) a entrada [ayntrada]
starving: I'm starving (said by man/woman) estou morto/ morta de fome [shtoh mohrtoo – di fohm]
state (country) o estado [shtadoo]
the States (USA) os Estados Unidos [shtadooz ooneedoosh]
station a estação [shtasowng]
statue a estátua [shtatwa]
stay: where are you staying? (to man/woman) onde está

hospedado/hospedada? [ohndshta oshpidadoo]
I'm staying at ... (said by man/ woman) estou hospedado/ hospedada em ... [shtoh – ayng]
I'd like to stay another two nights gostaria de ficar mais duas noites [gooshtaree-a di fikar mīsh doo-aJ noh-itsh]
steak o bife [beef]
steal roubar [rohbar]
my bag has been stolen roubaram-me a mala [rohbarowng m-ya mala]
steep (hill) íngreme [eengrim]
steering a direcção [direhsowng]
step: on the step no degrau [digrow]
stereo a aparelhagem (de som) [aparil-yaJayng (di song)]
sterling as libras esterlinas [leebraz ishtirleenash]
steward (on plane) o comissário de bordo [koomisar-yoo di bordoo]
stewardess a hospedeira [oshpidayra]
sticking plaster o adesivo [adizeevoo]
sticky tape a fita-cola [feeta kola]
still: I'm still here ainda estou aqui [a-eenda shtoh akee]
is he still there? ele ainda está aí? [ayl – shta a-ee]
keep still! fique quieto! [feek k-yehtoo]
sting: I've been stung (said by man/woman) fui picado/

picada [fwee pikadoo]
stockings as mcias [may-ash]
stomach o estômago
[shtohmagoo]
stomach ache a dor de
estômago [dohr dishtohmagoo]
stone (rock) a pedra [pehdra]
stop parar
  please, stop here (to taxi driver
  etc.) pare aqui, por favor [par
  akee poor favohr]
  do you stop near ...? pára
  perto de ...? [pehrtoo di]
  stop it! pare com isso! [kong
  eesoo]
stopover a paragem [parajayng]
storm a tempestade
[taympishtad]
straight (whisky etc) puro
[pooroo]
  it's straight ahead sempre em
  frente [saymprayng fraynt]
straightaway em seguida [ayng
sigeeda]
strange (odd) esquisito
[shkizeetoo]
stranger (man/woman) o
estranho [shtran-yoo], a
estranha
  I'm a stranger here sou de
  fora [soh di]
strap (on watch) a pulseira
[poolsayra]
  (on dress) a alça [alsa]
  (on suitcase) a correia [koorray-a]
strawberry o morango
[moorangoo]
stream o ribeiro [ribayroo]
street a rua [roo-a]

on the street na rua
streetmap o mapa da cidade
[sidad]
string o cordel [koordehl]
strong forte [fort]
stuck emperrado [aympirradoo]
  it's stuck está emperrado
  [shta]
student (male/female) o/a
estudante [shtoodant]
stupid estúpido [shtoopidoo]
suburb os arredores [arredorish]
subway (US) o metro [mehtroo]
suddenly subitamente
[soobitamaynt]
suede a camurça [kamoorsa]
sugar o açúcar [asookar]
suit o fato [fatoo]
  it doesn't suit me (jacket etc)
  não me fica bem [nowng mi
  feeka bayng]
  it suits you fica-lhe bem
  [feekal-yi]
suitcase a mala
summer o Verão [virowng]
  in the summer no Verão [noo]
sun o sol
  in the sun ao sol [ow]
  out of the sun à sombra
  [sohmbra]
sunbathe tomar banho de sol
[toomar ban-yoo di]
sunblock (cream) o creme écran
total [kraym ekran tootal]
sunburn a queimadura de sol
[kaymadoora di]
sunburnt queimado de sol
[kaymadoo]
Sunday domingo [doomeengoo]

111

sunglasses os óculos de sol [okooloosh di]

sun lounger a cadeira reclinável [kadayra reklinavil]

sunny: it's sunny está (a fazer) sol [shta (a fazayr) sol]

sunroof o tejadilho de abrir [tiJadeel-yoo dabreer]

sunset o pôr do sol [pohr doo]

sunshade o chapéu de sol [shapeh-oo di]

sunshine a luz do sol [looJ doo]

sunstroke a insolação [insoolasowng]

suntan o bronzeado [bronz-yadoo]

suntan lotion a loção de bronzear [loosowng di bronz-yar]

suntanned bronzeado [bronz-yadoo]

suntan oil o óleo de bronzear [ol-yoo di]

super óptimo [otimoo]

supermarket o supermercado [soopermerkadoo]

supper o jantar [Jantar]

supplement (extra charge) o suplemento [sooplimayntoo]

sure: are you sure? tem a certeza? [tayng a sirtayza]

sure! claro! [klaroo]

surname o apelido [apileedoo]

swearword a asneira [aJnayra]

sweater a camisola [kamizola]

sweatshirt a sweatshirt

Sweden a Suécia [swehs-ya]

Swedish (adj, language) sueco [swehkoo]

sweet (taste) doce [dohs]

(dessert) a sobremesa [sobrimayza]

sweets os rebuçados [riboosadoosh]

swelling o inchaço [inshasoo]

swim nadar

I'm going for a swim vou nadar [voh]

let's go for a swim vamos nadar [vamoosh]

swimming costume o fato de banho [fatoo di ban-yoo]

swimming pool a piscina [pish-seena]

swimming trunks os calções de banho [kalsoyngsh di ban-yoo]

Swiss (adj) suíço [sweesoo]

switch o interruptor [intirooptohr]

switch off (engine, TV) desligar [diJligar]

(lights) apagar

switch on (engine, TV) ligar [ligar]

(lights) acender [asayndayr]

Switzerland a Suíça [sweesa]

swollen inchado [inshadoo]

T

table a mesa [mayza]

a table for two uma mesa para duas pessoas [ooma – doo-ash pisoh-ash]

tablecloth a toalha de mesa [twal-ya di mayza]

table tennis o ténis de mesa [tehnish]

table wine o vinho de mesa [veen-yoo]

tailback (of traffic) a fila de carros [feela di karroosh]

tailor a alfaiataria [alfi-ataree-a]

take (lead) levar

(accept) aceitar [asaytar]

can you take me to the ...? pode levar-me ao ...? [pod levarmow]

do you take credit cards? aceita cartões de crédito? [aoayta kartoyngsh di krehditoo]

fine, I'll take it está bem, fico com ele [shta bayng feekoo kong ayl]

can I take this? (leaflet etc) posso levar isto? [posoo – eeshtoo]

how long does it take? quanto tempo leva? [kwantoo taympoo lehva]

it takes three hours leva três horas [trayzorash]

is this seat taken? este lugar está ocupado? [aysht loogar shta okoopadoo]

hamburger to take away o hamburger para levar

can you take a little off here? (to hairdresser) pode cortar um pouco aqui? [pod koortar oong pohkoo akee]

talcum powder o pó de talco [paw di talkoo]

talk falar

tall alto [altoo]

tampons os tampões [tampoyngsh]

tan o bronzeado [bronz-yadoo]

to get a tan bronzear-se [bronz-yarsi]

tank (of car) o depósito [dipozitoo]

tap a torneira [toornayra]

tape (for cassette) a fita [feeta]

tape measure a fita métrica [mehtrika]

tape recorder o gravador [gravadohr]

taste o sabor [sabohr]

can I taste it? posso provar? [posoo]

taxi o táxi

will you get me a taxi? pode chamar-me um táxi? [pod shamarmoong]

where can I find a taxi? onde posso encontrar um táxi? [ohnd poswaynkontrar]

dialogue

to the airport/Borges Hotel, please para o aeroporto/Hotel Borges, se faz favor [paroo-ayroopohrtoo/ohtehl borJish si fash favohr]

how much will it be? quanto vai custar? [kwantoo vī kooshtar]

ten euros dez euros [dehz ay-ooroosh]

that's fine right here, thanks aqui está bem, obrigado/obrigada [akee shta bayng obrigadoo]

taxi-driver o pracista
[pra**see**shta]

taxi rank a praça de táxis [p**ra**sa
di ta**xish**]

tea (drink) o chá [sha]

  tea for one/two, please chá
  para um/dois, por favor
  [oong/d**oh**-ish poor fa**voh**r]

  teabags os saquinhos de chá
  [sa**keen**-yooJ di sha]

teach: could you teach me?
  pode ensinar-me? [pod
  aynsin**ar**mi]

teacher (man/woman) o professor
  [proofes**ohr**], a professor**a**

team a equipa [e**kee**pa]

teaspoon a colher de chá [kool-
  yehr di sha]

tea towel o pano de cozinha
  [**pa**noo di koo**zeen**-ya]

teenager o/a adolescente
  [adoolish-s**aynt**]

telephone o telefone [tele**fohn**]
  see phone

television a televisão
  [televiz**ow**ng]

tell: could you tell him ...?
  pode dizer-lhe ...? [pod
  diz**ayr**l-yi]

temperature (weather) a
  temperatura [taympirat**oo**ra]
  (fever) a febre [**feh**br]

tennis o ténis [**teh**nish]

tennis ball a bola de ténis [di]

tennis court o campo de ténis
  [**kam**poo]

tennis racket a raqueta de
  ténis [rak**eh**ta]

tent a tenda (de campismo)

[**taynd**a (di kamp**ee**Jmoo)]

term (at school) o período
  escolar [pir**ee**-oodoo shk**oo**lar]

terminus (rail) o terminal
  [tir**minal**]

terrible terrível [tirr**ee**vil]

terrific (weather) esplêndido
  [shpl**aynd**idoo]
  (food, teacher) excelente [ish-
  sel**aynt**]

text (message) a mensajem de
  texto [mensa**J**ayng di t**ay**shtoo]

than* do que [doo ki]

  smaller than mais pequeno
  do que [mīsh pik**ay**noo]

thanks, thank you (said by man/
  woman) obrigado/
  obrig**ada** [obrig**a**doo]

  thank you very much
  muito obrigado/obrigada
  [m**wee**ngtoo]

  thanks for the lift obrigado/
  obrigada pela boleia [p**i**la
  bool**ay**-a]

  no thanks não obrigado/
  obrigada [n**ow**ng]

dialogue

> thanks (said by man/woman)
> obrigado/obrigada
> that's OK, don't mention it
> está bem, não se preocupe
> com isso [shta bayng nowng si
> pri-ook**oo**p kong **ee**soo]

that*: that ... esse/essa ... [**ays**/
ehsa]
  (further away) aquele/aquela ...

[akayl/akehla]

that one esse/essa/isso [**ee**soo]

(further away) aquele/aquela/
aquilo [a**kee**loo]

I hope that ... espero que ...
[shp**eh**ro ki]

that's nice! que bom! [bong]

is that ...? isso é ...? [eh]

that's it (that's right) certo
[**seh**rtoo]

the* o [oo], a

(pl) os [oosh], as [ash]

theatre o teatro [t-**ya**troo]

their* deles [**day**lish], delas
[**deh**lash]

theirs* deles, delas

them* os [oosh]

(feminine) as [ash]

for them para eles/elas [aylsh/
ehlash]

with them com eles/elas [kong]

to them para eles/elas

who? – them? quem? – eles/
elas [kayng]

then (at that time) então
[ayn**tow**ng]

(after that) depois [di**poh**-ish]

there ali [a**lee**], lá

over there ali adiante [ad-**yant**]

up there ali acima [a**see**ma]

is there/are there ...? há ...?
[a]

there is/there are ... há ...

there you are (giving something)
tome lá [tohm]

thermometer o termómetro
[tir**moh**mitroo]

Thermos flask® o termo
[**tayr**moo]

these*: these men estes
homens [**aysh**tiz**oh**mayngsh]

these women estas mulheres
[**eh**shtaJ mool-**yeh**rish]

I'd like these queria estes/
estas [ki**ree**-a **aysh**tish/**eh**shtash]

they* (male) eles [**ay**lish]

(female) elas [**eh**lash]

thick espesso [shp**ay**soo]

(stupid) estúpido [sh**too**pidoo]

thief (man/woman) o ladrão
[lad**row**ng], a ladra

thigh a coxa [**koh**sha]

thin fino [**fee**noo]

(person) magro [**ma**groo]

thing a coisa [**koh**-iza]

my things as minhas coisas [aJ
meen-yash koh-**iz**ash]

think pensar [payn**sar**]

I think so acho que sim [**a**shoo
ki seeng]

I don't think so acho que não
[**now**ng]

I'll think about it vou pensar
[voh]

third party insurance o seguro
contra terceiros [si**goo**roo
kohntra tirs**ay**roosh]

thirsty: I'm thirsty tenho sede
[**tayn**-yoo sayd]

this*: this boy este menino
[aysht min**ee**noo]

this girl esta menina [**eh**shta
min**ee**na]

this one este [aysht]/esta
[**eh**shta]/isto [**ees**htoo]

this is my wife esta é a minha
mulher [eh a **meen**-ya mool-**yehr**]

is this ...? isto é ...? [**ees**htweh]

English → Portuguese

those*: those ... esses/essas ...
[**ay**sish/**eh**sash]
(further away) aqueles/aquelas
... [a**kay**lish/a**keh**lash]
which ones? – those quais?
– esses/essas [kwish]
(further away) quais? – aqueles/
aquelas
thread o fio [**fee**-oo]
throat a garganta
throat pastilles as pastilhas
para a garganta [pash**teel**-yash]
through por, através de
[atra**vehJ** di]
does it go through ...? (train,
bus) passa em ...? [ayng]
throw atirar
throw away deitar fora [**day**tar]
thumb o polegar [poo**lig**ar]
thunderstorm a trovoada
[troo**wa**da]
Thursday quinta-feira [**keen**ta
fayra]
ticket o bilhete [bil-**yayt**]

dialogue

a return to Setúbal um
bilhete de ida e volta
para Setúbal [oong – **deed**ī
– sit**oo**bal]
coming back when?
quando volta? [**kwan**doo]
today/next Tuesday hoje/
na próxima terça-feira [ohJ/
na **pros**ima **tayr**sa **fay**ra]
that will be 6 euros são
seis euros [sowng sayz **ay**-
ooroosh]

ticket office (bus, rail) a
bilheteira [bil-yit**ay**ra]
tide a maré [**mareh**]
tie (necktie) a gravata
tight (clothes etc) apertado
[apir**ta**doo]
it's too tight está demasiado
apertado [shta dimaz-**ya**doo]
tights os collants [koo**lansh**]
till a caixa [**kī**sha]
time* o tempo [**taym**poo]
what's the time? que horas
são? [k-**yo**rash sowng]
this time esta vez [**eh**shta
vaysh]
last time a última vez [**oo**ltima]
next time a próxima vez
[**pro**sima]
three times três vezes [traysh
vayzish]
timetable o horário [oo orar-
yoo]
tin (can) a lata
tinfoil o papel de alumínio
[pap**ehl** daloo**meen**-yoo]
tin-opener o abre-latas
[abri**la**tash]
tiny minúsculo [min**oo**shkooloo]
tip (to waiter etc) a gorgeta
[goor**Jay**ta]
tired cansado [kan**sa**doo]
I'm tired (said by man/woman)
estou cansado/cansada [**shtoh**]
tissues os lenços de papel
[**layn**soosh di pap**ehl**]
to: to Lisbon/London para
Lisboa/Londres [liJb**oh**-a/
lohndrish]
to Portugal/England

Th

116

para Portugal/Inglaterra [poortoogal/inglatehrra]

we're going to the museum/ to the post office vamos ao museo/aos correios [vamooz ow moosay-oo/owsh koorray-oosh]

toast (bread) a torrada [toorrada]

today hoje [ohJ]

toe o dedo do pé [daydoo doo peh]

together juntos [Joontoosh]

we're together (in shop etc) viemos juntos [v-vaymoosh Joontoosh]

toilet a casa de banho [kaza di ban-yoo]

where is the toilet? onde é a casa de banho? [ohndeh]

I have to go to the toilet tenho de ir à casa de banho [tayn-yoo deer]

toilet paper o papel higiénico [papehl iJ-yehnikoo]

tomato o tomate [toomat]

tomato juice o sumo de tomate [soomoo di toomat]

tomato ketchup o ketchup

tomorrow amanhã [aman-yang]

tomorrow morning amanhã de manhã [aman-yang di man-yang]

the day after tomorrow depois de amanhã [dipoh-ish daman-yang]

toner (cosmetic) o tónico [tonikoo]

tongue a língua [leengwa]

tonic (water) a água tónica [agwa]

tonight esta noite [ehshta noh-it]

tonsillitis a amigdalite [ameegdaleet]

too (excessively) demasiado [dimaz-yadoo]

(also) também [tambayng]

too hot demasiado quente [kaynt]

too much demais [dimīsh]

me too eu também [ay-oo tambayng]

tooth o dente [daynt]

toothache a dor de dentes [dohr di dayntsh]

toothbrush a escova de dentes [shkohva]

toothpaste a pasta de dentes [pashta]

top: on top of ... em cima de ... [ayng seema di]

at the top no alto [noo altoo]

at the top of ... no topo de ... [tohpoo di]

top floor o piso superior [peezoo soopir-yohr]

topless topless

torch a lanterna [lantehrna]

total o total [tootal]

tour a excursão [shkoorsowng]

is there a tour of ...? há alguma excursão/visita guiada a ...? [algooma – vizeeta gee-ada]

tour guide (man/woman) o guia turístico [gee-a tooreeshtikoo], a guia turística

tourist (man/woman) o/a turista [tooreeshta]

117

tourist information office o turismo [tooreeJmoo]

tour operator o operador turístico [opiradohr tooreeshtikoo]

towards para

towel a toalha [twal-ya]

town a cidade [sidad]
in town na cidade
just out of town junto à cidade [joontwa]

town centre o centro da cidade [sayntroo]

town hall a câmara municipal [moonisipal]

toy o brinquedo [breenkaydoo]

track (US) o cais [kish]
see platform

tracksuit o fato de treino [fatoo di traynoo]

traditional tradicional [tradis-yoonal]

traffic o trânsito [tranzitoo]

traffic jam o engarrafamento [ayngarrafamayntoo]

traffic lights os semáforos [simafooroosh]

trailer (for carrying tent etc) o reboque [ribok]
(US) a roulotte [roolot]

trailer park o parque de campismo [park di kampeeJmoo]

train o comboio [komboy-oo]
by train de comboio [di]

dialogue

is this the train for Fátima?
é este o comboio para Fátima? [eh ayshtoo]

sure com certeza [kong sirtayza]
no, you want that platform there não, tem que ir à plataforma de lá [nowng tayng ki-eer – di]

trainers (shoes) os sapatos de treino [sapatoosh di traynoo]

train station a estação de comboios [shtasowng di komboy-oosh]

tram o eléctrico [elehtrikoo]

translate traduzir [tradoozeer]
could you translate that?
pode traduzir isto? [pod – eeshtoo]

translation a tradução [tradoosowng]

translator (man/woman) o tradutor [tradootohr], a tradutora

trash (waste) o lixo [leeshoo]

trashcan o caixote de lixo [kishot di leeshoo]

travel viajar [v-yaJar]
we're travelling around
estamos a viajar por aí [shtamooz – poor a-ee]

travel agent's a agência de viagens [aJaynsya di v-yaJayngsh]

traveller's cheque o cheque de viagem [shehk di v-yaJayng]

tray a travessa [travehsa]

tree a árvore [arvoori]

tremendous bestial [bisht-yal]

trendy à moda

trim: just a trim, please (to

hairdresser) queria só cortar as pontas, por favor [kir**ee**-a saw koort**ar** ash p**on**tash poor fav**ohr**]

trip (excursion) a excursão [shkoors**ow**ng]

I'd like to go on a trip to ... gostava de ir numa viagem a ... [goosht**ava** deer n**oo**ma v-ya**J**ayng]

trolley o carrinho [kar**ree**n-yoo]

trouble: I'm having trouble with ... tenho tido problemas com ... [**tayn**-yoo t**eed**oo proobl**ay**mash kong]

trousers as calças [k**al**sash]

true verdadeiro [virrdad**ayr**oo]

that's not true não é verdade [nowng eh vird**ad**]

trunk (US: of car) o porta-bagagens [p**or**ta-bag**aJ**ayngsh]

trunks (swimming) os calções de banho [kals**oyn**gsh di b**an**-yoo]

try tentar

can I try it? posso experimentar? [p**o**soo shpirimaynt**ar**]

(food) posso provar? [proov**ar**]

try on experimentar

can I try it on? posso experimentar? [p**o**soo shpirimaynt**ar**]

T-shirt a T-shirt

Tuesday terça-feira [t**ayr**sa f**ayr**a]

tuna o atum [at**oo**ng]

tunnel o túnel [t**oo**nil]

turn: turn left/right vire à esquerda/direita [v**ee**ra shk**ayr**da/dir**ay**ta]

turn off: where do I turn off? onde devo virar? [ohnd d**ay**voo]

can you turn the heating off? pode desligar o aquecimento? [pod diJlig**ar** oo akesim**ayn**too]

turn on: can you turn the heating on? pode ligar o aquecimento?

turning (in road) a curva [k**oor**va]

TV TV [tay-vay]

tweezers a pinça [p**een**sa]

twice duas vezes [d**oo**-aJ v**ay**zish]

twice as much o dobro [oo d**ohb**roo]

twin beds as camas separadas [k**am**ash sipar**ad**ash]

twin room o quarto com duas camas [kw**ar**too kong d**oo**-ash]

twist: I've twisted my ankle torci o meu tornozelo [toors**ee** oo m**ay**-oo toornooz**ay**loo]

type o tipo [t**ee**poo]

a different type of ... um tipo diferente de ... [oong – difir**ayn**t di]

typical típico [t**ee**pikoo]

tyre o pneu [p-n**ay**-oo]

U

ugly feio [f**ay**-oo]

UK Reino Unido [r**ay**noon**eed**oo]

ulcer a úlcera [**oo**lsira]

umbrella o guarda-chuva [gw**ar**da sh**oo**va]

uncle o tio [t**ee**-oo]

Un

unconscious inconsciente [inkonsh-syaynt]

under (in position) debaixo de [dibishoo di]
(less than) menos de [maynoosh di]

underdone (meat) mal passado [pasadoo]

underground (railway) o metro [mehtroo]

underpants as cuecas [kwehkash]

understand: I understand já percebi [Ja pirsibee]
I don't understand não percebo [nowng pirsayboo]
do you understand? está a compreender? [shta a kompr-ayndayr]

unemployed desempregado [dizaymprigadoo]

United States os Estados Unidos [shtadooz ooneedoosh]

university a universidade [oonivirsidad]

unleaded petrol a gasolina sem chumbo [gazooleena sayng shoomboo]

unlimited mileage quilometragem ilimitada [kilomitraJayng ilimitada]

unlock abrir [abreer]

unpack desfazer as malas [dishfazayr aJ malash]

until até a [ateh]

unusual pouco vulgar [pohkoo voolgar]

up acima [aseema]

up there lá em cima [ayng seema]

he's not up yet (not out of bed) ele ainda não está levantado [ayl a-eenda nowng shta levantadoo]

what's up? (what's wrong?) o que aconteceu? [oo ki akontisay-oo]

upmarket sofisticado [soofishtikadoo]

upset stomach o desarranjo intestinal [dizarranJoo intishtinal]

upside down de pernas para o ar [di pehrnash proo ar]

upstairs lá em cima [ayng seema]

urgent urgente [oorJaynt]

us* nos [noosh]
with us connosco [konohshkoo]
for us para nós [nosh]

USA os Estados Unidos [shtadooz ooneedoosh]

use usar [oozar]
may I use ...? posso usar ...? [posoo]

useful útil [ootil]

usual usual [oozwal]
the usual (drink etc) o de sempre [oo di saympr]

V

vacancy: do you have any vacancies? (hotel) têm vagas? [tay-ayng vagash]

vacation as férias [fehr-yash]
on vacation de férias [shtoh di]

vaccination a vacinação [vasinas**owng**]

vacuum cleaner o aspirador [ashpirad**ohr**]

valid (ticket etc) válido [**val**idoo]

how long is it valid for? até quando é válido? [at**eh** kw**ando**o]

valley o vale [val]

valuable (adj) valioso [val-**yoh**zoo]

can I leave my valuables here? posso deixar aqui os meus artigos de valor? [**po**soo daysh**ar** ak**ee** ooJ **may**-ooz arte**egoo**sh di val**ohr**]

value o valor

van a furgoneta [foorgoon**ayta**]

vanilla a baunilha [bown**eel**-ya]

a vanilla ice cream um gelado de baunilha [oong Jil**ado** di bown**eel**-ya]

vary: it varies varia [var**ee**-a]

vase a jarra [**Jarra**]

veal a vitela [vit**eh**la]

vegetables os legumes [lig**oo**mish]

vegetarian (man/woman) o vegetariano [viJitar-y**anoo**], a vegetariana

vending machine a máquina de venda [**ma**kina di **vay**nda]

very muito [m**wee**ngtoo]

very little for me muito pouco para mim [**poh**koo para meeng]

I like it very much gosto muito disso [**gosh**too – d**ee**soo]

vest (under shirt) a camisola interior [kami**zo**la intir-y**ohr**]

via via [**vee**-a]

video (film) o vídeo [**veed**-yoo]

video recorder o videogravador [**veed**-yoograva**dohr**]

view a vista [v**eesh**ta]

villa a vivenda [viv**aynda**]

village a aldeia [ald**ay**-a]

vinegar o vinagre [vin**agr**]

vineyard a vinha [v**een**-ya]

visa o visto [v**eesh**too]

visit visitar [vizit**ar**]

I'd like to visit ... gostaria de visitar ... [goosht**aree**-a di vizit**ar**]

vital: it's vital that ... é imprescindível que ... [eh impresh-sind**eevil** ki]

vodka o vodka

voice a voz [vosh]

voltage a tensão [taynso**wng**]

vomit vomitar [voomit**ar**]

W

waist a cintura [sint**oora**]

waistcoat o colete [kool**ayt**]

wait esperar [shpir**ar**]

wait for me espere por mim [shp**ehr** poor meeng]

don't wait for me não espere por mim [nowng]

can I wait until my wife/ partner gets here? posso esperar até a minha mulher/ companheira chegar? [pos shpir**ar** at**eh** a meen-ya mool-y**ehr**/ kompan-y**ayra** shig**ar**]

can you do it while I wait? pode fazer isso enquanto

espero? [pod fazayr eesoo
aynkwantoo shpehroo]
could you wait here for
me? pode esperar-me? [pod
shpirarmi]
waiter o empregado de mesa
[aympregadoo di mayza]
waiter! se faz favor! [si fash
favohr]
waitress a empregada de mesa
[aympregada di mayza]
waitress! se faz favor!
wake: can you wake me up
at 5.30? pode acordar-me às
cinco meia? [pod akoordarmi ash
seenkwee may-a]
wake-up call a chamada
para despertar [shamada para
dishpirtar]
Wales o País de Gales [pa-eeJ
di galish]
walk: is it a long walk?
é muito longe a pé? [eh
mweengtoo lohnJ a peh]
it's only a short walk é perto a
pé [pehrtoo]
I'll walk vou a pé [voh]
I'm going for a walk vou dar
um passeio [oong pasay-oo]
Walkman® o Walkman®
wall (outside) o muro [mooroo]
(inside) a parede [parayd]
wallet a carteira [kartayra]
wander: I like just wandering
around gosto de andar a ver
[goshtoo dandar a vayr]
want: I want a ... queria um ...
[kiree-a oong]
I don't want any ... não

quero ... [nowng kehroo]
I want to go home quero ir
para casa [eer para kaza]
I don't want to não quero
he wants to ele quer [ayl kehr]
what do you want? o que
deseja? [oo ki disayJa]
ward (in hospital) a enfermaria
[aynfirmaree-a]
warm quente [kaynt]
I'm so warm tenho tanto
calor [tayn-yoo tantoo kalohr]
was*: he was (ele) era [(ayl)
ehra]; (ele) estava [shtava]
she was (ela) era [(ehla)]; (ele)
estava
it was era; estava
wash lavar
(oneself) lavar-se [–si]
can you wash these? pode
lavar isto? [pod – eeshtoo]
washer (for bolt etc) a anilha
[aneel-ya]
washhand basin o lavatório
[lavator-yoo]
washing (clothes) a roupa para
lavar [rohpa]
washing machine a máquina
de lavar [makina di]
washing powder o detergente
[deterJaynt]
washing-up liquid o
detergente líquido [leekidoo]
wasp a vespa [vayshpa]
watch (wristwatch) o relógio (de
pulso) [riloJ-yoo (di poolsoo)]
will you watch my things for
me? pode tomar conta das
minhas coisas? [pod toomar

kohnta daJ meen-yash koh-izash]
watch out! cuidado! [kwidadoo]
watch strap a correia de
relógio [koorray-a di riloJ-yoo]
water a água [agwa]
  may I have some water? pode
  dar-me um pouco de água?
  [pod darmoong pohkoo dagwa]
waterproof (adj) à prova de
  água [dagwa]
waterskiing o esqui aquático
  [shkee akwatikoo]
wave (in sea) a onda [ohnda]
way: it's this way é por aqui
  [eh por akee]
  it's that way é por ali [alee]
  is it a long way to ...? é muito
  longe até ...? [mweengtoo lohnJ
  ateh]
  no way! de maneira nenhuma!
  [di manayra nin-yooma]

dialogue

could you tell me the
way to ...? pode indicar-
me o caminho para ...?
[podindikarmoo kameen-yoo]
go straight on until you
reach the traffic lights siga
em frente até chegar ao
semáforo [seegayng fraynt
ateh shigar ow semafooroo]
turn left vire à esquerda
[veera shkayrda]
take the first on the right
vire na primeira à direita
[veer na primayra dirayta]
see where

we* nós [nosh]
weak fraco [frakoo]
weather o tempo [taympoo]

dialogue

what's the weather
forecast? qual é a previsão
do tempo? [kwaleh a
privizowng doo taympoo]
it's going to be fine vai
estar bom [vī shtar bong]
it's going to rain vai chover
[shoovayr]
it'll brighten up later vai
melhorar mais tarde [mil-
yoorar mīsh tard]

wedding o casamento
  [kazamayntoo]
wedding ring a aliança [al-
  yansa]
Wednesday quarta-feira
  [kwarta fayra]
week a semana [simana]
  a week (from) today de hoje a
  uma semana [dohj a ooma]
  a week (from) tomorrow
  de amanhã a uma semana
  [daman-yang]
weekend o fim de semana
  [feeng di]
  at the weekend no fim de
  semana [noo]
weight o peso [payzoo]
weird esquisito [shkizeetoo]
  he's weird ele é esquisito [ayl
  eh]
welcome: welcome to ... bem

vindo a ... [bayng **vee**ndwa]
you're welcome (don't mention it) não tem de quê [nowng tayng di kay]
well: I don't feel well não me sinto muito bem [mi **see**ntoo m**wee**ngtoo bayng]
she's not well ela não está bem [**eh**la – shta]
you speak English very well fala inglês muito bem [ingl**ay**sh]
well done! muito bem!
this one as well este também [aysht tamb**ay**ng]
well well! (surprise) ah sim! [seeng]

dialogue

how are you? como está? [**koh**mo shta]
very well, thanks, and you? (said by man/woman) muito bem, obrigado/obrigada, e você? [obrig**a**doo – ee vos**ay**]

well-done (meat) bem passado [bayng pas**a**doo]
Welsh galês [gal**ay**sh]
I'm Welsh (man/woman) sou galês/galesa [soh – gal**ay**za]
were*: we were éramos [**eh**ramoosh]; estávamos [sht**a**vamoosh]
you were você era [vos**ay** **eh**ra]; você estava [sht**a**va]
they were (eles/elas) eram [(**ay**lsh/**eh**lash) **eh**rowng]; (eles/

elas) estavam [sht**a**vowng]
west o oeste [wesht]
in the west no oeste [noo]
West Indian (adj) antilhano [antil-**ya**noo]
wet molhado [mool-**ya**doo]
what? o quê? [oo kay]
what's that? o que é isso? [oo k-yeh **ee**soo]
what should I do? o que devo fazer? [oo kay d**ay**voo faz**ay**r]
what a view! que vista linda! [ki **vee**shta **lee**nda]
what bus do I take? que autocarro devo tomar? [ki owto**ka**rroo **day**voo too**ma**r]
wheel a r**o**da
wheelchair a cadeira de rodas [ka**day**ra di r**o**dash]
when? quando? [**kwa**ndoo]
when we get back quando nós voltarmos [nosh vool**ta**rmoosh]
when's the train/ferry? quando é o comboio/ferry? [**kwa**ndweh o komb**oy**-oo]
where? onde? [ohnd]
I don't know where it is não sei onde está [nowng say ohndsht**a**]

dialogue

where is the cathedral? onde fica a catedral? [ohnd **fee**ka]
it's over there fica ali adiante [**fee**kalee ad-**ya**nt]
could you show me where

it is on the map? pode mostrar-me onde está no mapa? [pod mooshtrarmi ohndshta noo mapa]
it's just here está bem aqui [shta bayng akee]
see **way**

which: which bus? qual autocarro? [kwal owtookarroo]

dialogue

which one? qual deles? [kwal daylish]
that one aquele [akayl]
this one? este? [aysht]
no, that one não aquele ali [nowng – alee]

while: while I'm here enquanto estou aqui [aynkwantoo shtoh akee]
whisky o whisky [weeshkee]
white branco [brankoo]
white wine o vinho branco [veen-yoo]
who? quem? [kayng]
who is it? quem é? [kayngeh]
the man who ... o homem que ... [ohmayng ki]
whole: the whole week toda a semana [tohda simana]
the whole lot tudo isto [toodoo eeshtoo]
whose: whose is this? de quem é isto? [di kayng eh eeshtoo]
why? porquê? [poorkay]

why not? porque não? [nowng]
wide largo [largoo]
wife: my wife a minha mulher [meen-ya mool-yehr]
will*: will you do it for me? fá-lo para mim? [faloo para meeng]
wind o vento [vayntoo]
window a janela [Janehla]
(of shop) a montra [mohntra]
near the window ao pé da janela [ow peh]
in the window (of shop) na montra
window seat o lugar ao pé da janela [loogar ow peh da Janehla]
windscreen o pára-brisas [para-breezash]
windscreen wiper o limpa pára-brisas [leempa]
windsurfing o windsurf
windy: it's so windy está muito vento [shta mweengtoo vayntoo]
wine o vinho [veen-yoo]
can we have some more wine? pode trazer mais vinho? [pod trazayr mīsh]
wine list a lista dos vinhos [leeshta dooJ veen-yoosh]
winter o Inverno [invehrnoo]
in the winter no Inverno [noo]
winter holiday as férias de inverno [fehr-yash dinvehrnoo]
wire o arame [aram]
(electric) o fio [fee-oo]
wish: best wishes com os melhores cumprimentos [kong ooJ mil-yorish koomprimayntoosh]
with com [kong]

I'm staying with ... estou na casa do/da ... [shtoh na kaza doo]

without sem [sayng]

witness a testemunha [tishtimoon-ya]

will you be a witness for me? quer ser minha testemunha? [kehr sayr meen-ya]

woman a mulher [mool-yehr]

wonderful (weather, holiday, person) maravilhoso [maravil-yohzoo]

(meal) excelente [ish-selaynt]

won't*: it won't start não pega [nowng pehga]

wood (material) a madeira [madayra]

woods (forest) o bosque [boshk]

wool a lã [lang]

word a palavra

work o trabalho [trabal-yoo]

it's not working não funciona [nowng foons-yohna]

I work in ... trabalho em ... [ayng]

world o mundo [moondoo]

worry: I'm worried (said by man/ woman) estou preocupado/ preocupada [shtoh pri-okoopadoo]

worse: it's worse está pior [shta p-yor]

worst o pior [oo]

worth: is it worth a visit? vale a pena uma visita? [val a payna ooma vizeeta]

would: would you give this to ...? pode dar isto a ...? [pod

dar eeshtwa]

wrap: could you wrap it up? pode embrulhá-lo? [aymbrool-yaloo]

wrapping paper o papel de embrulho [papehl daymbrool-yoo]

wrist o pulso [poolsoo]

write escrever [shkrivayr]

could you write it down? pode escrever isso? [pod – eesoo]

how do you write it? como é que escreve isso? [kohmoo eh kishkrehv]

writing paper o papel de carta [papehl di]

wrong: it's the wrong key não é esta a chave [nowng eh ehshta shav]

this is the wrong train este não é o comboio [aysht nowng eh oo komboy-oo]

the bill's wrong a conta está enganada [kohntashta aynganada]

sorry, wrong number desculpe, enganei-me no número [dishkoolp aynganaymi noo noomiroo]

sorry, wrong room desculpe, enganei-me no quarto [kwartoo]

there's something wrong with ... passa-se qualquer coisa com ... [pasasi kwalkehr koh-iza kong]

what's wrong? o que se passa? [oo ki si]

X

X-ray o raio X [ra-yoo shcesh]

Y

yacht o iate [yat]
yard* a jarda [Jarda]
year o ano [anoo]
yellow amarelo [amarehloo]
yes sim [seeng]
yesterday ontem [ohntayng]
  yesterday morning ontem de
  manhã [di man-yang]
  the day before yesterday
  anteontem [antiohntayng]
yet ainda [a-eenda], já [Ja]

dialogue

is it here yet? já está aqui?
[Ja shta akee]
no, not yet não, ainda não
[nowng a-eenda nowng]
you'll have to wait a little
longer yet ainda terá que
esperar um pouquinho [tira
kishpirar oong pohkeen-yoo]

yoghurt o iogurte [yoogoort]
you* (pol) você [vosay]
(more formal: to man/woman) o
senhor [oo sin-yohr], a senhora
(fam) tu [too]
this is for you isto é para si
[eeshtweh para see]
(fam) isto é para ti

with you consigo [konseegoo]
(fam) contigo [konteegoo]
young jovem [Jovayng]
your* (pol) seu [say-oo], sua
[soo-a]
(more formal: to man/woman) do
senhor [sin-yohr], da senhora
[sin-yora]
(fam) teu [tay-oo], tua [too-a]
yours* (pol) seu [say-oo], sua
[soo-a]
(more formal: to a man/woman)
do senhor [doo sin-yohr], da
senhora [sin-yora]
(fam) teu [tay-oo], tua [too-a]
youth hostel o albergue
da juventude [albehrg da
Joovayntood]

Z

zero zero [zehroo]
zip o fecho éclair®
[fayshwayklehr]
could you put a new zip on?
pode pôr um fecho éclair
novo? [pod pohr oong – nohvoo]
zipcode o código postal
[kodigoo pooshtal]
zoo o jardim zoológico
[Jardeeng zwoloJikoo]
zucchini a courgette

Portuguese

→

English

Colloquialisms

The following are words you might well hear. You shouldn't be tempted to use any of the stronger ones unless you are sure of your audience.

bestial! [bisht-yal] fantastic!
burro **m** [boorroo] thickhead
cabrão! [kabrowng] bastard!
está nas suas sete quintas [shta nash soo-ash seht keentash] he's/she's in his/her element
estou-me nas tintas [shtoh-mi nash teentash] I don't give a damn
filho da puta! [poota] son-of-a-bitch!
gajo **m** [gaJoo] bloke
grosso [grohsoo] pissed
imbecil [imbeseel] stupid
isso é canja [eesweh kanJa] piece of cake (literally: this is chicken soup)
louco [lohkoo] nutter
maçada [masada] bother
maluco [malookoo] barmy, nuts
merda! [mehrda] shit!
não faz mal [nowng faJ] it doesn't matter
não me diga! [nowng mi deega] you don't say!
ora essa! [ora ehsa] don't be stupid!
porreiro! [poorrayroo] bloody good!
que chatice! [ki shatees] oh no!, blast!
que disparate! [dishparat] rubbish!, nonsense!
que droga! [droga] blast!
raios o partam! [ra-yooz oo partowng] damn you!
rua! [roo-a] get out of here!
sacana! bastard!
tolo [tohloo] silly
vá à fava! go away!
vá para o caralho! [paroo karal-yoo] fuck off!
vá para o diabo! [d-yaboo] go to hell!
vá para o inferno! [infehrno] go to hell!

A

a the; to; her; it; to it; you
à to the
abaixo [abīshoo] below; down
 mais abaixo [mīz] further
 down
abcesso m [absehsoo] abscess
aberto [abehrtoo] open; opened
aberto até às 19 horas open
 until 7 p.m.
aberto das ... às ... horas open
 from ... to ... o'clock
abertura f [abirtoora] opening
aborrecer [aboorrisayr] to
 annoy; to bore
aborrecido [aboorriseedoo]
 annoying; bored; annoyed
abre-garrafas m [abrigarrafash]
 bottle-opener
abre-latas m [abrilatash] can-
 opener, tin-opener
Abril [abreel] April
abrir [abreer] to open; to
 unlock
 a abrir brevemente open soon
a/c c/o
acabar to finish
acalmar-se [–si] to calm down
acampar to camp
acaso: por acaso [poor akazoo]
 by chance
aceitar [asaytar] to accept; to
 take
acelerador m [asiliradohr]
 accelerator
acenda os médios switch on
 dipped headlights

acenda os mínimos switch on
 your parking lights
acender [asayndayr] to switch
 on; to light
acento m [asayntoo] accent
aceso [asayzoo] on, switched
 on
acesso m [asehsoo] access
acetona f [asitohna] nail polish
 remover
acho: acho que não [ashoo ki
 nowng] I don't think so
acho que sim [seeng] I think
 so
acidente m [asidaynt] accident;
 crash
acidente de viação [di v-ya-
 sowng] road accident
ácido [asidoo] sour; sharp
acima [aseema] up; above
acompanhar [akompan-yar] to
 accompany
aconselhar [akonsil-yar] to
 advise
acontecer [akontisayr] to
 happen
 o que aconteceu? [oo
 ki-akontisay-oo] what has
 happened?, what's up?, what's
 wrong?
 o que é que está a
 acontecer? [oo k-yeh kishta]
 what's happening?
acordado [akoordadoo] awake
acordar [akoordar] to wake, to
 wake up
 ele já acordou? [ayl Ja
 akoordoh] is he awake?
acordo: de acordo com [d-ya-

kohrdoo kong] according to
A.C.P. [a say pay] Portuguese Motoring Organization
acreditar to believe
acrílico m [akreelikoo] acrylic
actor m [atohr], actriz f [atreesh] actor; actress
adaptador m [adaptadohr] adapter
adega f cellar; old-style bar
adepta f [adehpta], adepto m [adehptoo] fan
adesivo m [adizeevoo] sticking plaster, Bandaid®
adeus [aday-oosh] goodbye
adeuzinho! [aday-oozeen-yoo] cheerio!
adiantado [ad-yantadoo] in advance
adiante: fica ali adiante [feekalee ad-yant] it's over there
adoecer [ad-wisayr] to fall ill
adolescente m/f [adoolish-saynt] teenager
adorar [adoorar] to adore
adorável [adooravil] lovely
adulta f [adoolta], adulto m [adooltoo] adult
advogada f [advoogada], advogado m [advoogadoo] lawyer
aeroporto m [a-ayroopohrtoo] airport
afiado [af-yadoo] sharp
afogador m choke
África f Africa
África do Sul [doo sool] South Africa
africano (m) [afrikanoo] African

afta f mouth ulcer
afundar [afoondar] to sink
agência f [aJayns-ya] agency
agência de viagens [di v-ya-Jayngsh] travel agency
agenda f [aJaynda] diary
agitar bem antes de usar shake well before using
agora [agora] now
agora não [nowng] not just now
Agosto [agohshtoo] August
agradável [agradavil] nice, pleasant
agradecer [agradisayr] to thank
agradecido [agradiseedoo] grateful
água f [agwa] water
aguaceiro m [agwasayroo] shower
água de colónia [di] eau de toilette
água destilada f [agwa dishtilada] distilled water
água fria [free-a] cold water
água potável [pootavil] drinking water
aguardar [agwardar] to wait for
agudo [agoodoo] sharp
agulha f [agool-ya] needle
aí [a-ee] there
ainda [a-eenda] yet, still
ainda mais ... [mīsh] even more ...
ainda não [nowng] not yet
ainda são só ... [sowng saw] it's only ...
ajuda f [aJooda] help
ajudar to help

al. avenue
alameda f [alamayda] avenue
alarme m [alarm] alarm
alarme de incêndios [dinsaynd-yoosh] fire alarm
alavanca f lever
alavanca das mudanças [daJ moodansash] gear lever
albergaria f [albirgaree-a] luxury hotel
albergue da juventude m [albehrg da Joovayntood] youth hostel
albergue juvenil youth hostel
alça f [alsa] strap
alcunha f [alkoon-ya] nickname
aldeia f [alday-a] village
aldeia de pescadores [di pishkadohrish] fishing village
além: além de [alayng di] apart from
para além de [paralayng] beyond
alemã (f) [alimang] German
Alemanha f [aliman-ya] Germany
alemão (m) [alimowng] German
alérgico a ... [alehrJikoo] allergic to ...
Alfa high-speed train
alfabeto m [alfabehtoo] alphabet
alfaiataria f [alfi-ataree-a], alfaiate m [alfi-at] tailor
alfândega f [alfandiga] Customs
alfinete m [alfinayt] brooch; pin
alfinete de segurança m [di sigooransa] safety pin
alforreca f [alfoorrehka] jellyfish
alga f seaweed

algodão m [algoodowng] cotton
algodão em rama [ayng] cotton wool
alguém [algayng] anybody; somebody, someone
algum [algoong], alguma [algooma] some; any
alguma coisa [koh-iza] something; anything
algumas [algoomash], alguns [algoonsh] some; any
ali [alee] (over) there
ali acima [aseema] up there
ali adiante [ad-yant] over there
é por ali [eh poor] it's that way
aliança f [al-vansa] wedding ring
alicate m [alikat] pliers
alicate de unhas [doon-yash] nail clippers
alimento m [alimayntoo] food
almoçar [almoosar] to have lunch
almoço m [almohsoo] lunch
almoço embalado [almohswaymbaladoo] packed lunch
almofada f [almoofada] cushion; pillow
alojamento m [alooJamayntoo] accommodation
alpinismo m [alpineeJmoo] mountaineering
altitude f [altitood] height
alto [altoo] high; tall; loud
no alto [noo] at the top
altura f [altoora] height
altura máxima maximum headroom

alugam-se quartos rooms to let, rooms for rent

alugar [aloogar] to hire, to rent

aluga-se [alooga-si] for hire, to rent

aluguer m [aloogehr] rent

aluguer de automóveis [dowtoomovaysh] car hire, car rental

aluguer de barcos boat hire

aluguer de barracas sunshades for hire

aluguer de cadeiras beach chairs for hire

aluguer de gaivotas pedal boat hire

aluguer de parassóis beach umbrellas for hire

alvorada f [alvoorada] dawn

ama f childminder

amanhã [aman-yang] tomorrow

amanhã à tarde [tard] tomorrow afternoon

amanhã de manhã [di man-yang] tomorrow morning

amar to love

amarelo [amarehloo] yellow

amargo [amargoo] bitter

amável [amavil] kind; generous

ambos [amboosh] both

ambulância f [amboolans-ya] ambulance

ameno [amaynoo] mild

América f America

americano [amirikanoo] American

amiga f [ameega] friend

amigdalite f [ameegdaleet] tonsillitis

amigo m [ameegoo] friend

amor m [amohr] love

amortecedor m [amoortisidohr] shock-absorber

amperes mpl [ampehrish] amps

ampliação f [ampl-yasowng] enlargement

ampolas bebíveis fpl [ampohlaJ bibeevaysh] ampoules

analgésicos mpl [analJehzeekoosh] painkillers

análises de sangue fpl [analiziJ di sang] blood tests

anca f hip

âncora f anchor

andar (m) floor, storey; to walk

andar à boleia [boolay-a] to hitchhike

andar a cavalo [kavaloo] horse-riding

andar a pé [peh] to walk

anel m [anehl] ring

anilha f [aneel-ya] washer

animado [animadoo] lively

aniversário de casamento m [anivirsar-yoo di kazamayntoo] wedding anniversary

aniversário natalício [nataleesyoo] birthday

ano m [anoo] year

Ano Novo [nohvoo] New Year

anteontem [anti-ohntayng] the day before yesterday

antepassado m ancestor

anterior: dia anterior m [dee-a antir-yohr] the day before

antes [antsh] before

antibióticos mpl [antib-yotikoosh]

134

antibiotics

antticongelante m [–konJilant] antifreeze

antigo [anteegoo] ancient, old

antiguidade f [antigweedad] antique

anti-histamínicos mpl [–eesh-tameenikoosh] antihistamines

antilaxante m [anti-lashant] medicine for diarrhoea

antiquado [antikwadoo] old-fashioned

anti-séptico m [–sehptikoo] antiseptic

anúncio m [anoons-yoo] advertisement

ao [ow] to the; at the
ao norte de north of

aos [owsh] to the; at the

apagar to switch off

apagar os máximos switch headlights off

apanhar [apan-yar] to get on, to catch; to pick up

apanhar banhos de sol [ban-yooJ di] to sunbathe

aparelhagem (de som) f [aparel-yaJayng (di song)] stereo; audio equipment

aparelho m [aparayl-yoo] device

aparelho auditivo hearing aid

aparelho para a surdez [soordaysh] hearing aid

aparelhos eléctricos mpl [aparayl-yooz elehtrikoosh] electrical appliances

apartamento m [apartamayntoo] apartment, flat

aparthotel m [apartohtehl] self-

catering apartment

apelido m [apileedoo] surname; family name

apendicite f [apendiseet] appendicitis

apertado [apirtadoo] tight

apertar to hold tight; to fasten

apertar o cinto de segurança fasten your seatbelt

apetecer [apitisayr] to feel like
apetece-me [apitehsimi] I feel like

apetite m [apiteet] appetite

aplnhado [apeen-yadoo] crowded

aprender [aprayndayr] to learn

apresentar [aprizentar] to introduce

apressar-se [aprisarsi] to hurry

aproximadamente [aproosimadamaynt] approximately, roughly

aquecedor m [akesidohr] heater

aquecedor eléctrico [elehtrikoo] electric fire

aquecimento m [akesimayntoo] heating

aquecimento central [sayntral] central heating

aquela [akehla], aquele [akayl] that, that one (further away)

aquelas [akehlash], aqueles [akaylish] those (further away)

aqui [akee] (over) here
aqui embaixo [aymbishoo] down here
aqui está/estão ... [shta/shtowng] here is/are ...

aqui mesmo [may**J**moo] just here

é por aqui [eh por] it's this way

aqui tem [tayng] here you are

aquilo [akeeloo] that; that one (further away)

ar m air

árabe [arabi] Arab; Arabic

os árabes the Arabs

arame m [aram] wire

aranha f [aran-ya] spider

arco-íris m [arkoo-**ee**reesh] rainbow

ar condicionado m [kondis-yoon**a**doo] air conditioning

arder [ard**ayr**] to burn

areia f [aray-a] sand

armário m [armar-yoo] cupboard

armazém m [armaz**a**yng] warehouse; big store

aroma artificial/natural artificial/natural fragrance

arq. architect

arqueologia f [ark-yoloo**J**ee-a] archaeology

arquitecto m [arkit**eh**too] architect

arraial m [arrī-**al**] local fair with fireworks, singing and dancing

arranhão m [arran-**yow**ng] scratch

arranjos mpl [arran**J**oosh] repairs

arredores mpl [arred**o**rish] suburb

arriscado [arrishk**a**doo] risky

arte f [art] art

artesanato m [artizan**a**too] handicrafts, crafts

artificial [artifis-y**al**] artificial

artigos de bébé mpl [art**ee**gooJ di beb**eh**] baby goods

artigos de campismo [kamp**ee**Jmoo] camping equipment

artigos de casa [k**a**za] household goods

artigos de desporto [dishp**oh**rtoo] sports goods

artigos de luxo [**loo**shoo] luxury goods

artigos de viagem [v-ya**J**ayng] travel goods

artigos em cabedal [ayng kabid**al**] leather goods

artigos em cortiça [koort**ee**sa] cork goods

artigos em pele [pehl] leather goods

artigos regionais regional goods, typical goods from the region

artista m/f [art**ee**shta] artist

árvore f [**a**rvoori] tree

as [ash] the; them; you

às to the; at the

asa f wing

asa-delta f [aza-d**eh**lta] hang-gliding

ascensor m [ashsayns**ohr**] lift, elevator

asma f [a**J**ma] asthma

asneira f [a**J**n**ay**ra] nonsense; swearword

aspirador m [ashpirad**ohr**] vacuum cleaner

aspirina f [ashpir**ee**na] aspirin

assaltado [asalt**a**doo] mugged

assar to bake; to roast

assento m [asayntoo] seat

assim [aseeng] this way

assim está bem [shta bayng] that'll do nicely

assim está bem? is that OK?

assinado signed

assinar to sign

assinatura f [asinatoora] signature

atacadores mpl [atakadohrish] shoelaces

atalho m [atal-yoo] shortcut

ataque m [atak] fit; attack

ataque cardíaco [kardee-akoo] heart attack

até [ateh] until

até amanhã [aman-yang] see you tomorrow

até já [Ja] see you soon

até logo! [logoo] see you!, see you later!

até mesmo ... [mayJmoo] even ...

atenção please note; caution; warning

atenção ao comboio beware of the train

atenção: portas automáticas warning: automatic doors

aterragem f [atirraJayng] landing

aterragem de emergência emergency landing

aterrar to land

atirar to throw

Atlântico m Atlantic

atletismo m [atleteeJmoo] athletics

atraente [atra-aynt] attractive

atrás [atrash] at the back, behind

atrás de ... [di] behind ...

atrasado [atrazadoo] late, delayed

estar atrasado [shtar] to be late

atraso m [atrazoo] delay

através de [atravehJ di] through

atravessar to go through, to cross

atravesse go, walk

atropelar [atropilar] to knock over, to knock down

auscultador m [owshkooltadohr] receiver

auscultadores mpl [owshkooltadohrish] headphones

australiano (m) [owshtral-yanoo] Australian

autobanco m [owtoobankoo] cash dispenser, ATM

autocarro m [owtookarroo] coach, bus

autocarro do aeroporto [dwayroopohrtoo] airport bus

autoestrada f [owtooohtrada] motorway, highway, freeway

automático [owtoomatikoo] automatic

automóvel m [owtoomovil] car

Automóvel Clube de Portugal Portuguese Motoring Organization

av. avenue

avance go, walk

avaria f [avaree-a] breakdown

avariado [avari-adoo] damaged; faulty; out of order

avariar [avari-**ar**] to damage; to break down

avarias [ava**ree**-ash] breakdown service

ave f [av**ï**] bird

avenida f [avin**ee**da] avenue

avião m [av-**yow**ng] plane, airplane

de avião [dav-**yow**ng] by plane; by air

aviso [av**ee**zoo] warning; notice

avô m [av**oh**] grandfather

avó f [av**aw**] grandmother

azedo [az**ay**doo] sour

azul [az**ool**] blue

azulejaria f [azoolayJar**ee**-a] tile maker's workshop

azul-marinho [az**ool** mar**een**-yoo] navy blue

B

bagagem f [baga**Jayng**] luggage, baggage

bagagem de mão f [di mowng] hand luggage

baía f [ba-**ee**-a] bay

baile m [b**ï**lï] dance

bairro m [b**ï**rroo] district

baixo [b**ï**shoo] low; short

balcão m [balk**ow**ng] counter

balcão de informações [dinfoormas**oy**ngsh] information desk

balcão da recepção [risehs**ow**ng] reception desk

balde m [b**ow**ld] bucket

banco m [b**ank**oo] bank; stool

banco de poupança [di pohp**ans**a] savings bank

banda f band

bandeira f [band**ay**ra] flag

banheira f [ban-**yay**ra] bathtub, bath

banheiro m [ban-**yay**roo] lifeguard

banheiros [ban-**yay**roosh] toilets

banho m [ban-yoo] bath

banho de sol: tomar banho de sol [toomar – di] to sunbathe

barata f cockroach

barato [bar**a**too] cheap, inexpensive

barba f beard

barbatanas fpl [barbat**a**nash] flippers

barbeiro m [barb**ay**roo] men's hairdresser's, barber's shop

barco m [b**ar**koo] boat

barco a motor [barkwa moot**ohr**] motorboat

barco a remos [r**ay**moosh] rowing boat

barco a vapor steamer

barco à vela sailing boat

barcos de aluguer boats for hire

barraca f beach hut

barro: louça de barro f [l**oh**sa di b**ar**roo] earthenware

barulhento [barool-y**ay**ntoo] noisy

barulho m [bar**ool**-yoo] noise

bastante [bash**tant**] fairly; rather; quite (a lot)

bata (à porta) knock

batechapas bodywork repairs

bater [batayr] to hit, to knock

bateria f [batiree-a] battery

baton m [batong] lipstick

baton para o cieiro [oo s-yayroo]
lip salve

bêbado [baybadoo] drunk

bebé m [bebeh] baby

beber [bibayr] to drink

bebida f [biheeda] drink

beco sem saída cul-de-sac,
dead end

bege beige

beijar [bayJar] to kiss

beijo m [bayJoo] kiss

beira: à beira do mar [bayra
doo] at/by the seaside

beira-mar: à beira-mar by
the sea

belga (m/f) Belgian

Bélgica f [behlJika] Belgium

beliche m [bileesh] berth,
bunk; couchette; bunk beds

belo [behloo] beautiful

bem [bayng] fine, well, OK;
properly

bem aqui [akee] right here

está bem [shta] that's fine

estás bem? [shtash] are you
all right?

bem-educado [bayng idookadoo]
polite

bem passado [pasadoo] well-
done

bem-vindo [veendoo] welcome

bem-vindo a ... welcome
to ...

bengaleiro m [bengalayroo]
cloakroom, checkroom

berço m [bayrsoo] cot

bestial! [bisht-yal] fantastic!,
tremendous!

bexiga f [bisheega] bladder

biberão m [bibirowng] baby's
bottle

biblioteca f [bibl-yootehka]
library

bicha f [beesha] queue, line

bicicleta f [bisiklehta] bicycle,
bike

bifurcação f [bifoorkasowng]
fork (in road)

bigode m [higod] moustache

bilha de gás f [beel-ya di gash]
gas cylinder

bilhete m [bil-yayt] ticket

bilhete de entrada [dayntrada]
admission ticket

bilhete de excursão
[dishkoorsowng] excursion
ticket

bilhete de ida [deeda] single
ticket, one-way ticket

bilhete de ida e volta [deedi]
return ticket, round trip
ticket

bilhete de lotaria [di lootaree-a]
lottery ticket

bilhete em aberto [bil-yaytayng
abehrtoo] open ticket

bilheteira f [bil-yitayra] box
office, ticket office

bilhetes tickets

bilhete simples m [bil-yayt
seemplish] single ticket, one-
way ticket

bloco de apartamentos m
[blokoo dapartamayntoosh]

apartment block
bloco de apontamentos
[dapontama**ayn**toosh] notebook
blusa f [b**loo**za] blouse
boa [b**oh**-a] good
boa noite [n**oh**-it] good
  evening; good night
Boas Festas! [b**oh**-ash f**eh**shtash]
  merry Christmas and a happy
  New Year!
boa sorte! [s**oh**rt] good luck!
boa tarde [tard] good
  afternoon; good evening
boate f [bwat] nightclub; disco
boa viagem! [v-ya**j**ayng] have a
  good journey!
boca f [b**oh**ka] mouth
bocadinho m [booka**deen**-yoo]
  little bit
bocado m [booka**doo**] piece
bochecha f [boosh**ay**sha] cheek
bóia f [b**o**-ya] buoy
boite f [bwat] nightclub; disco
bola f ball
bola de futebol [di f**oot**bol]
  football
boleia f [boo**lay**-a] lift; ride
dar (uma) boleia a to give a
  lift to
bolha f [b**ohl**-ya] blister
bolinha f [boo**leen**-ya] ball (small)
bolso m [b**ohl**soo] pocket
bom [bong] good; fine
bom apetite! [bong api**teet**]
  enjoy your meal!
bomba f [b**ohm**ba] bomb;
  pump
bomba de ar air pump
bomba de gasolina [di

gazoo**leen**a] garage, filling
  station, gas station; petrol
  pump
bombeiros mpl [bomb**ayr**oosh]
  fire brigade
bom dia [bong dee-a] good
  morning
boné m [boo**neh**] cap, hat
boneca f [boo**neh**ka] doll
bonito [boo**nee**too] beautiful;
  nice; pretty
borboleta f [borboo**layt**a]
  butterfly
borda f edge
borracha f [boo**rrash**a] rubber;
  eraser
bosque m [boshk] woods,
  forest
bota f boot (footwear)
botão m [boo**towng**] button
botas de borracha fpl
  wellingtons
bote de borracha m [bot di
  boo**rrash**a] dinghy
braço m [b**ras**oo] arm
branco [b**rank**oo] white
Brasil m [bra**zeel**] Brazil
brasileiro (m) [brazil**ayr**oo]
  Brazilian
breve [brev] brief
em breve soon
briga f [b**reeg**a] fight
brigar to fight
brilhante [breel-**yant**] bright;
  brilliant
brincadeira f [breenka**dayr**a]
  joke
brincos mpl [b**reenk**oosh]
  earrings

brinquedo m [breenkaydoo] toy

brisa f [breeza] breeze

britânico [britanikoo] British

brochura f [broshoora] leaflet

bronquite [bronkeet] bronchitis

bronzeado (m) [bronz-yadoo]
tan; suntan; suntanned

bronzeador m suntan lotion

bronzear [brohnz-yar] to tan

bronzear-se [–si] to get a tan

bugigangas mpl [booJigangash]
bric-a-brac

bule m [bool] teapot

buraco m [boorakoo] hole

burro (m) [boorroo] donkey;
thickhead; stupid

buscar [booshkar] to collect;
to fetch

bússola f [boosoola] compass

buzina f [boozeena] horn

C

c/ with

cá here

cabeça f [kabaysa] head

cabedais mpl [kabidash] leather
goods

cabedal m [kabidal] leather

cabeleireiro m [kabilayrayroo]
hairdresser's

cabeleireiro de homens
[dohmayngsh] men's hairdresser

cabeleireiro de senhoras [di
sin-yorash] ladies' hairdresser

cabeleireiro unisexo
[oonisehksoo] unisex salon

cabelo m [kabayloo] hair

cabide m [kabeed] coathanger

cabina f [kabeena] cabin

cabina de provas [di provash]
fitting room

cabina telefónica [kabeena
telefohnika] phone box, phone
booth

cabos para ligar a bateria mpl
[kaboosh – batiree-a] jump leads

cabra f goat

cabrão! [kabrowng] bastard!

cabrona! bastard!

caça f [kasa] game (meat);
hunting

caçarola f [kasarola] saucepan

cachimbo m [kasheemboo] pipe
(for smoking)

cacifo m [kaseefoo] locker

cada each; every

cadeado m [kad-yadoo] padlock

cadeia f [kaday-a] prison; chain

cadeira f [kadayra] chair

cadeira de bebé [di bebeh]
highchair

cadeira de lona [lohna]
deckchair

cadeira de rodas [rodash]
wheelchair

cadeira reclinável [reklinavil]
sun lounger

cadeirinha de bebé f
[kadayreen-ya di bebeh]
pushchair, buggy

caderneta f [kadayrnayta] book
of tickets

café m [kafeh] café; coffee

café de esplanada [dishplanada]
pavement café

cãibra f [kaymbra] cramp

cair [ka-**eer**] to fall

cais **m** [kīsh] quay; quayside; platform, (US) track

caixa **f** [kīsha] box; cash desk, till; cashier; cashpoint, ATM; savings bank; building society

caixa automático [owtoo**mat**eekoo] cashpoint, ATM

caixa de fusíveis [di foo**zee**vaysh] fusebox

caixa de mudanças [moo**dan**sash] gearbox

caixa de primeiros socorros [pri**may**roosh soo**ko**rroosh] first-aid kit

caixa de velocidades [viloosi**dad**sh] gearbox

caixa do correio [doo koo**rray**-oo] postbox; mailbox

caixa fechada till closed

caixote de lixo **m** [kī**sho**t di **lee**shoo] bin, dustbin, trashcan

calçado **m** [kal**sa**doo] footwear

calcanhar **m** [kalkan-**yar**] heel (of foot)

calças **fpl** [**kal**sash] trousers, (US) pants

calções **mpl** [kal**soy**ngsh] shorts

calções de banho [di **ban**-yoo] swimming trunks

calculadora **f** [kalkoola**doh**ra] calculator

caldeira **f** [kal**day**ra] boiler

calendário **m** [kalen**dar**-yoo] calendar

cale-se! [**kal**si] quiet!; shut up!

calmo [**kal**moo] calm

calor **m** [ka**lohr**] heat

está imenso calor [shta i**mayn**soo] it's hot

ter calor [tayr] to be hot

cama **f** bed

cama de bebé [di be**beh**] cot

cama de campanha [kampan-ya] campbed

cama de casal [di ka**zal**] double bed

cama de solteiro [sool**tay**roo] single bed

cama dupla [**doo**pla] double bed

cama individual **f** [individwal] single bed

câmara **f** camera

câmara de ar **f** [dar] inner tube

câmara de vídeo **f** [di **veed**-yoo] camcorder

câmara municipal **f** [**moo**nisipal] town hall

camarim **m** [kama**reeng**] dressing room

camarote **m** [kama**rot**] cabin

camas separadas **fpl** [**ka**mash sipa**ra**dash] twin beds

câmbio **m** [**kamb**-yoo] bureau de change; exchange rate

câmbio do dia [doo **dee**-a] current exchange rate

camião **m** [kam-**yowng**] truck

caminho **m** [ka**meen**-yoo] path

caminho de ferro railway

Caminhos de Ferro Portugueses Portuguese Railways

camioneta **f** [kam-yoo**nay**ta] coach, bus; light truck

camisa f [kameeza] shirt

camisa de dormir [di doormeer] nightdress

camisaria f [kamizaree-a] shirt shop

camisola f [kamizola] jersey, jumper, sweater

camisola interior [intir-yohr] vest (under shirt)

campainha f [kampa-een-ya] bell

campismo m [kampeeJmoo] camping

campo m [kampoo] field; countryside, country

campo de futebol [di footbol] football ground

campo de golfe [golf] golf course

campo de ténis [tehnish] tennis court

camurça f [kamoorsa] suede

canadiano (m) [kanad-yanoo] Canadian

canal m canal; channel

Canal da Mancha English Channel

canalizador m [kanalizadohr] plumber

canção f [kansowng] song

cancelado [kansiladoo] cancelled

cancelar [kansilar] to cancel

candeeiro m [kand-yayroo] lamp

caneca f [kanehka] mug

caneta f [kanayta] pen

caneta de feltro [di fayltroo] felt-tip pen

caneta esferográfica [shfiroografika] ballpoint pen

canhoto [kan-yohtoo] left-handed

canivete m [kaniveht] penknife

cano m [kanoo] pipe (for water)

canoa f [kanoh-a] canoe

canoagem m [kanwaJayng] canoeing

cano de esgoto m [kanoo diJgohtoo] drain

cansado [kansadoo] tired

cantar to sing

canto m [kantoo] corner

no canto [noo] in the corner

cantor m [kantohr], cantora f singer

cão m [kowng] dog

cão de guarda [gwarda] guard dog

capacete m [kapasayt] helmet

capaz: não seria capaz de ... [siree-a kapaJ di] I wouldn't be able to ...

capela f [kapehla] chapel

capelista f [kapeleeshta] haberdasher

capô m [kapoh] bonnet (of car), (US) hood

cápsula f capsule

cara f face

caranguejo m [karangayJoo] crab

caravana f caravan, (US) trailer

carburador m [karbooradohr] carburettor

careca [karehka] bald

carga máxima maximum load

carnaval m carnival

caro [karoo] expensive

carpete f [karpeht] carpet

carrinho **m** [karr**ee**n-yoo] trolley, (US) cart

carrinho de bagagem [di baga**J**ayng] luggage trolley, (US) baggage cart

carrinho de bebé [beb**eh**] pushchair; pram

carro **m** [k**a**rroo] car

de carro [di] by car

carroçaria **f** [karroosar**ee**-a] bodywork

carro de aluguer **m** [k**a**rroo daloog**ehr**] rented car

carro de mão [di mowng] trolley

carros de aluguer [daloog**ehr**] car hire, car rental

carruagem **f** [karrwa**J**ayng] carriage, coach

carruagem-cama **f** sleeper, sleeping car

carruagem para não fumadores **f** [**now**ng foomad**oh**rish] nonsmoking carriage

carruagem restaurante [ristowr**ant**] buffet car; restaurant car

carta **f** letter

carta de condução [di kondoos**ow**ng] driver's licence

carta de embarque [daymb**a**rk] boarding pass

carta de identidade [didentid**a**d] ID card

cartão **m** [kart**ow**ng] card; pass; identity card; business card; cardboard

cartão bancário [bank**a**r-yoo] cheque card

cartão de crédito [di kr**eh**deetoo] credit card

cartão de débito [d**eh**beetoo] charge card

cartão de embarque [daymb**a**rk] boarding pass

cartão de garantia [di garant**ee**-a] cheque card

cartão de telefone [di telef**oh**n] phonecard

cartão de visitas [di viz**ee**tash] business card

cartão Eurocheque Eurocheque card

carta por correio expresso [poor koorr**ay**-oo shpr**eh**soo] express letter

cartas letters

carta verde [v**a**yrd] green card (car insurance)

cartaz **m** [kart**a**sh] poster

carteira **f** [kart**a**yra] purse; wallet

carteirista **m/f** [kartayr**ee**shta] pickpocket

carteiro **m** postman

casa **f** [k**a**za] home; house

em casa [**a**yng] at home

na sua casa [**soo**-a] at your place

estar na casa do/da [shtar ... doo] to stay with

ir para casa to go home

casaco **m** [kaz**a**koo] jacket; coat

casaco de malha [di m**a**l-ya] cardigan

casa de antiguidades **f** [k**a**za dantigweed**a**dsh] antique shop

casa de banho [di b**a**n-yoo]

144

bathroom; toilet, rest room

casa de banho dos homens [dooz **oh**mayngsh] gents' toilet, men's room

casa de banho privativa [privat**ee**va] private bathroom

casa de banho pública [**poo**blika] public convenience

casa de fados [di f**a**doosh] restaurant where traditional Portuguese fado songs are sung

casa de hóspedes [**do**shpidsh] guesthouse

casa de jantar [di **ja**ntar] dining room

casa de pasto [**pa**shton] canteen-style eating place, usually open at lunchtime and serving a cheap three-course menu

casa de saúde [disa-**ood**] clinic; nursing home

casado [kaz**a**doo] married

casal m [kaz**a**l] couple

casamento m [kazam**ay**ntoo] wedding

casar-se [kaz**a**rsi] to get married

casas de banho mpl [ka**za**J di **ba**n-yoo] toilets, rest rooms

caseiro [kaz**ay**roo] home-made

caso m [k**a**zoo] case

 em caso de in case of

castanho [kash**ta**n-yoo] brown

castelo m [kash**teh**loo] castle

catarata f waterfall; cataract

catedral f [kati**dra**l] cathedral

categoria f [katigoor**ee**-a]

category

católico (m) [kat**o**likoo] Catholic

catorze [kat**ohr**z] fourteen

causa f [k**ow**za] cause

 por causa de [poor – di] because of

cautela take care

cavaleiro m [kaval**ay**roo] horseman

cavalheiro m [kaval-y**ay**roo] gentleman

cavalheiros mpl [kaval-y**ay**roosh] gents' toilet, men's room

cavalo m [kav**a**loo] horse

cave f [k**a**v] cellar; basement

caveira f [kav**ay**ra] skull

caverna f [kav**eh**rna] cave

cavilha f [kav**ee**l-ya] tent peg

c/c current account

CE f [say eh] EC

cedo [s**ay**doo] early

 mais cedo [mish] earlier

cego [s**eh**goo] blind

cem [sayng] hundred

cemitério m [simit**ehr**-yoo] cemetery

centígrado m [sentee**gra**doo] centigrade

centímetro m [sent**ee**mitroo] centimetre

cento e ... [s**ay**ntwee] one hundred and ...

central [sen-tr**a**l] central

central de correios f [di koorray-**oo**sh] main post office

centro m [s**ay**ntroo] centre

centro comercial [komayrs-y**a**l] shopping centre

centro da cidade [sid**a**d] city

centre, town centre

centro de enfermagem [dingfirmaJayng] clinic

centro de informação turística [dinfoormasowng tooreestika] tourist information office

centro de turismo [di tooreeJmoo] tourist information

cerâmicas fpl [siramikash] ceramics

cerca f [sayrka] fence

cerimónia f [sirimohn-ya] ceremony

de cerimónia [di] formal

certamente [sirtamaynt] certainly

certamente que não [ki nowng] certainly not

certeza: de certeza [di sirtayza] definitely

de certeza que não [ki nowng] definitely not

tem a certeza? [tayng] are you sure?

com certeza [kong] certainly, of course, sure

certidão f [sirtidowng] certificate

certo [sehrtoo] correct, right; sure

cervejaria f [sirvayJaree-a] beer house serving food

cesto m [sayshtoo] basket

cesto de compras [di komprash] shopping basket

céu m [seh-oo] sky

chaleira f [shalayra] kettle

chamada f [shamada] call

chamada de longa distância [di lohnga dishtans-ya] long-distance call

chamada internacional [internas-yoonal] international call

chamada interurbana [interoorbana] long-distance call

chamada local [lookal] local call

chamada paga no destinatário [noo dishtinatar-yoo] collect call, reverse charge call

chamada para despertar [dishpirtar] wake-up call

chamar [shamar] to call

chamar-se [–si] to be called

como se chama? [kohmoo si shama] what's your name?

champô m [shampoh] shampoo

chão m [showng] ground; floor

no chão [noo] on the floor; on the ground

chapa da matrícula f [shapa da matreekoola] licence plate

chapelaria f [shapilaree-a] hat shop

chapéu m [shapeh-oo] hat

chapéu de sol [di] beach umbrella, sunshade

charcutaria f [sharkootaree-a] delicatessen

charuto m [sharootoo] cigar

chateado [shat-yadoo] bored

chave f [shav] key

chave de fendas [di fayndash] screwdriver

chave de porcas [porkash]

spanner

chave inglesa [inglayza] wrench; spanner

chaveiro m [shavayroo] keyring

check-in: fazer o check-in to check in

chávena f [shavena] cup

chefe da estação m [shehf dishtas-owng] station master

chega [shayga] that's plenty; that's enough

chegada f [shigada] arrival

chegadas arrivals

chegar [shigar] to arrive, to get in; to reach

cheio [shay-oo] full

cheirar [shayrar] to smell

cheiro m [shayroo] smell

cheque de viagem m [shehk di v-yajayng] traveller's cheque

chinês (m) [shinaysh] Chinese

chique [sheek] posh; chic

chocante [shookant] shocking

choque m [shok] shock

chorar [shoorar] to cry

chover [shoovayr] to rain
está a chover it's raining

chumbo m [shoomboo] lead; filling

chupa-chupa m [shoopa-shoopa] lollipop

chupeta f [shoopayta] dummy

churrascada f [shoorrashkada] barbecue

chuva f [shoova] rain

Cia. company

ciclismo m [sikleejmoo] cycling

ciclista m/f [sikleeshta] cyclist

cidadã/cidadão de terceira idade f/m [sidadang/sidadowng di tirsayra idad] senior citizen

cidade f [sidad] town; city; town centre
fora da cidade out of town

cidade antiga [anteega] old town

ciência f [s-yayns-ya] science

cigarro m [sigarroo] cigarette

cima: em cima de ... [ayng seema di] on top of ...
lá em cima up there; upstairs

cinco [seenkoo] five

cinquenta [sinkwaynta] fifty

cinto m [seentoo] belt

cinto de salvação [di salvasowng] lifebelt

cinto de segurança [sigooransa] seatbelt

cintura f [sintoora] waist

cinzeiro m [sinzayroo] ashtray

cinzento [sinzayntoo] grey

circuito turístico m [sirkoo-eetoo tooreeshtikoo] sightseeing tour

circule pela direita/esquerda keep right/left

círculo m [seerkooloo] circle

ciumento [s-yoomayntoo] jealous

claro [klaroo] pale; light; clear; claro! sure!, of course!
claro que não [ki-nowng] of course not
é claro [eh] of course

classe f [klas] class

classe económica [ekoonohmika] economy class

clima m [kleema] climate

clínica f [kleenika] clinic

CI

147

clínica médica clinic
clínica veterinária veterinary
 clinic
clube m [kloob] club
clube de golfe [di golf] golf
 club
clube de ténis [di tehnish]
 tennis club
cobertor m [koobirtohr] blanket
cobra f snake
cobrar to cash
cobrir to cover
código m [kodigoo] code
código da estrada highway
 code
código postal m [pooshtal], cod.
 postal postcode, zip code
coelho m [kwayl-yoo] rabbit
cofre m safe
coisa f [koh-iza] thing
cola f glue
colar m [koolar] necklace
colarinho m [koolareen-yoo]
 collar
colchão m [koolshowng]
 mattress
colchão de praia [di prī-a]
 beach mat
colecção f [koolehsowng]
 collection
colégio m [koolehJ-yoo] college
colete m [koolayt] waistcoat
colete de salvação [di
 salvasowng] life jacket
colher f [kool-yehr] spoon
colher de chá f [di sha]
 teaspoon
colisão f [kooleezowng] crash
collants mpl [koolansh] tights,

pantyhose
com [kong] with
comandante m [koomandant]
 captain
combinação f [kombinasowng]
 combination; slip, underskirt
comboio m [komboy-oo] train
 de comboio [di] by train
comboio rápido express train
começar [koomesar] to begin,
 to start
começo m [koomaysoo] start,
 beginning
comédia f [koomehd-ya]
 comedy
comer [koomayr] to eat
comerciante m/f [koomayrs-yant]
 business person
comichão f [koomishowng] itch
comida f [koomeeda] food;
 meal
comida congelada [konJilada]
 frozen food
comida de bebé f [di bebeh]
 baby food
comidas fpl food; meals
comissão m [koomisowng]
 commission
comissário de bordo m
 [koomisar-yoo di bordoo] steward
como [kohmoo] how; like;
 since, as
 como? what?, pardon (me)?,
 sorry?
 como é? [eh] what's it like?
 como está? [shta] how are
 you?, how do you do?
 como este [kohmwaysht] like
 this

como vai? [vi] how are things?

companheira f [kompan-**yay**ra] partner, girlfriend

companheiro m [kompan-**yay**roo] partner, boyfriend

companhia f [kompan-**yee**-a] company

companhia aérea [a-**ehr**-ya] airline

compartimento m [kompartim**ayn**too] compartment

completamente [komplitam**aynt**] completely

completo [kompl**eh**too] full

complicado [komplik**a**doo] complicated

compra f [**koh**mpra] purchase

comprar [kompr**ar**] to buy

compras fpl [**koh**mprash] shopping

ir às compras [eer ash] to go shopping

compreender [kompr-yaynd**ayr**] to understand

comprido [kompr**ee**doo] long

comprimento m [komprim**ayn**too] length

comprimido m [komprim**ee**doo] tablet

comprimido para dormir [doorm**eer**] sleeping pill

computador m [kompootad**ohr**] computer

Comunidade Europeia European Community

concerto m [kons**ayr**too] concert

concessionário m [konsis-yoonar-yoo] agent

concha f [**koh**nsha] shell

concha do mar [doo] seashell

concordar [konkord**ar**] to agree

concordo [konk**or**doo] I agree

condições fpl [kondis**oy**ngsh] conditions, terms

condução f [kondoos**ow**ng] driving; transport

condução enquanto embriagado [aynkw**an**too aymbr-yag**a**doo] drunken driving

condutor m [kondoot**ohr**], condutora f driver

conduza com cuidado drive carefully

conduzir [kondooz**eer**] to lead, to drive

cone de gelado m [kohn di Jil**a**doo] ice-cream cone

confecções de criança fpl [konfehs-**oy**ngsh di kr-yansa] children's wear

confecções de homem [**doh**mayng] menswear

confecções de senhora [di sin-yora] ladies' wear

confeitaria [konfaytar**ce**-a] sweet shop, candy store

conferência f [konfir**ayns**-ya] conference

confirmar [konfirm**ar**] to confirm

confortável [konfoort**a**vil] comfortable

confusão f [konfooz**ow**ng] confusion, mix-up

congelador m [konJilad**ohr**] freezer

congestionamento m

[konJisht-yoonamayntoo] traffic congestion

conhecer [kon-yisayr] to know

connosco [konohshkoo] with us

consciente [konsh-syaynt] conscious

consertar [konsirtar] to fix, to mend

conservar afastado da luz solar directa store away from direct sunlight

conservar no frio store in a cold place

consigo [konseegoo] with you

constipação f [konshtipasowng] cold

constipado: estou constipado [shtoh konshtipadoo] I have a cold

consulado m [konsooladoo] consulate

consulta f [konsoolta] appointment

consultório m [konsooltor-yoo] surgery, doctor's office

consultório dentário dental surgery

consumir dentro de ... dias to be consumed within ... days

conta f [kohnta] bill; account

conta bancária [bankar-ya] bank account

contactar to contact

contaminado [kontaminadoo] polluted

conta-quilómetros m [konta-kilohmitroosh] speedometer

contar to count; to tell

contente [kontaynt] happy; glad, pleased

contigo [konteegoo] with you

conto m [kohntoo] tale, story; a thousand escudos

contra against

contraceptivo m [kontrasipteevoo] contraceptive

contra-indicações fpl contraindications

contrário m [kontrar-yoo] opposite

controlo de passaportes passport control

contusão f [kontoozowng] bruise

conveniente [konvin-yaynt] convenient

convento m [konvayntoo] convent

conversação f [konversasowng] conversation

convés m [konvehsh] deck

convidada f [konvidada], convidado m [konvidadoo] guest

convidar [konvidar] to invite

convir [konveer] to suit; to be convenient

convite m [konveet] invitation

copo m [kopoo] glass; cup

cor f [kohr] colour

coração m [koorasowng] heart

corajoso m [kooraJohzoo] brave

corda f rope

cordeiro m [koordayroo] lamb

cordel m [koordehl] string

cor de laranja [kohr di laranJa] orange (colour)

cor de rosa [roza] pink

corpo m [kohrpoo] body

corredor m [koorridohr] corridor

correia f [koorray-a] strap

correia da ventoinha [da ventooween-ya] fan belt

correia de relógio [di riloJ-yoo] watch strap

correio m [koorray-oo] post, mail; post office

pôr no correio [pohr noo] to post, to mail

correio aéreo [a-ehr-yoo] airmail

correio azul [azool] express mail

correio expresso [shprehsoo] express mail, special delivery

correio registado [ri.lishtadoo] registered mail

correios mpl [koorray-oosh] post office

Correios de Portugal S.A. National Mail Service

corrente f [koorraynt] chain; current

corrente de ar [koorraynt dar] draught

correr [koorrayr] to run

correspondente m/f [koorrishpondaynt] penfriend

corrida f [koorreeda] race

cortado [koortadoo] cut; blocked

cortar to cut

corte m [kort] cut

corte de cabelo [di kabayloo] haircut

corte de energia [denirJee-a] power cut

corte e brushing [ee] cut and blow-dry

cortiça f [koorteesa] cork

cortiças fpl [koorteesash] cork goods

cortina f [koorteena] curtain

cortinados mpl [koortinadoosh] curtains

coser [koozayr] to sew

cosméticos mpl [kooJmehtikoosh] cosmetics, make-up

costa f [koshta] coast

na costa on the coast

costas fpl [kushtash] back (of body)

costela f [kooshtehla] rib

cotação cambial f [kootasowng kamb-yal] exchange rate

cotovelo m [kootoovayloo] elbow

couro m [kohroo] leather

coxa f [kohsha] thigh

coxia f [kooshee-a] aisle

cozer [koozayr] to cook

cozinha f [koozeen-ya] kitchen

cozinhar [kozeen-yar] to cook

cozinheiro m [kozeen-yayroo] cook

CP [say pay] Portuguese Railways

crédito m [krehditoo] credit

creme m [kraym] cream, lotion

creme amaciador [amas-yadohr] conditioner

creme de barbear [di barb-yar] shaving cream

creme de base [baz] foundation cream

creme de limpeza [leempayza] cleansing lotion

creme écran total [ekrang tootal] sunblock

creme hidratante [kraymeedratant] moisturizer

crer [krayr] to believe

criada f [kr-yada] maid

criada de quarto [di kwartoo] chambermaid

criança f [kr-yansa] child

crianças children; children crossing

cru, crua [kroo, kroo-a] raw

cruzamento m [kroozamayntoo] junction, crossroads

cruzamento perigroso dangerous junction

cruzar [kroozar] to cross

cruzeiro m [kroozayroo] cruise

cruzeta f [kroozayta] coathanger

Cruz Vermelha Red Cross

CTT [say tay tay] National Mail Service

cuecas fpl [kwehkash] underpants; pants, panties

cuecas de mulher [kwehkaJ di mool-yehr] pants, panties

cuidado m [kwidadoo] care

cuidado! look out!, be careful!, take care!

cuidado com o cão beware of the dog

cuidadoso [kwidadohzoo] careful

cujo [kooJoo] of which; whose

culpa f [koolpa] fault

é culpa minha/dele it's my/his fault

culpado [koolpadoo] guilty

cumprimento m

[koomprimayntoo] compliment

com os melhores cumprimentos with best wishes

cunhada f [koon-yada] sister-in-law

cunhado m [koon-yadoo] brother-in-law

curar [koorar] to cure

curso m [koorsoo] course

curso de línguas [di leengwash] language course

curto [koortoo] short

curva f [koorva] turning; bend

curva perigosa dangerous bend

custar [kooshtar] to charge; to cost

cutelaria f [kootilaree-a] cutlery shop

c/v basement

D

d. right

da of the; from the

dá he/she/it gives; you give

damas f [damash] ladies' toilets, ladies' room

damos [damoosh] we give

dança f [dansa] dance

dança folclórica [foolklorika] folk dancing

dançar [dansar] to dance

dão [downg] they give; you give

daqui [dakee] from now

dar to give

das [dash] of the; from the
dás you give
data f date
data de validade [di validad]
  expiry date
de [di] from; of; by; in
  de autocarro [dowtookarroo] by
  bus
  de avião [dav-yowng] by air
  de carro [di karroo] by car
  de manhã [di man-yang] in the
  morning
debaixo de ... [dibīshoo di]
  under ...
decepcionado [disips-yoonadoo]
  disappointed
decepcionante [disips-yonant]
  disappointing
decidir [disideer] to decide
décimo [dehsimoo] tenth
decisão f [disizowng] decision
declaração f [diklarasowng]
  statement
dedo m [daydoo] finger
dedo do pé [doo peh] toe
defeito m [difaytoo] fault, defect
deficiente [difis-yaynt] disabled
deficientes físicos mpl disabled
degrau m [digrow] step
deitar fora [daytar] to throw
  away
deitar-se [daytarsi] to lie down;
  to go to bed
deixar [dayshar] to leave
  (behind); to let
deixar cair [ka-eer] to drop
dela [dehla] her; hers
delas [dehlash] their; theirs
dele [dayl] his

deles [daylish] their; theirs
delicioso [dilis-yohzoo] lovely,
  delicious
demais [dimīsh] too much
demasiado [dimaz-yadoo] too
  demasiado grande too big
dê-me [daymi] give me
demora f delay
dentadura postiça f [dentadoora
  pooshteesa] dentures
dente m [daynt] tooth
dentista m/f [denteeshta] dentist
dentro de ... [dayntroo]
  inside
  dentro de ... dias [di ... dee-ash]
  in ... days' time
  dentro de um momento [doong
  moomayntoo] in a minute
  dentro de casa [di kaza]
  indoors
departamento m
  [dipartamayntoo] department
depende [dipaynd] it depends
  depende de ... [di] it depends
  on ...
depois [dipoh-ish] then, after
  that; afterwards
  depois de ... [di] after ...
  depois de amanhã [daman-
  yang] the day after tomorrow
depósito m [dipozitoo] deposit;
  tank
  depósito de bagagem [di
  bagaJayng] left luggage (office),
  baggage checkroom
depósitos mpl deposits
depressa [diprehsa] quickly
deprimido [diprimeedoo]
  depressed

dê prioridade give way, yield

derrubar [dirroobar] to knock over

desafio de futebol m [dizafee-oo di footbol] football match

desagradável [dizagradavil] unpleasant

desaparecer [dizaparisayr] to disappear

desapontado [dizapontadoo] disappointed

desarranjo intestinal m [dizarranJoo intishtinal] upset stomach

descansar [dishkansar] to relax

descanso m [dishkansoo] rest

descer [dishsayr] to go down; to get off

descobrir [dishkoobreer] to find out, to discover

descolagem f [dishkoolaJayng] take-off

descolar [dishkoolar] to take off, to unglue

descontar [dishkontar] to cash

desconto m [dishkohntoo] discount

descrição f [dishkrisowng] description

desculpar-se [dishkoolparsi] to apologize

desculpas fpl [dishkoolpash] apologies

desculpe [dishkoolp] I'm sorry, excuse me, pardon (me)

desde [dayJdi] since; from

desejar [disayJar] to want

que deseja? [ki disayJa] how can I help you?

desempregado [dizaymprigadoo] unemployed

desenho m [disayn-yoo] drawing; pattern

desenvolver [disaynvolvayr] to develop

desfazer as malas [dishfazayr aJ malash] to unpack

desfiladeiro m [dishfiladayroo] pass

desfolhada f [disfool-yada] party held at threshing time

desgarradas fpl [diJgarradash] improvised popular songs

cantar à desgarrada to sing impromptu in competition

desinfectante m [dizinfetant] disinfectant

desligado [diJligadoo] off, switched off

desligar [diJligar] to turn off; to switch off

desligue o motor switch off your engine

desmaiar [diJmī-ar] to faint; to collapse

desmaquilhador de olhos m [dishmakil-yadohr dol-yoosh] eye make-up remover

desocupar antes das ... vacate before ...

desodorizante m [dizohdoorizant] deodorant

despacha-te! [dishpashat] hurry up!

despertador m [dishpirtadohr] alarm clock

desporto m [dishpohrtoo] sport

desportos náuticos mpl

[dishpohrtoosh nowtikoosh] water sports

destinatário m addressee

destino m [dishteenoo] destination

desvio m [dijvee-oo] detour, diversion

detergente m [deterJaynt] soap powder, washing powder

detergente líquido [leekidoo] washing-up liquid

detergente para lavar a louça [lohsa] washing-up liquid

detestar [ditishtar] to hate

detestável [ditishtavil] obnoxious

Deus [day-oosh] God

devagar [divagar] slow; slowly

deve [dehv] you must, you have to

dever (m) [divayr] duty; to owe; to have to

devia [divee-a] you should

devolver [divolvayr] to give back

dez [dehsh] ten

dezanove [dizanov] nineteen

dezasseis [dizasaysh] sixteen

dezassete [dizaseht] seventeen

Dezembro [dezaymbroo] December

dezoito [dizoh-itoo] eighteen

dia m [dee-a] day

diabética (f) [d-yabehtika], diabético (m) [d-yabehtikoo] diabetic

dia de anos m [dee-a danoosh] birthday

dialecto m dialect

diamante m [d-yamant] diamond

diapositivo m [d-yapooziteevoo] slide

diária f [d-yar-ya] cost per day

diariamente [d-yar-yamaynt] daily

diário (m) [d-yar-yo] diary; daily

diarreia f [d-yarray-a] diarrhoea

dias de semana weekdays

dias verdes cheap travel days

dicionário m [dis-yoonar-yoo] dictionary

dieta f [d-yehta] diet

diferença f [difiraynsa] difference

diferente [difiraynt] different

difícil [difeesil] difficult, hard

dificuldade f [difikooldad] difficulty

digo I say

diluir num pouco de água dissolve in a little water

Dinamarca f [dinamarka] Denmark

dinamarquês [dinamarkaysh] Danish

dinheiro m [deen-yayroo] money; cash

dirá [dira] he/she will say; you will say

dirão [dirowng] they will say; you will say

dirás [dirash] you will say

direcção f [direhsowng] direction; steering

directo [direhtoo] direct

direi [diray] I will say

Di

direita: à direita [dir**ay**ta] on the right

à direita (de) [di] on the right (of)

vire à direita [veer] turn right

direito [dir**ay**too] straight; right (not left)

direitos **mpl** [dir**ay**toosh] rights

livre de direitos [leevr di] duty-free

diremos [dir**ay**moosh] we will say

disco **m** [d**ee**shkoo] disco; record

discoteca **f** [dishkoot**eh**ka] disco; record shop

disjuntor principal **m** [diJoont**ohr** preensip**al**] mains switch

disquete **f** [dishk**eht**] disk, diskette

disse [dees] I/he/she/it/you said

dissemos [dis**ay**moosh] we said

disseram [dis**eh**rowng] you/they said

disseste [dis**ehsh**t] you said

distância **f** [disht**ans**-ya] distance

distribuição **f** [dishtribwees**owng**] delivery

distribuidor **m** [dishtribweed**ohr**] distributor

dito [d**ee**too] said

DIU **m** [d**ee**-oo] IUD, coil

divertido [divirt**ee**doo] fun, amusing, enjoyable

divertir-se [divirt**eer**si] to enjoy oneself

divisas **fpl** foreign currency

divorciado [divoors-y**a**doo] divorced

dizer [diz**ayr**] to say; to tell

o que quer dizer? [oo ki kehr] what do you mean?

do of the; from the

dobro [d**oh**broo] twice as much

doce [dohs] sweet

documento **m** [dookoom**ay**ntoo] document

doença **f** [dw**ay**nsa] disease, illness

doente [dw**ay**nt] ill, sick, unwell

doer [dw**ay**r] to hurt

doido [d**oh**-idoo] crazy, mad

dois [d**oh**-ish] two

doloroso [dooloor**oh**zoo] painful

domingo [doom**ee**ngoo] Sunday

domingos e dias feriados Sundays and public holidays

Dona Mrs

dona **f** [d**oh**na] owner; respectful way of addressing a woman, precedes the first name

donde [d**oh**nd] where from

donde é? [dohnd**eh**] where do you come from?

dono **m** [d**oh**noo] owner

do que [doo ki] than

dor **f** [dohr] ache, pain

dor de cabeça [di kab**ay**sa] headache

dor de dentes [d**ay**ntsh] toothache

dor de estômago [disht**oh**magoo] stomach ache

dor de garganta [di garg**a**nta] sore throat

dor de ouvidos [dohveedoosh] earache

dormidas rooms to let (in a private house)

dormir [doormeer] to sleep
a dormir asleep

dor nas costas f [dohr nash koshtash] backache

dos of the; from the

dose f [doz] portion

dose para crianças f [doz kr-yan-sash] children's portion

dou [doh] I give

doutor m [dohtohr], doutora f [dohtora] doctor

doutro modo [dohtroo modoo] otherwise

doze [dohz] twelve

droga f [droga] drugs, narcotics

drogaria f [droogaree-a] drugstore, shop selling toiletries

dto. right

duas vezes [doo-aJ vayzish] twice

duche m [doosh] shower
com duche [kong] with shower

dunas fpl [doonash] sand dunes

duplo [dooploo] double

durante [doorant] during

duro [dooroo] hard; stale

duzentas [doozayntash], duzentos [doozayntoosh] two hundred

dúzia f [dooz-ya] dozen

E

e [ee] and

e. left

é [eh] he/she/it is; you are
é ...? is he/she/it ...?; are you ...?

écran m [ekrang] screen

edifício m [idifees-yoo] building

edredão m [idridowng] duvet

efervescente [ifirvish-saynt] effervescent, sparkling

oh! hey!

eixo m [ayshoo] axle

ela [ehla] she; her; it

elas [ehlash] they; them

elástico m [ilashtikoo] elastic; elastic band

ele [ayl] he; him; it

electricidade f [eletrisidad] electricity

electricista m [eletriseeshta] electrician

eléctrico (m) [elehtrikoo] electric; tram, streetcar

electro-domésticos mpl [doomehshtikoosh] electrical appliances

eles [aylish] they; them

elevador m [elevadohr] lift, elevator

em [ayng] in; at; on

embaixada f [aymbishada] embassy

embaixo [aymbishoo] down, downstairs; underneath

embaixo de ... [di] under-neath ...

lá embaixo down there

embalagem económica f economy pack

embalagem familiar family pack

embaraçoso [aymbarasohzoo] embarrassing

embora [aymbora] although

ir embora to go away

embraiagem f [aymbrī-aJayng] clutch

embrulhar [aymbrool-yar] to wrap

embrulho m [aymbrool-yoo] parcel

ementa f [emaynta] menu

ementa fixa [feeksa] set menu

ementa turística [tooreestika] today's menu, set menu

emergência f [emirjayns-ya] emergency

emergências casualty, emergencies

emocionante [emoos-yoonant] exciting

emperrado [aympirradoo] stuck

empoeirado [aympoo-ayradoo] dusty

empolha f [aympohl-ya] blister

empregada f [aympregada] waitress

empregada de balcão [di balkowng] barmaid

empregada de mesa [mayza] waitress

empregada de quarto [kwartoo] chambermaid, maid

empregado [aympregadoo] m employee

empregado (de mesa) m [di mayza] waiter

emprego m [aympraygoo] job

empresa f [aymprayza] company, firm

emprestado: pedir emprestado [pideer aymprishtadoo] to borrow

emprestar [aymprishtar] to lend

empurrar [aympoorrar] to push

E.N. national highway

encantador [aynkantadohr] lovely

encaracolado [aynkarakooladoo] curly

encerrado [aynsayrradoo] closed

encher [aynshayr] to fill up, to fill

encomenda f [aynkoomaynda] package; parcel

encomendas fpl parcels, parcels counter

encontrar [aynkontrar] to find; to meet

encravado [aynkravadoo] jammed

endereço m [ayndiraysoo] address

enevoado [inivwadoo] foggy; misty; cloudy

enfarte m [aynfart] heart attack

enfermaria f [aynfirmaree-a] hospital ward

enfermeira f [aynfirmayra], enfermeiro m [aynfirmayroo] nurse

enganado [aynganadoo] wrong

enganar-se [aynganarsi] to be wrong, to make a mistake

estavas [shtavash] you used to be

este [aysht] this; this one

este m [ehsht] east

estendal m [shtendal] clothes line

estes [ayshtish] these

esteve [shtayv] he/she/it was; you were

estive [shteev] I was

estivemos [shtivaymoosh] we were

estiveram [shtivehrowng] they were; you were

estiveste [shtivehsht] you were

estômago m [ahtohmngoo] stomach

estou [shtoh] I am

estrada f [shtrada] road

estrada nacional [nas-yoonal] national highway

estrada principal [preensipal] main highway

estragado [shtragadoo] faulty; out of order

estragar [shtragar] to damage

estrangeira (f), estrangeiro (m) [shtranJayroo] foreign; foreigner

no estrangeiro [noo] abroad

estranha (f) [shtran-ya], estranho (m) [shtran-yoo] stranger; peculiar; funny; strange

estreia f [shtray-a] first showing

estreito [shtraytoo] narrow

estrela f [shtrayla] star

estudante m/f [shtoodant]

student

estupendo [shtoopayndoo] amazing

estúpido [shtoopidoo] stupid

etiqueta f [etikayta] label

eu [ay oo] I

EUA USA

eu mesmo [ay-oo mayJmoo] myself

Europa f [ay-ooropa] Europe

europeia (f) [ay-ooroopay-a], europeu (m) [ay-ooroopay-oo] European

exactamente! [ezatamaynt] exactly!

exacto [ozatoo] accurate, correct

exagerar [ezaJirar] to exaggerate

exame m [ezam] exam, test

exausto [ezowshtoo] exhausted, tired

excelente [ish-selaynt] excellent; lovely

excepto [ish-sehtoo] except

excepto aos domingos Sundays excepted

excesso de bagagem m [ish-sehsoo di bagaJayng] excess baggage

excursão f [shkoorsowng] coach trip; trip

excursão com guia [kong] guided tour

excursão organizada [organizada] package holiday

excursões fpl [shkoorsoyngsh] excursions

exemplo m [ezaymploo]

enganei-me [aynganaym] I've made a mistake

engarrafamento m [ayngarrafamayntoo] traffic jam

engolir [ayngooleer] to swallow

engraçado [ayngrasadoo] funny, amusing

enjoado [aynJwadoo] seasick

enorme [enorm] enormous

enquanto [aynkwantoo] while

ensinar [aynsinar] to teach

então [ayntowng] then, at that time

entrada f [ayntrada] entrance, way in; starter, appetizer; admission charge

entrada livre admission free

entrada proibida no entry

entrar [ayntrar] to go in, to enter

entre! come in!

entre [ayntr] among; between

entrega ao domicílio delivery service

entregar [ayntrigar] to deliver

entrevista [ayntriveeshta] appointment

entupido [ayntoopeedoo] blocked

envelope m [aynvilop] envelope

envelope de avião m [dav-yowng] airmail envelope

envergonhado [aynvirgoon-yadoo] ashamed

enviar [aynv-yar] to send

enviar posteriormente to forward

enxaqueca f [aynshakayka] migraine

época f [ehpooka] season; age

equipa f [ekeepa] team

equipamento m [ekipamayntoo] equipment

era [ehra] I was; he/she/it was; you were

eram [ehrowng] they were; you were

éramos [ehramoosh] we were

eras [ehrash] you were

ermida f [ermeeda] chapel

errado [erradoo] wrong

erro m [ayrroo] mistake, error

erupção f [eroopsowng] rash

ervanário m [ervanar-yoo] herbalist

és [ehsh] you are

esc. escudo (Portuguese unit of currency)

escada f [shkada] ladder; stairs

escadas fpl [shkadash] stairs

escadas rolantes [roolantsh] escalator

escala f [shkala] intermediate stop

escalar [shkalar] to climb

escocês (m) [shkoosaysh] Scottish; Scotsman

escocesa (f) [shkoosayza] Scottish; Scots woman

Escócia f [shkos-ya] Scotland

escola f [shkola] school

escola de línguas f [di leengwash] language school

escolher [shkool-yayr] to choose

esconder [shkondayr] to hide

escorregadio [shkoorrigadee-oo] slippery

escova f [shkohva] brush

escova de cabelo [di kabayloo] hairbrush

escova de dentes [dayntsh] toothbrush

escova de unhas [doon-yash] nailbrush

escrever [shkrivayr] to write

escrito por ... [shkreetoo poor] written by ...

por escrito in writing

escritório m [shkritor-yoo] office

escudo m [shkoodoo] escudo (Portuguese unit of currency)

escurecer [shkooresayr] to get dark

escuro [shkooroo] dark

escutar [shkootar] to listen (to)

esferográfica f [shfiroografika] ballpoint pen

Espanha f [shpan-ya] Spain

espanhóis: os espanhóis [shpan-oysh] the Spanish

espanhol [shpan-yol] Spanish

espantoso [shpantohzoo] amazing, astonishing

especialidade f [shpis-yalidad] speciality

especialmente [shpis-yalmaynt] especially

espectáculo m [shpitakooloo] show

espelho m [shpayl-yoo] mirror

espelho retrovisor [ritroovizohr] rearview mirror

esperar [shpirar] to expect; to hope; to wait

espero que não [shpehroo ki nowng] I hope not

espero que sim [seeng] I hope

so

espere [shpehr] wait

espere pelo sinal wait for the tone

esperto [shpehrtoo] clever

espesso [shpaysoo] thick

espetáculo m [shpitakooloo] show

espigados mpl [shpigadoosh] split ends

espingarda f [shpeengarda] gun

espirrar [shpirrar] to sneeze

espirro m [shpeerroo] sneeze

esplanada f [shplanada] esplanade; pavement café

esplêndido [shplayndidoo] terrific

esposa f [shpohza] wife

espuma de barbear f [shpooma di barb-yar] shaving foam

esq. left

esquadra da polícia f [shkwarda da poolees-ya] police station

esquecer [shkisayr] to forget

esqueci-me [shkiseemi] I forget

esquerda: à esquerda [shkayrda] on the left (of), to the left

vire à esquerda [veera] turn left

esquerdo [shkayrdoo] left

esqui aquático m [shkee akwatikoo] waterskiing

esquisito [shkizeetoo] weird, odd, strange

essa [ehsa] that; that one

essas [ehsash] those

esse [ays] that

essencial [esayns-yal] essential

esses [aysish] those

esta [ehshta] this; this one

está [shta] hello (on the phone); he/she/it is; you are

ele está? [ayl] is he in?

está ... it is ...

está ...? is it ...?; hello? (on the telephone)

está bem [bayng] that's fine, all right

estação f [shtasowng] station; season

estação alta high season

estação baixa [bisha] low season

estação de autocarros [dowtookarroosh] bus station

estação de caminho de ferro [di kameen-yoo di fehrroo] railway station

estação de camionetas [kam-yoonaytash] bus station, coach station

estação de comboios [komboy-oosh] train station

estação de serviço [di sirveesoo] service station

estação dos autocarros [dooz owtookarroosh] bus station, coach station

estacionamento m [shtas-yoonamayntoo] car park, parking lot

estacionamento privado [privadoo] private parking

estacionamento proibido no parking

estacionamento reservado

aos hóspedes parking reserved for patrons, patrons only

estacionar [shtas-yoonar] to park

estadia f [shtadee-a] stay

estádio m [shtad-yoo] stadium

estado m [shtadoo] state

Estados Unidos (da América) mpl [shtadooz ooneedooJ (damehrika)] United States (of America)

estafado [shtafadoo] shattered, exhausted

estalagem f [shtalaJayng] luxury hotel

estamos [shtamoosh] we are

estância f [shtans-ya] timber yard

estão [shtowng] they are; you are

estar [shtar] to be

estará [shtara] he/she/it/you will be

estarão [shtarowng] you/they will be

estarás [shtarash] you will be

estarei [shtaray] I will be

estaremos [shtaraymoosh] we will be

estas [ehshtash] these

estás [shtash] you are

estátua f [shtatwa] statue

estava [shtava] I/he/she/it/you used to be

estavam [shtavam] you/they used to be

estávamos [shtavamoosh] we used to be

example
por exemplo [poor] for example
exigir [eziJeer] to demand
Exmo. Sr. (Excelentíssimo Senhor) Dear Sir
experiente [shpir-yaynt] experienced
experimentar [shpirimayntar] to try; to try on
explicar [shplikar] to explain
exposição f [shpoozisowng] exhibition
extensão f [shtensowng] extension; extension lead
extintor m [shtintohr] fire extinguisher
extraordinário [shtra-ohrdinar-yoo] extraordinary
extremamente [shtremamaynt] extremely

F

F cold
fábrica f [fabrika] factory
fabricado em ... made in ...
faca f [faka] knife
fácil [fasil] easy
faço [fasoo] I do
factor de protecção m [fatohr di prootesowng] protection factor
factura f [fatoora] invoice
fadista m/f [fadeeshta] singer of traditional Portuguese fado songs
fado m [fadoo] traditional Portuguese song, usually sad

and romantic
faiança f [fi-ansa] glazed earthenware
faixa f [fisha] lane
falar to speak; to talk
fala ...? do you speak ...?
não falo inglês I don't speak English
falido [faleedo] broke; bankrupt
falso [falsoo] fake; false
falta missing
faltar to be lacking; to be missing
família f [fameel-ya] family
famoso [famohzoo] famous
fantástico [fantashtikoo] fantastic
fará [fara] he/she/it/you will do
farão [farowng] you/they will do
farás [farash] you will do
farei [faray] I will do
faremos [faraymoosh] we will do
farmácia f [farmas-ya] pharmacy, chemist's
farmácias de serviço fpl [di sirveesoo] emergency pharmacies, duty chemists
faróis máximos mpl [faroyJ masimoosh] headlights
faróis médios dipped headlights
faróis mínimos [meenimoosh] sidelights
farol m headlight; lighthouse
farto [fartoo] fed up
fato m [fatoo] suit

fato de banho [di ban-yoo] swimming costume

fato de treino [traynoo] tracksuit

favorito [favooreetoo] favourite

favor: por favor [favohr] please

se faz favor [si fash] please

é favor fechar a porta please close the door

favor não incomodar please do not disturb

fazem-se chaves keys cut here

fazer [fazayr] to do; to make

fazer a barba to shave

fazer amor [amohr] to make love

fazer as malas [aJ malash] to pack

fazer bicha [beesha] to queue, to stand in line

fazer brushing to blow-dry

fazer mudança [moodansa] to change (trains)

fazer surf to surf

fazer vela [vehla] to sail

fazer windsurf to windsurf

faz favor [fash favohr] please, excuse me

febre f [fehbr] temperature, fever

febre dos fenos [fehbr doosh faynoosh] hayfever

febril [febreel] feverish

fechado [fishadoo] shut, closed; reserved; overcast

fechado à chave [fishadwa shav] locked

fechado até ... closed until ...

fechado para balanço closed for stocktaking

fechado para férias closed for holidays

fechado para obras closed for repairs

fechadura f [fishadoora] lock

fechar [fishar] to close; to shut

fechar à chave [shav] to lock

fecho m [fayshoo] handle

fecho éclair® [fayshoo] zip, zipper

feio [fay-oo] ugly

feira f [fayra] funfair; trade fair

feiras das vilas local village fairs

feito [faytoo] made; done

feito à mão [faytwa mowng] hand-made

feliz [fileesh] happy

feliz aniversário! [fileez anivirsar-yoo] happy birthday!

Feliz Ano Novo! [anoo nohvoo] Happy New Year!

felizmente [filiJmaynt] fortunately

Feliz Natal! [fileeJ] Merry Christmas!

feminista (f) [femineeshta] feminist

feriado m [fir-yadoo] public holiday

férias fpl [fehr-yash] holiday; vacation

de férias [di] on holiday; on vacation

férias de inverno fpl [dinvehrnoo] winter holiday

férias grandes fpl [grandsh] summer holidays

ferida f [fireeda] wound

ferido [fireedoo] injured
ferragens fpl [firraJayngsh] ironmongery, hardware
ferramenta f [firramaynta] tool
ferro m [fehrroo] iron
ferro de engomar m [dayngoomar] iron
festa f [fehshta] party
  Boas Festas! [boh-ash fehshtash] merry Christmas and a happy New Year
festas dos santos populares feast days of saints
Fevereiro [fivrayroo] February
fez [faysh] he/she/it did, he/she/it has done; you did, you have done
fibras naturais natural fibres
ficar [fikar] to remain, to stay
  ficam dois [feekowng doh-ish] there are two left
  onde fica ...? [feeka] where is ...?
ficar com [kong] to keep
fígado m [feegadoo] liver
filha f [feel-ya] daughter
filho m [teel-yoo] son
  filho da puta! [poota] son-of-a-bitch!
filme m [feelm] film; movie
filme colorido m [koolooreedoo] colour film
filtro m [feeltroo] filter
filtros de café mpl [feeltroosh di kafeh] filter papers
fim m [feeng] end
  no fim de ... [noo – di] at the end of ...
  no fim eventually

fim de autoestrada end of motorway/highway
fim de estaçao end of season
fim de semana [di simana] weekend
finalmente [finalmaynt] at last
fino [feenoo] thin; fine
fio m [fee-oo] lead; thread; wire
fio de fusivel m [di foozeevil] fuse wire
fio dentário m [dentar-yoo] dental floss
fita f [feeta] tape, cassette
fita-cola f sticky tape
fita elástica f [elashtika] rubber band
fita gomada [goomada] Sellotape®, Scotch tape®
fita métrica [mehtrika] tape measure
fiz [feesh] I did, I have done
fizemos [fizaymoosh] we did, we have done
fizeram [fizehrowng] you/they did, they have done
fizeste [fizehsht] you did, you have done
flertar [flirtar] to flirt
flor f [flohr] flower
floresta f [floorehshta] forest
fluentemente [flwentimaynt] fluently
fogão m [foogowng] cooker
fogo m [fohgoo] fire
fogos de artifício mpl [fogoosh dartifees-yoo] fireworks
fogueira f [foogayra] fire, campfire

foi [**foh**-i] it was, he/she went, he/she has left

folha f [**fohl**-ya] leaf; sheet

folha de prata silver foil

folheto m [fool-**yay**too] brochure; leaflet

fome [fohm] hunger

tenho fome [**tayn**-yoo] I'm hungry

tens fome? [**taynsh**] are you hungry?

fomos [**foh**moosh] we were, we have been; we went, we have gone

fonte f [fohnt] fountain

fora: lá fora outside

do lado de fora [doo ladoo di] outside

fora de casa [di kaza] outdoors

foram [**foh**rowng] you/they were, you/they have been; you/they went, you/they have gone

forcados mpl [foork**a**doosh] group of men who wrestle with the bull during a bullfight

forma: em forma [ayng **for**ma] fit

de qualquer forma [di kwalk**ehr**] anyway

formiga f [foorm**ee**ga] ant

forno m [**foh**rnoo] oven

forte [fort] strong; rich

fósforos mpl [**fo**shfooroosh] matches

foste [fohsht] you were, you have been; you went, you have gone

fotocópias fpl [footook**o**p-yash] photocopies

fotografar [footoografar] to photograph

fotografia f [footoografee-a] photograph; photographic goods

fotógrafo m [foot**o**grafoo] photographer

fraco [fra**koo**] weak

fractura f [frat**oo**ra] fracture

frágil [fra**j**il] fragile

fralda f [fralda] nappy, diaper

fraldas descartáveis fpl [dishkart**a**vaysh] disposable nappies/diapers

França f [fransa] France

francês (m) [frans**aysh**] French; Frenchman

francesa (f) [frans**ay**za] French; French woman

franquia f [frank**ee**-a] postage

free-shop f duty-free shop

frente f [fraynt] front

em frente [ayng] in front

em frente a [fraynta] opposite; in front of

na frente at the front

frequência f [frikw**ay**ns-ya] frequency

frequentado [frikwaynt**a**doo] busy

frequente [frikw**ay**nt] frequent

frequentemente [frikwayn-tem**ay**nt] frequently

fresco [fray**shkoo**] fresh; cool

frigideira f [friji**day**ra] frying pan

frigorífico m [frigoor**ee**fikoo]

fridge

frio [**free**-oo] cold

  tenho frio [**tayn**-yoo] I'm cold

fritar [fri**tar**] to fry

fronha da almofada f [**froh**n-ya dalmoo**fada**] pillow case

fronteira f [front**ayra**] border, frontier

frutaria f [froota**ree**-a] fruit shop

fuga f [**foo**ga] leak

fui [fwee] I went, I have gone; I was, I have been

fumadores mpl [foomad**oh**rish] smokers, smoking

fumar [foo**mar**] to smoke

  fuma? [**foo**ma] do you smoke?

  não fumo [nowng] I don't smoke

fumo m [**foo**moo] smoke

funcionar [foons-yo**nar**] to work

  não funciona [nowng] out of order

fundo (m) [**foon**doo] deep; bottom

funil m [foo**neel**] funnel

furado [foo**ra**doo] flat (tyre)

furgão m [foor**gowng**] van

furgoneta f [foorgoon**ayta**] van

furioso [foor-y**oh**zoo] furious

furo m [**foo**roo] puncture

fusível m [foo**zee**vil] fuse

futebol m [foot**bol**] football

futuro m [foot**oo**roo] future

  no futuro [noo] in future

G

gado m [**ga**doo] cattle

gajo m [**ga**Joo] guy

galão m [ga**lowng**] gallon; milky coffee in a tall glass

galeria de arte f [gali**ree**-a dart] art gallery

Gales m [**ga**lish] Wales

galês (m) [ga**laysh**] Welsh; Welshman

galesa (f) [ga**layza**] Welsh; Welsh woman

gama f range

ganhar [gan-**yar**] to win; to earn

ganso m [**gan**soo] goose

garagem f [gara**Jayng**] garage

garantia f [garan**tee**-a] guarantee

garfo m [**gar**foo] fork

garganta f throat

garrafa f bottle

garraiadas fpl [garrī-**a**dash] bull-running

gás m [gash] gas

gás Cidla® m camping gas

gasóleo m [ga**zol**-yoo] diesel

gasolina f [gazoo**leena**] petrol, gasoline

gasolina-normal three-star petrol, regular gas

gasolina sem chumbo [sayng sh**oom**boo] unleaded petrol

gasolina-super [**soo**per] four-star petrol

gás para campismo m [gash para kam**pee**Jmoo] camping gas

gastar [gashtar] to spend

gato m [gatoo] cat

gaveta f [gavayta] drawer

G.B. [Jay bay] Great Britain

geada f [J-yada] frost

gelado (m) [Jiladoo] frozen; ice cream; ice lolly

gelataria f [Jilataree-a] ice-cream parlour

gel de duche m [Jehl di doosh] shower gel

gelo [Jayloo] ice

gel para o cabelo m [Jehl par-oo kabayloo] hair gel

gémeos mpl [Jaym-yoosh] twins

gengiva f [JenJeeva] gum

genro m [Jaynroo] son-in-law

gente f [Jaynt] people

toda a gente [tohda] everyone

genuíno [Jinweenoo] genuine

geral [Jeral] general

geralmente [Jeralmaynt] usually

gerente m/f [Jeraynt] manager; manageress

gesso m [Jaysoo] plaster cast

ginásio m [Jinaz-yoo] gym

gira-discos m [Jeera-deeshkoosh] record player

glutão [glootowng] greedy

G.N.R. [Jay en err] branch of the Portuguese police

golfe m [golf] golf

Golfo da Biscáia m [gohlfoo da bishkī-a] Bay of Biscay

gordo [gohrdoo] fat

gorduroso [goordoorohzoo] greasy

gorgeta f [goorJayta] tip

gostar [gooshtar] to like

gosta de ...? [goshta di] do you like ...?

gosto [goshtoo] I like, I like it

gostoso [gooshtohzoo] tasty; pleasant; nice

gota f [gohta] drop

gotas para os olhos fpl [gohtash parooz ol-yoosh] eye drops

governo m [goovayrnoo] government

Grã-Bretanha f [gran britan-ya] Great Britain

gradualmente [gradwalmaynt] gradually

grama m gram(me)

gramática f [gramatika] grammar

grande [grand] large, big

grandes armazéns mpl [grandz armazayngsh] department store

granizo m [graneezoo] hail

gratuito [gratoo-eetoo] free (of charge)

gravador (de cassetes) m [gravadohr (di kasehtsh)] tape recorder

gravata f tie, necktie

grave [grav] nasty

grávida pregnant

graxa para sapatos f [grasha para sapatoosh] shoe polish

Grécia f [grehs-ya] Greece

grego (m) [graygoo] Greek

grelhador m [gril-yadohr] grill

gripe f [greep] flu

gritar [gritar] to shout

grosseiro [groosayroo] rude

grosso [grohsoo] pissed

grupo m [groopoo] group, party

grupo de sange [di sang] blood group

guarda m/f [gwarda] caretaker

guarda-chuva m [gwarda shoova] umbrella

Guarda Fiscal Customs police

Guarda Nacional Republicana branch of the Portuguese police

guardanapo m [gwardanapoo] napkin, serviette

guardar [gwardar] to keep

guerra f [gehrra] war

guia f [gee-a] guide, courier

guia turística f [tooreeshtika], guia turístico m [tooreeshtikoo] tour guide

guichet m [geeshay] window; ticket window

H

h is not pronounced in Portuguese

H gents', men's room

há ... [a] there is ..., there are ...

há ...? is there...?, are there ...?

há uma semana [ooma simana] a week ago

há pouco [pohkoo] recently

há vagas vacancies, rooms free

hábito m [abeetoo] custom; habit

hall m lobby

H.C. state hospital

hemorróidas fpl [emoorroydash] piles

hepatite f [epateet] hepatitis

hipermercado m [eepermerkadoo] hypermarket

história f [ishtor-ya] history; story

hoje [ohJ] today

Holanda f [olanda] Netherlands, Holland

holandês (m) [olandaysh] Dutch; Dutchman

holandesa (f) [olandayza] Dutch; Dutch woman

homem m [ohmayng] man

homens mpl [ohmayngsh] men; gents' toilet, men's room

honesto [onehshtoo] honest

hora f [ora] hour; time

hora de chegada [di shigada] arrival time

hora de partida [parteeda] departure time

hora de ponta [pohnta] rush hour

hora local local time

horário m [orar-yoo] timetable, (US) schedule

horário das consultas [dash konsooltash] surgery hours, (US) office hours

horas fpl [orash] hours; o'clock

às seis horas [ash sayz orash] at six o'clock

que horas são? [k-yorash sowng] what's the time?

horas de abertura fpl [orash dabirtoora] opening times

horas de visita fpl [di vizeeta] visiting hours

horrível [orreevil] awful, dreadful, horrible

hortelã-pimenta f [ortilang pimaynta] peppermint

hospedado [oshpidadoo]: estar hospedado em [shtar – ayng] to be a guest at, to stay at

hospedaria f [oshpidaree-a] guesthouse

hospedar-se [oshspidarsi] to stay

hóspede m/f [oshpidi] guest

hospedeira (de bordo) f [oshpidayra (di bordoo)] stewardess, air hostess

Hospital Civil m state hospital

hospitalidade f [oshpitalidad] hospitality

houve [ohv] there has been

húmido [oomeedoo] damp; humid

humor m [oomohr] mood; humour

hydroplano m [idrooplanoo] hydrofoil

I

iate m [yat] yacht

ida: bilhete de ida [bil-yayt deeda] single ticket, one-way

ticket

idade f [eedad] age

que idade tem? [keedad tayng] how old are you?

ideia f [iday-a] idea

idiota m [id-yota] stupid

ignição f [ignisowng] ignition

igreja f [igrayJa] church

igual [igwal] same

ilha f [eel-ya] island

imediatamente [imid-yatamaynt] immediately, at once

imenso [imaynsoo] immensely, a lot

imitação f [imitasowng] imitation

impermeável m [impirm-yavil] raincoat

importante [impoortant] important

importar to matter, to be important; to import

importa-se de ...? [importasi] will you ...?

importa-se se ...? [si] do you mind if ...?

não me importo [nowng mimportoo] I don't mind

importuno [importoonoo] annoying

impossível [impooseevil] impossible

imprescindível [impresh-sindeevil] vital

impressionante [impris-yoonant] impressive

impresso m [imprehsoo] form, document

impressos mpl [imprehsoosh]

printed matter

incêndio m [insaynd-yoo] fire

inchaço m [inshasoo] lump, swelling

inchado [inshadoo] swollen

incluído [inklweedoo] included

incluir [inklweer] to include

inconsciente [inkonsh-syaynt] unconscious

inconstante [inkonshtant] changeable

incrível [inkreevil] incredible

indiano (m) [Ind-yanoo] Indian

indicações indications

indicador m [indikadohr] indicator

indicativo m [indikateevoo] dialling code, area code

indigestão f [indiJishtowng] indigestion

indústria f [indooshtr-ya] industry

infecção f [infehsowng] infection

infeccioso [infehs-yohzoo] infectious

infectado [infehtadoo] septic

infelizmente [infiliJmayngt] unfortunately

inflamação f [inflamasowng] inflammation

inflamável inflammable

informação f [infoormasowng] information, piece of information

informações fpl [infoorm-asoyngsh] directory enquiries; information

Inglaterra f [inglatehrra] England

inglês (m) [inglaysh] English; Englishman

em inglês [ayng] in English

inglesa (f) [inglayza] English; English woman

ingleses: os ingleses [inglayzish] the English

ingredientes mpl [ingrid-yayntsh] ingredients

íngreme [eengrim] steep

início m [inees-yoo] beginning

no início [noo] at the beginning

início de autoestrada start of motorway/highway

injecção f [inJehsowng] injection

inocente [inoosaynt] innocent

insecto m [insehtoo] insect

insistir [insishteer] to insist

insolação f [insoolasowng] sunstroke

insónia f [inson-ya] insomnia

Instituto do Vinho do Porto m Port Wine Institute

inteiro [intayroo] whole

inteligente [intiliJaynt] intelligent, clever

Intercidades fast train, Intercity train

interdito a menores de ... anos no admission to those under ... years of age

interessado [intrisadoo] interested

interessante [intrisant] interesting

internacional [internas-yoonal] international

interpretar [interpritar] to interpret

intérprete m/f [intehrprit] interpreter

interruptor m [intirooptohr] switch

interruptor de ligar/desligar m [di ligar/diJligar] on/off switch

intervalo m [intervaloo] interval

intoxicação alimentar f [intoksikasowng] food poisoning

introduza a moeda na ranhura insert coin in slot

inundação f [inoondasowng] flood

Inverno m [invehrnoo] winter

ir [eer] to go

ir buscar [booshkar] to get, to fetch

Irlanda f [eerlanda] Ireland

Irlanda do Norte f [eerlanda doo nort] Northern Ireland

irlandês (m) [eerlandaysh] Irish; Irishman

irlandesa (f) [eerlandayza] Irish; Irishwoman

irmã f [eermang] sister

irmão m [eermowng] brother

isqueiro m [ishkayroo] cigarette lighter

isso [eesoo] that; that one

isso é ... [eh] that's ...

isso é ...? is that ...?

isto [eeshtoo] this; this one

isto é ...? [eeshtweh] is this ...?

Itália f [ital-ya] Italy

italiana (f) [ital-yana] Italian, italiano (m) [ital-yanoo] Italian

J

já [Ja] ever; already

Janeiro [Janayro] January

janela f [Janehla] window

jantar (m) [Jantar] evening meal, dinner; supper; to have dinner

jarda f [Jarda] yard

jardim m [Jardeeng] garden

jardim público [pooblikoo] park

jardim zoológico [zwoloJikoo] zoo

jarra f [Jarra] vase

jarro m [Jarroo] jug; jar

joalharia f [Jwal-yaree-a] jewellery

joalheiro m [Jwal-yayroo] jeweller

joelho m [Jwayl-yoo] knee

jogar [Joogar] to play

jogar fora to throw away

jogo m [Johgoo] game, match

jóias fpl [Jo-yash] jewellery

jornal m [Joornal] newspaper

jovem [Jovayng] young

jovens mpl [Jovayngsh] young people

judaico [JoodIkoo] Jewish

Julho [Jool-yoo] July

Junho [Joon-yoo] June

junta da culatra f [Joonta da koolatra] cylinder head gasket

junto da ... [Joontoo da] beside the ...

juntos [Joontoosh] together

justo [Jooshtoo] just, fair

L

lá over there, there

lã f [lang] wool

lábios mpl [lab-yoosh] lips

laca f hair spray

lado m [ladoo] side
  do outro lado [doo-ohtroo] opposite
  do outro lado de ... [doo ohtroo ladoo di] across the ...

ladra f, **ladrão** m [ladrowng] thief

lago m [lagoo] lake; pond

lama f mud

lamentar [lamayntar] to regret, to be sorry

lâminas para barbear fpl [laminash para barb-yar] razor blades

lâmpada f light bulb

lanterna f [lantehrna] torch, flashlight

lápis m [lapsh] pencil

lápis para as sobrancelhas [parash sobransayl-yash] eyebrow pencil

lápis para os olhos [parooz ol-yoosh] eyeliner

largo (m) [largoo] wide; square

lata f [lapsh] can; tin

lata de gasolina f [di gazooleena] petrol can

lavabos mpl [lavaboosh] toilets, rest rooms

lavagem a seco f [lavaJayng a saykoo] dry-cleaning

lavagem automática [owtoomatika] carwash

lavagem e mise [ee meez] shampoo and set

lava-louça f [lava lohsa] sink

lavandaria f [lavandaree-a] laundry (place)

lavandaria automática [owtoomatika] launderette

lavar to wash

lavar à mão [mowng] to handwash

lavar a roupa [rohpa] to do the washing

lavar e pentear [paynt-yar] wash and set

lavar na máquina machine wash

lavar-se [-si] to wash (oneself)

lavatório m [lavator-yoo] washhand basin

lavrador m [lavradohr] farmer

laxativo m [lashateevoo] laxative

lei f [lay] law

leitaria f [laytaree-a] shop selling dairy products

leite de limpeza m [layt di leempayza] skin cleanser

leitor de CDs m [laytohr di say daysh] CD-player

lembrança f [laymbransa] gift; souvenir

lembrar-se [-si] to remember
  lembra-se? [laymbrasi] do you remember?
  não me lembro [nowng mi laymbroo] I don't remember

lenço m [laynsoo] handkerchief

lenço de cabeça [di kabaysa] headscarf

lenço de pescoço [pishk**oh**soo] scarf (for neck)

lençol m [layns**ol**] sheet

lenços de papel mpl [**lay**nsoosh di pap**ehl**] tissues, paper handkerchiefs, Kleenex®

lentes de contacto fpl [layntsh di kont**a**too] contact lenses

lentes gelatinosas [Jilatin**o**zash] soft lenses

lentes rígidas [**ree**Jidash] hard lenses

lentes semi-rígidas [simir**ee**Jidash] gas permeable lenses

lento [**lay**ntoo] slow

leque m [lehk] fan (handheld)

ler [layr] to read

lésbica f [**leh**Jbika] lesbian

leste m [lehsht] east

no leste [noo] in the east

letra f [**lay**tra] letter

letra de imprensa block letters

levada m country walkway along irrigation channels on Madeira

levantar-se [livant**a**rsi] to get up

levante o auscultador lift the receiver

levar to take; to carry

para levar to take away, to go (food)

leve [lehv] light (not heavy)

Lg. square

lhe [l-yi] (to) him; (to) her; (to) you

lhes [l-yaysh] (to) them; (to) you

libra f [**lee**bra] pound

libras esterlinas fpl [**lee**braz ishtirl**ee**nash] pounds sterling

lição f [lis**ow**ng] lesson

licença f [lis**a**ynsa] licence; permit

com licença [kong] excuse me

licenciatura f [lisayns-yat**oo**ra] degree

liceu m [lis**ay**-oo] secondary school, high school

ligação f [ligas**ow**ng] connection

ligação com ... connects with ...

ligadura f [ligad**oo**ra] bandage

ligar to turn on, to switch on

lima de unhas f [**lee**ma d**oo**n-yash] nailfile

limite de velocidade m [lim**ee**t di viloosid**ad**] speed limit

limpa pára-brisas m [**lee**mpa parabr**ee**zash] windscreen wiper

limpar [leemp**a**r] to clean

limpeza a seco f [leemp**ay**za a s**ay**koo] dry-clean; dry-cleaning

limpo [l**ee**mpoo] clean

língua f [**lee**ngwa] language; tongue

linha f [l**ee**n-ya] line

liquidação sale

liquidação total clearance sale

Lisboa [liJb**oh**-a] Lisbon

liso [l**ee**zoo] plain

lista f [l**ee**shta] list

lista telefónica [telef**oh**nika] phone book, telephone directory litro m [**lee**troo] litre

livraria f [livraree-a] bookshop, bookstore

livre [**lee**vr] free, vacant

livro m [**lee**vroo] book

livro de cheques [di shehksh] cheque book

livro de expressões [dishpris**oy**ngsh] phrasebook

livro de moradas [di moo**ra**dash] address book

livro-guia m [gee-a] guidebook

lixívia f [lish**ee**v-ya] bleach

lixo m [**lee**shoo] rubbish, trash; litter

local de encontro m [lookal daynk**oh**ntroo] meeting place

localidade f [look**ali**dad] place

loção f [loos**ow**ng] lotion

loção de bronzear f [di bronz-yar] suntan lotion

loção écran total f [ekrang t**oo**tal] sunblock

loção para depois do sol f [dip**oh**-ish doo] aftersun cream

locomotiva f [loknomoot**ee**va] engine

logo [**lo**goo] immediately, at once

logo que possível [ki poos**ee**vil] as soon as possible

loiça f [**loh**-isa] crockery

loiça de barro [di b**a**rroo] pottery

loja f [**lo**Ja] shop

loja de aluguer de automóveis [daloog**ehr** dowtoom**o**vaysh] car hire, car rental

loja de antiguidades f

[dantigweed**adsh**] antique shop

loja de artesanato [dartizan**a**too] craft shop, handicrafts shop

loja de artigos fotográficos [dart**ee**goosh fotografik**oo**sh] camera shop

loja de brinquedos [di breenk**ay**doosh] toyshop

loja de desportos [dishp**o**rtoosh] sports shop

loja de ferragens [di firraJ**ay**ngsh] hardware store

loja de fotografia [fotografee-a] photography shop

loja de lembranças [laymbr**a**nsash] gift shop

loja de malas [m**a**lash] handbag shop

loja de peles [p**eh**lsh] furrier

loja de produtos naturais [prood**oo**toosh nat**oo**rīsh] health food shop

Londres [**loh**ndrish] London

longe [**loh**nJ] far

ao longe [ow] in the distance

fica longe? [**fee**ka] is it far away?

lotação esgotada all tickets sold

louça: lavar a louça [**loh**sa] to wash the dishes

louça de barro f [di b**a**rroo] earthenware

louco [**loh**koo] nutter

louro [**loh**roo] blond

lua f [**loo**-a] moon

lua-de-mel f [**loo**-a di m**eh**l] honeymoon

lugar m [loog**ar**] greengrocer's;

seat; place

em outro lugar [ayng **oh**troo] elsewhere

lugar ao pé da janela [ow peh da Ja**neh**la] window seat

lugar de corredor [di kooridohr] aisle seat

lugar de vegetais [di vigi**tish**] greengrocer's

lugares em pé standing room

lugares reservados a cegos, inválidos, grávidas e acompanhantes de crianças com menos de 4 anos seats reserved for the blind, disabled, expectant mothers and those with children under four

lume m [loom] light; fire

luvas fpl [loovash] gloves

luxo m [looshoo] luxury

de luxo [di] de luxe

luxuoso [loosh-wohzoo] luxurious

luz f [loosh] light

luz do sol f [looJ doo] sunshine

luzes de presença fpl [looziJ di pri**zay**nsa] sidelights

luzes de trânsito traffic lights

luzes de trás [loozish di trash] rear lights

Lx Lisbon

M

M. underground, (US) subway

má bad; nasty

macaco m [maka**koo**] jack

maçada f [masada] bother

maçador [masadohr] boring

maçaneta f [masanayta] door knob

machão m [mashowng] macho

machista [masheeshta] sexist

maço m [masoo] packet

madeira f [madayra] wood

madrasta f [madrashta] stepmother

madrugada f [madroogada] dawn

de madrugada [di] at dawn

maduro [madooroo] ripe

mãe f [mayng] mother

magricela f [magrisehla] skinny

magro [magroo] slim; thin

Maio [**mī**-oo] May

maior [mī-**or**] greater; bigger, larger

o maior the biggest

a maior parte (de) [part (di)] most (of)

maioria: a maioria dos/das ... [mī-ooree-a doosh/dash] most ...

mais [mīsh] more

mais alguma coisa? [mīz algooma koh-iza] anything else?

mais de ... [mīJ di] more than ..., over ...

mais ... do que ... more ... than ...

mais um/uma [mīz oong/ooma] an extra one

não há mais [nowng a mīsh] there's none left

mais longe [mīJ lohnJ] further

mais nada no more; nothing else

mais ou menos [mīz oh **may**noosh] about, approximately, more or less; average, so-so

mais tarde [mīsh tard] later, later on

mal hardly; badly

mala f bag; suitcase; handbag

fazer as malas [fa**zayr** aJ **ma**lash] to pack one's bags

mala de mão [di mowng] handbag, (US) purse

mal cozido [koo**zee**doo] not cooked, undercooked

mal-entendido m [malayntayn**dee**doo] misunderstanding

maluco [ma**loo**koo] barmy, nuts

mamã f [ma**mang**] mum

mamar: dar de mamar a to breastfeed

mancha f spot

mandar to send

manga f sleeve

manhã f [man-**yang**] morning

às sete da manhã [ash seht] at seven a.m.

de manhã [di] in the morning

esta manhã [**eh**shta] this morning

manivela do motor f [mani**veh**la doo mo**tohr**] crankshaft

manta f blanket

mantenha-se à direita, caminhe pela esquerda (cars) keep to the right, (pedestrians) walk on the left

mão f [mowng] hand

mapa m map

mapa da cidade m [si**dad**] street map

mapa das estradas m [daz shtr**adash**] road map

maquilhagem f [makil-ya**Jayng**] make-up

máquina f [**ma**kina] machine

máquina de barbear [di barb-**yar**] electric shaver

máquina de lavar [**lavar**] washing machine

máquina de venda [di **vay**nda] vending machine

máquina fotográfica [footoogr**afika**] camera

mar m sea

maravilhoso [maravil-**yoh**zoo] wonderful

marca f make, brand name

marcação f [marka**sow**ng] appointment

marcar to dial

marca registada registered trademark

marcha f [**mar**sha] candlelit procession

marcha atrás [**marsha**trash] reverse gear

Março [**mar**soo] March

marco de correio m [**mar**koo di koo**ray**-oo] letterbox, mailbox

maré f [mareh] tide

margem f [mar**Jay**ng] shore

marido m [ma**ree**doo] husband

marisqueira f [marish**kay**ra] seafood restaurant

marque o número desejado dial the number you require

Marrocos m [marro**koosh**]

Morocco
martelo m [marte**hl**oo] hammer
mas [mash] but
matar to kill
maternidade f [maternidad]
maternity hospital
matrícula f [matree**k**oola]
registration number
mau [mow] bad; nasty
maxila f [mak**seela**] jaw
me me; to me; myself
mecânico m [me**k**anikoo]
mechanic
média: em média [ayng me**hd**-ya] on average
médica f [me**hd**ika] doctor
medicamento m [midika**m**ayntoo]
drug
médico m [me**hd**ikoo] doctor
medida f [mi**deed**a] size
médio [me**hd**-yoo] medium;
medium-rare
de tamanho médio [di taman-yoo] medium-sized
Mediterrâneo m [miditirran-yoo]
Mediterranean
medo m [may**d**oo] fear

meia dúzia f [may-a d**oo**z-ya]
half a dozen
meia hora f [ora] half an hour
meia-noite f [n**oh**-it] midnight
meia pensão f [payns**ow**ng] half
board, American plan
meias fpl [may-ash] stockings;
socks
meias collants stockings
meias de vidro [di **veed**roo]
hosiery
meio m [may-oo] middle; half

no meio [noo] in the middle
meio bilhete m [bil-**yayt**] half
fare
meio-dia m [may-oo dee-a]
midday, noon
ao meio-dia [ow] at midday
mel m [meh**l**] honey
melhor [mil-**yor**] best; better
melhorar [mil-yorar] to improve
mencionar [mayns-yoonar] to
mention
menina f [mi**neena**] girl; young
lady
menino m [mi**neena**] boy
menor [mi**nor**] smaller
menos [may**noosh**] less
menos de [di] under, less than
menos do que [doo ki] less
than
pelo menos at least
mentir [mayn**teer**] to lie
menu de preço fixo [di pray**soo**
feeksoo] fixed-price menu
menu turístico [tooree**sh**tikoo]
tourist menu
mercado m [mir**k**adoo] market
mercearia f [mirs-yaree-a]
grocery store
merceeiro m [mirs-**yay**roo]
grocery store
merda! [me**hrd**a] shit!
mergulhar [mirgool-yar] to dive
mergulho m [mir**gool**-yoo] skin-
diving
mês m [maysh] month
mesa f [may**z**a] table
mesma [may**J**ma], **mesmo**
[may**J**moo] same; myself
o/a mesmo/mesma the same

ele mesmo himself

mesmo se ... [may**J**mo si] even if ...

metade f [mitad] half

metade do preço [doo praysoo] half price

metro m [**meh**troo] metre; underground, (US) subway

metropolitano m underground, (US) subway

meu [**may**-oo] my; mine

meu próprio ... [**pro**pr-yoo] my own ...

meus [**may**-oosh] my; mine

mexer [mi**shayr**] to move

microondas f [mikroo-**ohn**dash] microwave (oven)

mil [meel] thousand

milha f [**meel**-ya] mile

milhão m [mil-**yow**ng] million

milímetro m [mil**ee**mitroo] millimetre

mim [meeng] me

minha [**meen**-ya], minhas [**meen**-yash] my; mine

ministério m [minish**tehr**-yoo] ministry, government department

minúsculo [min**oo**shkooloo] tiny

minuto m [min**oo**too] minute

míope [mee-**oo**pi] shortsighted

miradouro m scenic view, vantage point

missa m [**mee**sa] mass

misturar [mish**too**rar] to mix

mobília f [moo**beel**-ya] furniture

mochila f [moo**shee**la] rucksack, backpack

moda f fashion

na moda fashionable

modas para senhoras fpl [**mo**dash para sin-**yo**rash] ladies' fashions

moderno [moo**deh**rnoo] modern

moeda f [**mweh**da] coin

moinho (m) [moo-**een**-yoo] mill; dull (pain)

mola f [**mo**la] spring (in seat); peg

mola de roupa [di **roh**pa] clothes peg

mola para o cabelo [paroo kab**ay**loo] hairgrip

mole [mol] soft

molhado [mool-**ya**doo] wet

momento m [moo**mayn**too] moment

um momento [oong] hold on, just a moment

montanha f [mon**tan**-ya] mountain

montar a cavalo [kava**loo**] to go horse-riding

monte m [mohnt] hill

montra f [**moh**ntra] shop window

monumento m [moonoo**mayn**too] monument

monumento nacional national monument

morada f [moo**ra**da] address

morar [moo**rar**] to live

mordedura f [moorded**oo**ra] bite

morrer [moo**rrayr**] to die

morte f [mort] death

morto [**moh**rtoo] dead

morto de fome [di fohm] starving

mosca f [**moh**shka] fly

mosquito m [mooshk**ee**too] mosquito

mosteiro m [moosh**tay**roo] monastery

mostrar [moosh**trar**] to show

mota f, motocicleta f [mootoosikl**eh**ta] motorbike

motor m [moot**ohr**] engine

motor de arranque [dar**rank**] starter motor

motoreta f [mootoor**ay**ta] scooter

motorista m/f [mootoor**ee**shta] driver; motorist

motorizada f [mootooriz**a**da] moped

mourisco [mohr**ee**shkoo] Moorish

mouro m [**moh**-ooroo] Moor
os mouros the Moors

móveis de cozinha mpl kitchen furniture

muçulmano [moosool**ma**noo] Muslim

mudança f [mood**an**sa] gear(s)

mudar [**moo**dar] to move

mudar de roupa [di **roh**pa] to get changed

mudar em ... change at ...

muitas vezes [mw**ee**ngta**J** v**ay**zish] often

muito [mw**ee**ngtoo] a lot, lots; plenty of; much; very (much); quite

muito mais [mīsh] a lot more

não muito [n**ow**ng] not (very) much; not a lot; not too much

muito tempo [t**ay**mpoo] a long time

muito bem [b**ay**ng] very well

muito bem! well done!

muito prazer [pra**zayr**] how do you do?, nice to meet you

muito prazer em conhecê-lo [**ay**ng koon-yis**ay**loo] very pleased to meet you

muitos mpl [mw**ee**ngtoosh] many

muletas fpl [mool**ay**tash] crutches

mulher f [mool-**yeh**r] woman; wife

mulher-polícia f [pool**ee**s-ya] policewoman

multa f [**moo**lta] fine

multa por uso indevido penalty for misuse

multidão f [moolti**dow**ng] crowd

mundo m [**moo**ndoo] world

muro m [**moo**roo] wall

músculo m [**moo**shkooloo] muscle

museu m [moo**zay**-oo] museum

música f [**moo**zika] music

música folclórica [foolk**lo**rika] folk music

música pop pop music

música rock rock (music)

músico m [**moo**zikoo] musician

N

n. number

na in the; at the; on the
na casa do Américo at Américo's

na quinta-feira by Thursday

na televisão on television

nacional [nas-yoonal] national

nacionalidade f [nas-yoonalidad] nationality

nada nothing

mais nada [miɪ] nothing else

de nada my pleasure, don't mention it

nada a declarar nothing to declare

nadador salvador f [nadadohr salvadohr] lifeguard

nadar to swim

nalguma parte [nalgooma part] somewhere

namorada f [namoorada] girlfriend

namorado m [namooradoo] boyfriend

não [nowng] no; not

não aconselhável a menores de ... anos not recommended for those under ... years of age

não beber do not drink

não congelar do not freeze

não contém ... does not contain ...

não engolir do not swallow

não engomar do not iron

não exceder a dose indicada do not exceed the dose indicated

não faz mal [faɪ mal] it doesn't matter, never mind; it's OK

não fumar no smoking

não funciona out of order

não há vagas no vacancies

não ingerir do not swallow

não me diga! [mi deega] you don't say!

não mexer do not touch

não ... nada nothing; not ... anything

não ... nenhum [nin-yoong] none; not ... any

não ... ninguém [ningayng] nobody, no-one; not ... anybody, not ... anyone

não ... nunca [noonka] never

não pendurar do not hang, dry flat

não pisar a relva please keep off the grass

não secar na máquina do not spin-dry

não sei [say] I don't know

não tem de quê [tayng di kay] don't mention it, you're welcome

não torcer do not wring

nariz m [nareesh] nose

nas [nash] in the; at the; on the

nascer [nash-sayr] to be born

nasci em ... [nash-see ayng] I was born in ...

Na. Sra. (Nossa Senhora) Our Lady

natação f [natasowng] swimming

Natal m Christmas

natural [natooral] natural

natureza f [natoorayza] nature

náuseas fpl [nowz-yash] nausea

navio m [navee-o] ship

de navio [di] by ship

necessário [nisisar-yoo] necessary

negativo m [nigateevoo] negative

negócio m [nigos-yoo] deal; business

nem eu [nayng ay-oo] nor do I

nem ... nem ... [nayng] neither ... nor ...

nenhum [nin-yoong], nenhuma [nin-yooma] none; no ...
de maneira nenhuma! [di manayra] no way!
de nenhum modo [modoo] not in the least
nenhum deles [daylsh] neither of them

neo-zelandês m [neh-o zilandaysh], neo-zelandesa f [zilandayza] New Zealander

nervoso [nirvohzoo] nervous

neta f [nehta] granddaughter

neto m [nehtoo] grandson

nevar [nivar] to snow

neve f [nehv] snow

névoa f [nehvwa] mist

nevoeiro m [nivwayroo] fog

ninguém [ningayng] nobody, no-one

nível de óleo m [neevil dol-yoo] oil level

no [noo] in; in the; at the; on the
no alto at the top
no fundo de at the bottom of
no hotel at the hotel
no sábado on Saturday
no. number

nódoa f [nodwa] stain

noite f [noh-it] evening; night
à noite in the evening; at night
de noite at night
esta noite [ehshta] this evening; tonight

noite de Santo António 13th June: Saint's day with music, fireworks and processions

noite de São João 24th June: Saint's day with music, fireworks and processions

noite de São Pedro 29th June: Saint's day with music, fireworks and processions

noiva (f) [noh-iva] engaged; fiancée

noivo (m) [noh-ivoo] engaged; fiancé

nojento [nooJayntoo] disgusting; filthy

nome m [nohm] name

nome de solteira [di sooltayra] maiden name

nome próprio [propr-yoo] Christian name, first name

nono [nohnoo] ninth

nora f daughter-in-law

nordeste m [noordehsht] northeast

noroeste m [noorwehsht] northwest

norte m [nort] north
ao norte [ow] to the north
no norte [noo] in the north

Noruega f [noorwehga] Norway

norueguês (m) [noorwegaysh], norueguesa (f) [noorwegayza] Norwegian nos [noosh] in the; at the; on the; us; to us; ourselves

nós [nosh] we; us

No. Sr. (Nosso Senhor) Our Lord

nossa, nossas [nosash], nosso [nosoo], nossos [nosoosh] our; ours

nota f note; banknote, (US) bill

notas falsas fpl [notash falsash] forged banknotes

notícias fpl [nootees-yash] news

noutro [nohtroo] in another; on another

nova morada f [moorada] forwarding address

Nova Zelândia [ziland-ya] New Zealand

nove [nov] nine

novecentas [novesayntash], novecentos [novesayntoosh] nine hundred

Novembro [noovaymbroo] November

noventa [noovaynta] ninety

novidades fpl [noovidadsh] news

novo [nohvoo] new

nu [noo], nua [noo-a] naked

num [noong], numa [nooma] in a

número m [noomiroo] number

número de telefone [di telefohn] phone number

número de voo [noomiroo di voh-oo] flight number

nunca [noonka] never

nuvem f [noovayng] cloud

O

o [oo] the; him; it; to it; you

objectiva f [objeteeva] lens (of camera)

objectos de escritório mpl office supplies

objectos perdidos lost property, lost and found

obliterador m [oblitiradohr] ticket-stamping machine

obra f work

obras (na estrada) fpl roadworks

obrigada, obrigado [obrigadoo] thanks, thank you

muito obrigado/obrigada [mweengtoo] thank you very much

observar [obsirvar] to watch

obturador m [obtooradohr] shutter

óbvio [obv-yoo] obvious

Oceano Atlântico [os-yanoo atlantikoo] Atlantic Ocean

oculista m [okooleeshta] optician

óculos mpl [okooloosh] glasses, spectacles

óculos de sol [di] sunglasses

óculos protectores [prootetohrish] goggles

ocupado [okoopadoo] engaged; busy; occupied

oeste m [wesht] west

no oeste [noo] in the west

ofender [ofayndayr] to offend

ofensivo [ofaynseevoo] offensive

oferecer [ofrisayr] to get; to offer

oferta especial special offer

oiço [oh-isoo] I hear

oitavo [oh-itavoo] eighth

oitenta [oh-itaynta] eighty

oito [oh-itoo] eight

oitocentas [oh-itoosayntash], oitocentos [oh-itoosayntoosh] eight hundred

olá! [oola] hi!, hello!

óleo m [ol-yoo] oil

óleo de bronzear [di brohnz-yar] suntan oil

oleoso [ol-yohzoo] oily

olhar para [ol-yar] to look at

olho m [ohl-yoo] eye

ombro m [ohmbroo] shoulder

onda f [ohnda] wave

onde? [ohnd] where?

onde é? [ohndeh] where is it?

onde está? [ohnd shta] where is it?

onde vai? [vī] where are you going?

de onde? [dohnd] where from?

de onde é? [dohnd-eh] where are you from?

ontem [ohntayng] yesterday

ontem à noite [noh-it] last night

ontem de manhã [di man-yang] yesterday morning

onze [ohnz] eleven

operação f [opirasowng] operation

operador turístico m [opiradohr tooreeshtikoo] tour

operator

oposto [opohshto] opposite

optimista [otimeeshta] optimistic

óptimo [otimoo] super

óptimo! great!, good!, excellent!

o que [oo kay] what

o que é isso? [oo k-yeh eesoo] what's this?

ora essa! [ora ehsa] don't be stupid!

orelha f [orayl-ya] ear

organizar [organizar] to organize

orgulhoso [orgool-yohzoo] proud

orquestra f [orkehshtra] orchestra

os [oosh] the; them; you

osso m [ohsoo] bone

otorrinolaringologista ear, nose and throat specialist

ou [oh] or

ou ... ou ... either ... or ...

ouriço-do-mar m [ohreesoo doo] sea urchin

ourivesaria f [ohrivezaree-a] jeweller's

ouro m [ohroo] gold

ousar [ohzar] to dare

Outono [ohtohnoo] autumn, (US) fall

no Outono [noo] in the autumn, in the fall

outra coisa [ohtra koh-iza] something else

outras localidades [ohtraɹ lookalidadsh] other places

outra vez [ohtra vaysh] again

outro [**oh**troo] different, another; other

Outubro [ohto**o**broo] October

ouvir [oh**veer**] to hear

ao ouvir o sinal... when you hear the tone ...

ovelha f [o**vay**l-ya] sheep

P

P. square

pá f spade

pacote m [pa**kot**] carton; pack

padaria f [pada**ree**-a] bakery

padeiro m [pa**day**roo] baker

padrasto m [pa**drash**too] stepfather

padre m [padr] priest

pagamento m [paga**mayn**too] payment

pagamento a pronto cash payment

pagar to pay

pagar em dinheiro [ayng deen-**yay**roo] to pay cash

página f [**pa**Jina] page

páginas amarelas [**pa**Jinaz ama**reh**lash] yellow pages

pai m [pī] father

painel m [pī**nehl**] dashboard; panel

país m [pa-**eesh**] country; nation; homeland

pais mpl [pīsh] parents

paisagem f [pīza**J**ayng] scenery

País de Gales m [pa-**ee**J di **ga**lish] Wales

palácio m [pa**las**-yoo] palace

palavra f word

palco m [**pal**koo] stage

pálido [**pa**lidoo] pale

panela f [pa**neh**la] pan, saucepan

panfleto m [pan**flay**too] leaflet

pano m [**pa**noo] fabric, cloth

pano de cozinha [di koo**zeen**-ya] tea towel

pano de loiça [**loh**-isa] dishcloth

pantufas fpl [pan**too**fash] slippers

papá m dad

papeira f [pa**pay**ra] mumps

papéis waste paper

papel m [pa**pehl**] paper

papelaria f [papela**ree**-a] stationer

papel de alumínio [daloo**meen**-yoo] aluminium foil

papel de carta [di] writing paper, notepaper

papel de embrulho [**daym**brool-yoo] wrapping paper

papel higiénico [i.i-**yeh**nikoo] toilet paper

par m pair

um par de ... [oong par di] a couple of ...; a pair of ...

para into; for; to; towards

para onde? [**ohn**d] where to?

para alugar [para**loo**gar] for hire; to rent

parabéns! [para**bayng**sh] congratulations!; happy birthday!

pára-brisas m [para**bree**zash] windscreen

185

pára-choques m [parashoksh] bumper

parafuso m [parafoozoo] screw

paragem f [paraJayng] stop

paragem do autocarro f [doo owtookarroo] bus stop

parapentismo m [parapaynteeJmoo] para-gliding

parar to stop

pare! [par] stop!

  pare com isso! [kong eesoo] stop it!

parecer [paresayr] to look like

parede f [parayd] wall

páre, escute e olhe stop, look and listen

parente m/f [paraynt] relative

parque de campismo m [park di kampeeJmoo] campsite; caravan site, (US) trailer park

parque de estacionamento [shtas-yonamayntoo] car park, parking lot

parque de estacionamento subterrâneo [soobtirran-yoo] underground car park/ parking lot

parque para roulotes [roolotsh] caravan site, (US) trailer park

parque recreativo [rekr-yateevoo] amusement park

parte f [part] part

  em parte nenhuma [nin-yooma] nowhere

  em toda a parte [tohda] everywhere

parte posterior [pooshteriohr] back (part)

particular [partikoolar] private

partida f [parteeda] departure

partido (m) [parteedoo] broken; party (political)

partilhar [partil-yar] to share

partir [parteer] to break; to leave

  a partir de [di] from

Páscoa f [pashkwa] Easter

passadeira de peões f [pasadaira di p-yoyngsh] pedestrian crossing, (US) crosswalk

passado (m) [pasadoo] past

  no ano passado [noo anoo] last year

  semana passada [simana] last week

passageira f [pasaJayra], **passageiro m** [pasaJayroo] passenger

passagem de nível m [pasaJayng] level crossing, (US) grade crossing

passagem de peões pedestrian crossing, (US) crosswalk

passagem subterrânea underpass

passaporte m [pasaport] passport

passar to pass

  o que se passa? [oo ki si] what's happening?; what's wrong?

passar a ferro [a fehrroo] to iron

pássaro m [pasaroo] bird

passatempo m [–taympoo] hobby

passe (m) go, walk, cross now;
weekly or monthly ticket
passeio m [pasay-oo]
pavement, sidewalk; walk
ir a dar um passeio to go for
a walk
pasta f [pashta] briefcase
pasta de dentes [di dayntsh]
toothpaste
pastelaria f [pashtilaree-a] cake
shop, café selling cakes
pastilha elástica f [pashteel-ya
elashtika] chewing gum
pastilhas de mentol fpl
[pashteel-yas di] mints
pastilhas para a garganta
throat pastilles
patinar [patinar] to skid; to
skate
patins de gelo mpl [pateenj di
Jayloo] ice skates
pátio de recreio m [pat-yoo di
rikray-oo] playground
patrão m [patrowng] boss
pavilhão desportivo sports
pavilion
Pç. square
pé m [peh] foot
a pé on foot
ir a pé to walk
estar de pé [di] to stand
ao pé de [ow ... di] near
peão m [p-yowng] pedestrian
peça de teatro f [pehsa di t-
yatroo] play
peça sobresselente f
[sobrisilaynt] spare part
pechincha f [pisheensha]
bargain

pedaço m [pidasoo] piece
pedir [pideer] to ask; to order
pedir emprestado
[aymprishtadoo] to borrow
pedra f [pehdra] stone, rock
pega f [pehga] handle; action
of wrestling with the bull
during a bullfight
pegar [pigar] to catch
peito m [paytoo] breast; bust;
chest
peixaria f [paysharee-a]
fishmonger's
pela [pila] through the; by the;
about the
pelas [pilash] through the; by
the, about the
pelas três horas by three
o'clock
pele f [pehl] skin; leather;
suede; fur
peleiro m [pilayroo] furrier
película aderente f [pileekoola
adiraynt] clingfilm
pelo [piloo] through the; by
the; about the
pelos [piloosh] through the; by
the; about the
pena: é uma pena [eh ooma
payna] it's a pity
que pena! [ki] what a pity!
não vale a pena [nowng val-ya]
there's no point
tenho muita pena [mweengta]
I'm so sorry
pensão f [paynsowng]
guesthouse
pensão completa [komplehta]
full board

187

pensar [paynsar] to think
penso m [paynsoo] dressing; Elastoplast®, Bandaid®
pensos higiénicos mpl [paynsooz iJ-yehnikoosh] sanitary napkins/towels
pente m [paynt] comb
peões mpl [p-yoyngsh] pedestrians
pequeno [pikaynoo] little, small
pequeno almoço m [almohsoo] breakfast
perceber [pirsibayr] to understand
percebo [pirsayboo] I understand, I see
perdão [pirdowng] sorry
perder [pirdayr] to lose; to miss
perdido [pirdeedoo] lost
perdidos e achados lost property, lost and found
perfeito [pirfaytoo] perfect
perfumaria f [pirfoomaree-a] perfume shop
pergunta f [pirgoonta] question
perguntar [pirgoontar] to ask
perigo m [pireegoo] danger
perigo de desmoronamento danger of landslides
perigo de incêndio beware of starting fires
perigo de morte extreme danger
perigo, parar danger: stop
perigoso [pirigohzoo] dangerous
período m [piree-oodoo] period
período escolar [shkoolar] term
permanente f [pirmanaynt] perm
permitido [pirmiteedoo] allowed

permitir to allow
perna f [pehrna] leg
(de) pernas para o ar [(di) pehrnash proo ar] upside down
persianas fpl [pirs-yanash] blinds
pertencer [pirtaynsayr] to belong
perto [pehrtoo] near
perto daqui [dakee] nearby, near here
perto de [di] next to
perturbar [pirtoorbar] to disturb
peruca f [pirooka] wig
pesadelo m [pizadayloo] nightmare
pesado [pizadoo] heavy
pesca f [pehshka] fishing
pescar [pishkar] to fish
pesca submarina f [soobmareena] underwater fishing
pescoço m [pishkohsoo] neck
peso m [payzoo] weight
peso líquido net weight
peso neto net weight
pessoa f [pisoh-a] person
pessoal m [pisoo-al] staff, employees
peúga f [p-yooga] sock
piada f [p-yada] joke
picada f [pikada] bite; sting
picada de insecto [dinsehtoo] insect bite
picado [pikadoo] stung
picante [pikant] hot, spicy
picar [pikar] to sting; to chop finely
picar o bilhete stamp/punch your ticket

pijama **m** [piJama] pyjamas

pilha **f** [peel-ya] battery

pílula **f** [peeloola] pill

pinça **f** [peensa] tweezers

pincel **m** [peensehl] paintbrush

pintado de fresco wet paint

pintar [peentar] to paint

pintura **f** [peentoora] picture

pior [p-yor] worse; worst

o pior the worst

piquenique **m** [pikineek] picnic

pires **m** [peersh] saucer

piscina **f** [pish-seena] swimming pool

piscina coberta [koobehrta] indoor pool

piscina infantil [infanteel] children's pool

piso **m** [peezoo] floor, storey; surface

piso escorregadio slippery road surface

piso irregular uneven road surface

piso superior [soopir-yohr] top floor

pista **f** runway

pistola **f** [pishtola] gun

plano (**m**) [planoo] plan; flat (adj)

planta **f** plant

plástico **m** [plashtikoo] plastic

plataforma **f** [plataforma] platform, (US) track

plateia **f** [platay-a] audience; ground floor of auditorium

platinados **mpl** [platinadoosh] points

P.M.P. (por mão própria) deliver by hand

pneu **m** [pnay-oo] tyre

pneu sobresselente [soobrisilaynt] spare tyre

pó **m** [paw] dust; powder

pobre [pobr] poor

pode [pod] you can/he/she can

pode (você) ...? [vosay] can you ...?

pode-se ...? [podsi] is it OK to ...?

pode dar-me ...? [pod darmi] can I have a ...?, may I have ...?

poder [poodayr] to be able to

pó de talco **m** [paw di talkoo] talcum powder

podia ...? [poodee-a] could you ...?

podre [pohdr] rotten

põe [poyng] he/she/it puts; you put

põem [poh-ayng] you/they put

pões [poyngsh] you put

polegada **f** [pooligada] inch

polegar **m** [pooligar] thumb

polícia **m** [poolees-ya] police; policeman

Polícia de Segurança Pública branch of the Portuguese police responsible for public order

polícia de trânsito traffic warden

Polícia Judiciária branch of the police force responsible for investigating crime

poliéster polyester

política **f** politics

político political

189

polvo m [pohlvoo] octopus

pomada f [poomada] ointment

pomada para calçados [kalsadoosh] shoe polish

pomos [pohmoosh] we put

pónei m [ponay] pony

ponho [pohn-yoo] I put

pontão m [pontowng] jetty

ponte f [pohnt] bridge; crown

ponto de encontro meeting point

população f [poopoolasowng] population

por [poor] through; by
por avião by airmail
por noite [noh-it] per night

pôr [pohr] to put

porca f [porka] nut (for bolt)

porção f [poorsowng] portion

porcaria f [poorkaree-a] dirt; mess

porcelana f [poorsilana] china

por cento [sayntoo] per cent

porco m [pohrkoo] pig

pôr do sol m [pohr doo] sunset

por favor [poor favohr] please

porque [poorkay] because; why
porque não? [nowng] why not?

porreiro! [poorrayroo] bloody good!

porta f door; gate

porta-bagagens m [bagaJayngsh] boot, (US) trunk

porta-bagagens na capota, porta-bagagens no tejadilho [noo tiJadeel-yoo] roof rack

porta-bebés m [bebehsh] carry-cot

porta de embarque f [daymbark] gate

portagem toll

porta-moedas m [mwehdash] purse

porta nº ... gate number ...

portão m [poortowng] gate

portão de embarque [daymbark] gate (at airport)

porteiro m [poortayroo] doorman, porter

porteiro da noite [noh-it] night porter

Porto m [pohrtoo] Oporto

porto m harbour, port

Portugal Telecom National Telecommunications Service

português (m) [poortoogaysh] Portuguese; Portuguese man
em português in Portuguese
os portugueses the Portuguese

portuguesa (f) [poortoogayza] Portuguese; Portuguese woman

posologia f dose

possível [pooseevil] possible

posso [posoo] I can
posso ...? can I ...?
posso ter ...? [tayr] can I have ...?

postal m [pooshtal] postcard

posta-restante f [poshta rishtant] poste restante, (US) general delivery

poste indicador m [posht indikadohr] signpost

posterior: parte posterior f [pooshtir-yohr] back (part)

postigos **mpl** [pooshteegoosh] shutters

Posto da Polícia **m** [pohshtoo da poolees-ya] police station

posto de enfermagem first-aid post

posto de socorros first-aid centre

pouco [pohkoo] a little
um pouco [oong] a little bit
um pouco caro [karoo] a bit expensive
um pouco disto [deeshtoo] some of this

pouco vulgar [voolgar] unusual

poucos [pohkoosh] few; a few

pouquinho: um pouquinho [oong pohkeen-yoo] a little bit

pousada **f** [pohsada] state-owned hotel, often a historic building

praça **f** [prasa] square; market

praça de táxis [di taxish] taxi rank

praça de touros [tohroosh] bullring

pracista **m** [praseeshta] taxi-driver

praia **f** [prī-a] seafront; beach
na praia on the beach

prancha à vela **f** [pransha vehla] sailboard

prancha de saltos [di saltoosh] diving board

prancha de windsurf sailboard

prata **f** [prata] silver

prateleira **f** [pratilayra] shelf

praticar [pratikar] to practise

praticar jogging to go jogging

praticar windsurf to windsurf

prático [pratikoo] practical

prato **m** [pratoo] course, dish; plate

prazer: (muito) prazer em conhecê-lo/conhecê-la [(mweengtoo) prazayr aing koon-yisayloo] pleased to meet you

precipício **m** [prisipees-yoo] cliff

precisar [prisizar] to need
preciso de ... [priseezoo di] I need ...

preço **m** [praysoo] price; charge

pré-comprado bought in advance

preço de custo cost price

preço por dia [poor dee-a] price per day

preço por pessoa [pisoh-a] price per person

preço por semana [simana] price per week

preços reduzidos reduced prices

preencher [pri-aynshayr] to fill in

preferir [prifireer] to prefer
prefiro ... [prifeeroo] I prefer ...

prego **m** [prehgoo] nail (metal); roll with a thin slice of meat

preguiçoso [prigisohzoo] lazy

prendas **fpl** [prayndash] gifts

prender [prayndayr] to arrest

preocupação **f** [pri-ookoo-pasowng] worry

preocupado [pri-ookoopadoo] worried

preocupar-se com to worry about

pré-pagamento choose your food, drink etc then pay at the cash desk before being served

preparar [priparar] to prepare

presente m [prizaynt] present, gift

preservativo m [prizirvateevoo] condom

presidente m/f [prizidaynt] president

pressa: estou com pressa [shtoh kong prehsa] I'm in a hurry

não há pressa [nowng a] there's no hurry

pressão f [prisowng] tyre pressure

pressão arterial [artiri-al] blood pressure

presta: não presta [nowng prehshta] it's no good

prestável [preshtavil] helpful

preto [praytoo] black

preto e branco black and white

previsão do tempo f [privizowng doo taympoo] weather forecast

prima f [preema] cousin

Primavera f [primavehra] spring

primeira: a primeira vez [primayra vaysh] the first time

primeira à esquerda [a-shkayrda] first on the left

primeira classe [klas] first class

primeiro [primayroo] first

primeiro andar m first floor, (US) second floor

primeiro ministro m [primayroo mineeshtroo] prime minister

primeiro piso first floor, (US) second floor

primeiros socorros mpl [primayroosh sookorroosh] first aid

primo m [preemoo] cousin

princesa f [preensayza] princess

principal [preensipal] main

principalmente [preensipalmaynt] mostly

príncipe m [preensipi] prince

principiante m/f [preensip-yant] beginner

princípio: ao princípio [ow preenseep-yoo] at first

prioridade f right of way; priority

dar prioridade give way, yield

prisão f [prizowng] jail

prisão de ventre [di vayntr] constipation

privado [privadoo] private

problema m [prooblayma] problem

procissão f [proosisowng] candlelit procession held to celebrate feast days and Good Friday

procurar [prookoorar] to look for; to search

produto m [proodootoo] product

produtos alimentares [alimayntarish] foodstuffs

produtos de beleza [di belayza] beauty products

produtos de limpeza [leempayza] household cleaning materials

professor m [proofes**ohr**],
professora f [proofes**ohr**a]
teacher

programa m [pro**gra**ma]
program(me)

proibida a entrada a ... no
admittance to ...

proibida a entrada a cães no
dogs

proibida a entrada a menores
de ... anos no admittance to
those under ... years of age

proibida a inversão de marcha
no U-turns

proibida a paragem no
stopping

proibida a passagem no access

proibido [proo-i**bee**doo]
forbidden

proibido ... no ...

proibido acampar no camping

proibido a pessoas estranhas
ao serviço personnel only

proibido estacionar no
parking

proibido fazer lume no
campfires

proibido fumar no smoking

proibido nadar no swimming

proibido pescar no fishing

proibido tirar fotografias no
photography

proibido tomar banho no
bathing

proibido ultrapassar no
overtaking

prometer [proomit**ayr**] to
promise

pronto [**prohn**too] ready

pronto a vestir ready-to-wear

pronto-socorro m [**prohn**too
sook**ohr**roo] breakdown service

pronunciar [proonoons-**yar**] to
pronounce

propósito: de propósito [di
proop**oz**itoo] deliberately

própria: a sua própria [**soo**-a
propr-ya], o seu próprio [oo
say-oo propr-yoo] his/her/its/
your/their own

propriedade privada private
property

proteger [prootiJ**ayr**] to protect

proteger do calor e humidade
store away from heat and
damp

protestante (m/f) [prootisht**ant**e]
Protestant

prova: à prova de água [**da**gwa]
waterproof

provar [proo**var**] to try; to try
on; to taste

provavelmente [proovavilm**aynt**]
probably

próxima sessão às ... horas
next showing at ... o'clock

próximo [**pros**imoo] near; next

o/a ... mais próximo/próxima
[mīJ] the nearest ...

próximo de [di] next to

ps. weight

P.S.P. branch of the
Portuguese police

pua f [**poo**-a] splinter

público (m) [**poo**blikoo]
audience; public

pular [poo**lar**] to jump

pulga f [**pool**ga] flea

pulmões **mpl** [poolmoyngsh] lungs

pulseira **f** [poolsayra] bracelet; watchstrap

pulso **m** [poolsoo] wrist

pura lã pure wool

pura lã virgem pure new wool

puxar [pooshar] to pull

puxar (a alavanca) em caso de emergência pull (lever) in case of emergency

puxe pull

Q

Q hot

quais? [kwish] which?; which ones?

qual? [kwal] which?

qual deles? [daylsh] which one?

qualidade **f** [kwalidad] quality

qualquer [kwalkehr] any

qualquer coisa [koh-iza] anything

qualquer medicamento deve estar fora do alcance das crianças keep all medicines out of the reach of children

quando? [kwandoo] when?

quantia **f** [kwantee-a] amount

quanto? [kwantoo] how much?

quanto custa? [kooshta] how much does it cost?

quanto é? [kwantweh] how much is it?

quantos? [kwantoosh] how many?

quarenta [kwaraynta] forty

quarentena **f** [kwarayntayna] quarantine

quarta-feira **f** [kwarta fayra] Wednesday

quarta parte **f** [part] quarter

quarto (**m**) [kwartoo] bedroom; room; quarter; fourth

quarto andar fourth floor, (US) fifth floor

quarto com duas camas [kong doo-ash kamash] twin room

quarto de banho das senhoras [di ban-yoo dash sin-yorash] ladies' toilets, ladies' room

quarto de casal [di kazal] double room

quarto de hotel [dohtehl] hotel room

quarto duplo [dooploo] double room

quarto individual [individwal] single room

quarto para duas pessoas [doo-ash pisoh-ash] double room

quarto para uma pessoa [ooma] single room

quase [kwaz] almost, nearly

quase nunca [noonka] hardly ever

quatro [kwatroo] four

quatrocentas [kwatrosayntash], quatrocentos [kwatrosayntoosh] four hundred

que that; than

o que? what?

o que é isso? [oo k-yeh eesoo] what's that?

que ...! what a ...!
que bom! [kI bong] that's nice!
quê? [kay] what?
quebrar [kibrar] to break
quebre em caso de
  emergência break in case of
  emergency
queda f [kehda] fall
queda de pedras falling stones
queda de rochas falling rocks
queimado [kaymado] burnt
queimado de sol [di] sunburnt
queimadura f [kaymadoora]
  burn
queimadura de sol f sunburn
queimar [kaymar] to burn
queixas complaints
queixo m [kayshoo] chin
quem? [kayng] who?
  de quem? [di] whose?
  de quem é isto? [eh eeshtoo]
  whose is this?
  quem é? [kayngeh] who is it?
  quem fala? who's calling?
quente [kaynt] warm; hot
quer ...? [kehr] would you
  like ...?, do you want...?
querer [kirayr] to want
queria [kiree-a] I want; I'd like
  queria ...? could I have ...?
quero [kehroo] I want
  não quero I don't want (to)
  não quero nada I don't want
  anything
quieto [k-yehtoo] still
quilo m [keeloo] kilo
quilometragem ilimitada
  [kilomitraJayng ilimitada]
  unlimited mileage

quilómetro m [kilomitroo]
  kilometre
quinhentas [keen-yayntash],
  quinhentos [keen-yayntoosh]
  five hundred
quinta f [keenta] farm
quinta-feira f [keenta fayra]
  Thursday
quinto [keentoo] fifth
quinze [keenz] fifteen
quinzena f [keenzayna]
  fortnight
quiosque m [k-yoshk] kiosk
quiosque de jornais [di
  Joornish] newspaper kiosk

R

R. street
rabo m tail; backside, behind
radiador m [rad-yadohr] radiator
Radiodifusão Portuguesa
  Portuguese Radio
radiografia f [rad-yoografee-a]
  X-ray
Radiotelevisão Portuguesa
  Portuguese Television
rainha f [ra-een-ya] queen
raio m [rī-oo] ray, beam; spoke
raio X m [ra-yoo sheesh] X-ray
rapariga f [rapareega] girl
rapaz m [rapash] boy
Rápido m [rapidoo] express
  (train)
rápido fast, quick
raqueta f [rakehta] racket
raqueta de ténis tennis racket
raro [raroo] rare, uncommon

ratazana f [ratazana] rat

rato m [ratoo] mouse

razão f [razowng] reason
tinhas razão [teen-yaJ razowng]
you were right

razoável [razwavil] reasonable

r/c ground floor, (US) first
floor

R.D.P. Portuguese Radio

realmente [r-yalmaynt] really

reaver [r-yavayr] to get back

rebentado [ribentado] burst

reboque m [ribok] trailer (for
carrying tent etc)

rebuçado m [riboosadoo] sweet,
candy

recado m [rikadoo] message
deixar um recado [dayshar
oong] to leave a message

receber [risibayr] to receive

receita f [risayta] recipe;
prescription

recepção f [risehsowng]
reception

recepcionista m/f [risehs-
yooneeeshta] receptionist

recibo m [riseeboo] receipt

reclamação f [riklamasowng]
complaint

reclamação de bagagens [di
bagaJayngsh] baggage claim

reclamações complaints

reclamar [riklamar] to complain

recomendar [rikoomayndar] to
recommend

reconhecer [rikoon-yisayr] to
recognize

rede f [rayd] net; hammock

redondo [ridohndoo] round

reembolsar [ri-aymboolsar] to
refund

reembolso m [ri-aymbohlsoo]
refund

refeição f [rifaysowng] meal

reformada (f) [rifoormada]
pensioner; retired

reformada de terceira idade f
[di tirsayra idad] senior citizen

reformado (m) [rifoormadoo]
pensioner; retired

reformado de terceira idade m
senior citizen

refugo m [rifoogoo] rubbish

reg. registered

região f [riJ-yowng] region; area
da região local

Regional local train, usually
stopping at most stations

registado [riJishtadoo]
registered

registos registered mail

reg.to. regulation

regulamento m regulation

rei m [ray] king

Reino Unido m [raynooneedoo]
United Kingdom

relâmpago m [rilampagoo]
lightning

religião f [riliJ-yowng] religion

relógio m [riloJ-yoo] clock;
watch, wristwatch

relógio de pulso [di poolsoo]
watch, wristwatch

relojoaria f [rilooJwaree-a]
watchmaker's shop

relva f [rehlva] grass

relvado m [relvadoo] lawn

rem. sender

196

remar to row

remédio m [rimehd-yoo] medicine

remetente m/f sender

renda f [raynda] lace

reparar [riparar] to fix, to repair

repele-insectos m [ripehl insehtoosh] insect repellent

repele-mosquitos m [mooshkeetoosh] mosquito repellent

repelente de insectos eléctrico m [ripilaynt dinsehtoosh elehtrikoo] electric mosquito killer

repetir [ripiteer] to repeat

repousar [ripohzar] to rest

repouso m [ripohzoo] rest

representante m/f [riprizayntant] agent

repugnante [ripoognant] revolting

rés de chão m [rehJ doo showng] ground floor, (US) first floor

reserva f [rizehrva] reservation

reserva de lugares [di loogarish] seat reservation

reservado [rizirvadoo] reserved

reservar [rizirvar] to book, to reserve

reservas reservations

residencial m [rizidayns-yal] bed and breakfast hotel

respirar [rishpirar] to breathe

responder [rishpondayr] to answer

responsável [rishponsavil] responsible

resposta f [rishposhta] answer

ressaca f [risaka] hangover

restaurante m [rishtowrant] restaurant

resto m [rehshtoo] rest, remainder

retalho m [rital yoo] oddment

retirado [ritiradoo] secluded

retrato m [ritratoo] portrait

retretes fpl [ritrehtsh] toilets, rest rooms

retrosaria f [ritroozaree-a] haberdasher

reumatismo m rheumatism

reunião f [r-yoon-yowng] meeting

revelação de filmes f [rivilasowng di feelmsh] film processing

revisor m [rivizohr] ticket inspector

revista f [riveeshta] magazine

ribeiro m [ribayroo] stream

rico [reekoo] rich

ridículo [rideekooloo] ridiculous

rímel m [reemil] mascara

rinque de patinagem m [reenk di patinaJayng] ice rink

rins mpl [roongsh] kidneys

rio m [ree-oo] river

rir [reer] to laugh

R.N. National bus/coach service

rocha f [rosha] rock

rochedo m [rooshaydoo] cliff

roda f [roda] wheel

rodada f [roodada] round

Rodoviária Nacional National bus/coach service

rolha f [rohl-ya] cork

romance m [roomans] novel

roncar [ronkar] to snore

rosa f [roza] rose
rótulo m [rotooloo] label
rotunda f [rootoonda] roundabout
roubado [rohbadoo] robbed
roubar [rohbar] to steal
roubo m [rohboo] burglary; theft; rip-off
roulotte f [roolot] caravan, (US) trailer
roupa f [rohpa] clothes
roupa de cama [di kama] bed linen
roupa de homens [dohmayngsh] menswear
roupa de senhoras [sin-yorash] ladies' wear
roupa interior [intir-yohr] underwear
roupão m [rohpowng] dressing gown
roupa para lavar laundry, washing
roxo [rohshoo] purple
R.T.P. Portuguese Television
rua f [roo-a] road; street
rua! get out of here!
rua principal [preensipal] main road
rua secundária [sikoondar-ya] side street
rua sem saída cul-de-sac, dead end
rubéola f [roobeh-ola] German measles
ruínas fpl [rweenash] ruins
ruivo [roo-ivoo] red-headed

S

S ladies' toilets, ladies' room
S. saint
S/ without
sábado [sabadoo] Saturday
saber [sabayr] to know; to be able to
sabia [sabee-a] I knew
   não sabia [nowng] I didn't know
sabonete m [saboonayt] soap
sabor m [sabohr] taste; flavour
saboroso [saboorohzoo] tasty, delicious
sacana! bastard!
saca-rolhas m [sakarrohl-yash] corkscrew
saco m [sakoo] bag
saco de compras [di kohmprash] shopping bag
saco de dormir [doormeer] sleeping bag
saco (de) plástico [plashtikoo] plastic bag
sacos de lixo mpl [sakoosh] bin liners
saia f [sī-ya] skirt
saia! get out!
saída f [sa-eeda] departure; exit
saída de emergência [demirjAyns-ya] emergency exit
saio [sī-oo] I get off; I go out; I leave
sair [sa-eer] to get off, to get out; to go out; to leave
sais de banho mpl [sīJ di ban-

yoo] bath salts

saiu [sa-**ee**-oo] he/she is out;
he/she has gone out

sala f lounge

sala de chá tea room

sala de convívio [di kon**veev**-yoo]
lounge

sala de embarque [daym**bark**]
departure lounge

sala de espera [dish**peh**ra]
lounge, departure lounge

sala de estar [dish**tar**] living
room

sala de jantar [di **jan**tar] dining
room

salão de beleza m [sal**owng** di
bel**ay**za] beauty salon

salão de cabeleireiro [di
kabilayr**ayr**oo] hairdressing
salon

saldos mpl [sal**doosh**] sale

salgado [sal**ga**doo] savoury;
salty

salto m [**sal**too] heel (of shoe)

sandálias fpl [sandal-**yash**]
sandals

sangrar to bleed

sangue m [sang] blood

santinho! [santeen-yoo] bless
you!

são [sowng] healthy; they are;
you are

sapataria f [sapatar**ee**-a] shoe
shop

sapateira f [sapat**ay**ra] crab

sapateiro m [sapat**ayr**oo] shoe
repairer's

sapateiro rápido [**ra**pidoo] heel
bar

sapatos mpl [sapa**toosh**] shoes

sapatos de treino [di **tray**noo]
trainers

sarampo m [sa**rampoo**] measles

sardinhada f [sardin-**ya**da] party
where grilled sardines are
eaten

S.A.R.L. (Sociedade Anónima
de Responsabilidade
Limitada) limited company

satisfeito [satisf**ay**too] satisfied,
full

saudável [sowd**avll**] healthy

saúde [sa-**ood**] health

saúde! cheers!

à sua saúde! [**soo**-a] your
health!

se [si] if; yourself; himself;
herself; themselves;
yourselves; itself; oneself

secador de cabelo m [sika**dohr**
di kab**ay**loo] hairdryer

secador de roupa [di **roh**pa]
spin-dryer

secar [si**kar**] to dry

secar com secador (de mão)
[kong sika**dohr** (di **mowng**)] to
blow-dry

secção f [sehk**sowng**] section;
department

secção de crianças [di kry-
ansash] children's department

secção de perdidos e achados
[di pird**ee**dooz ee-a**sha**doosh]
lost property office, lost and
found

seco [**say**koo] dry

secreto [sik**reh**too] secret

século m [**sehk**ooloo] century

seda f [**say**da] silk

sede: ter sede [tayr sayd] to be thirsty

se faz favor [si fash fa**vohr**] please; excuse me

seguida: em seguida [ayng si**gee**da] straight away

seguinte [si**gee**ngt] following; next

dia seguinte m the day after

seguir [si**gee**r] to follow

seguir pela direita [pila di**rayt**a] keep to your right

seguir pela esquerda [pilash**kayr**da] keep to your left

segunda classe [si**goo**nda klas] second class

segunda-feira f [si**goo**nda **fayr**a] Monday

segunda mão: em segunda mão [si**goo**nda mowng] second-hand

segundo (m) [si**goo**ndoo] second

segundo andar m second floor, (US) third floor

segurar [si**goo**rar] to hold

seguro (m) [si**goo**roo] insurance; safe; sure

seguro de viagem [di v-ya**Jay**ng] travel insurance

sei [say] I know

seis [saysh] six

seiscentas [saysh**sayn**tash], seiscentos [saysh**sayn**toosh] six hundred

sela f [**seh**la] saddle

selo m [**say**loo] stamp

selvagem [silva**Jay**ng] wild

sem [sayng] without

semáforos mpl [sima**foo**roosh] traffic lights

semana f [si**mana**] week

na próxima semana [**pro**sima] next week

Semana Santa Easter

sem chumbo [sayng sh**oo**mboo] leadfree, unleaded

sem conservantes does not contain preservatives

sem corantes does not contain artificial colouring

sem corantes nem conservantes does not contain artificial colouring or preservatives

semelhante [simil-**yant**] similar

sem pensão no meals served

sempre [**saympr**] always

sempre em frente [**say**mprayng fraynt] straight ahead

sem preservativos does not contain preservatives

senha f [**sayn**-ya] ticket; receipt

Senhor [sin-**yohr**] Mr

senhor (m) sir; gentleman; you

o senhor [oo] you

os senhores [oosh sin-**yohr**ish] you

do senhor [doo] your; yours

dos senhores [doosh sin-**yohr**ish] your; yours

Senhora [sin-**yora**] Mrs

senhora madam; lady; you

a senhora you

as senhoras [ash sin-**yora**sh] you

da senhora, das senhoras your; yours

senhoras ladies' toilet, ladies' room
sensato [saynsatoo] sensible
sensível [saynseevil] sensitive
sentar-se [sayntarsi] to sit, to sit down
como se sente? [kohmoo si saynt] how are you feeling?
sente-se [sayntsi] sit down
sentido proibido no entry
sentido único one way
sentimento m [sayntimayntoo] feeling
sentir [saynteer] to feel
separadamente [siparadamaynt] separately
separado [siparadoo] separate; separated
ser [sayr] to be
será [sira] he/she/it/you will be
serão [sirowng] you/they will be
serás [sirash] you will be
serei [siray] I will be
seremos [siraymoosh] we will be
sério [sehr-yoo] serious
serve-se ... das ... horas às ... horas ... served from ... o'clock until ... o'clock
serviço m [sirveesoo] service
serviço automático direct dialling
serviço de quartos [di kwartoosh] room service
serviço de urgências [doorJayns-yash] casualty department

serviço expresso express service
serviço incluído service included
serviço internacional international service
serviço permanente 24-hour service
servir [sirveer] to serve
sessenta [sesaynta] sixty
sete [seht] seven
setecentas [setesayntash], **setecentos** [setesayntoosh] seven hundred
Setembro [sitaymbroo] September
setenta [cetaynta] seventy
setentrional [setayntr-yoonal] northern
sétimo [sehtimoo] seventh
seu [say-oo], **seus** [say-oosh] his; her; hers; its; your; yours; their; theirs
sexo m [sehxoo] sex
sexta-feira f [sayshta fayra] Friday
Sexta-Feira Santa Good Friday
sexto [sayshtoo] sixth
S.f.f. please
si [see] you
SIDA f [seeda] AIDS
siga-me [seegami] follow me
significar [signifikar] to mean
silêncio m [silayns-yoo] silence
silencioso [silayns-yohzoo] quiet
sim [seeng] yes; it is
sim? really?
ah sim! [seeng] well well!

simpático [simpatikoo] friendly

simples [seemplish] simple, easy

sinagoga f [sinagoga] synagogue

sinal m sign; signal; roadsign

sinal de alarme [dalarm] emergency alarm

sincero [sinsehroo] sincere

sino m [seenoo] bell

sintético [sintehtikoo] synthetic

sinto-me [seentoomi] I feel

sinto-me bem [bayng] I'm OK, I'm fine

sítio m [seet-yoo] place

noutro sítio [nohtroo] somewhere else

só [saw] alone; just; only

sobrancelha f [soobransayl-ya] eyebrow

sobre [sohbr] about, concerning; on

sobretudo m [soobritoodoo] overcoat

sobrinha f [soobreen-ya] niece

sobrinho m [soobreen-yoo] nephew

sóbrio [sobr-yoo] sober

sociedade f [soos-yaydad] society; company

socorro! [sookohrroo] help!

sofá m [soofa] sofa; couch

sofisticado [soofishtikadoo] sophisticated; upmarket

sogra f mother-in-law

sogro m [sohgroo] father-in-law

sogros mpl [sogroosh] in-laws

soirée evening performance

sol m sun

ao sol [ow] in the sun

está (a fazer) sol [shta (a fazayr)] it's sunny

solteiro (m) [sooltayroo] single; bachelor

solto [sohltoo] loose

solução de limpeza f [sooloosowng di leempayza] cleaning solution

solução para as lentes de contacto [paraJ layntsh di kontaktoo] soaking solution

soluços mpl [sooloosoosh] hiccups

sombra f [sohmbra] shade; shadow

à sombra in the shade

sombra para os olhos [parooz ol-yoosh] eye shadow

somente [somaynt] only; just

somos [sohmoosh] we are

sonho m [sohn-yoo] dream

sonífero m [sooneefiroo] sleeping pill

sono m [sohnoo] sleep

estar com sono [shtar kong] to be sleepy

sopé: no sopé do ... [noo soopeh doo] at the bottom of ...

só pode vender-se mediante receita médica available only on prescription

sorrir [soorreer] to smile

sorriso m [soorreezoo] smile

sorte f [sort] luck

sou [soh] I am

sou de ... [di] I am from ...

soutien m [soot-yang] bra

sozinha [sozeen-ya], sozinho [sozeen-yoo] by myself

Sr. Mr

Sra. Mrs

Sto. saint

sua [soo-a] his; her; hers; its; your; yours; their; theirs

suar [soo-ar] to sweat

suas [soo-ash] his; her; hers; its; your; yours; their; theirs

suave [swav] delicate; mild

subir [soobeer] to go up

subitamente [soobitamaynt] suddenly

sucesso m [soosehsoo] success

sudeste m [soodehsht] southeast

sudoeste m [soodwehsht] southwest

Suécia f [swehs-ya] Sweden

sueca (f) [swehka], sueco (m) [swehkoo] Swedish; Swede

suficiente [soofis-yaynt] enough

suficientemente [soofis-yayntimaynt] enough

Suíça f [sweesa] Switzerland

suíça (f) [sweesa], suíço (m) [sweesoo] Swiss

sujidade f [sooJidad] dirt

sujo [sooJoo] dirty

sul m [sool] south

no sul [noo] in the south

sul-africana (f) [soolafrikana], sul-africano (m) [soolafrikanoo] South African

supermercado m [soopermerkadoo] supermarket

suplemento m [sooplimayntoo] supplement, extra charge

supositório m [soopoozitor-yoo] suppository

surdo [soordoo] deaf

surpreendente [soorpr-yayndaynt] surprising

surpresa f [soorprayza] surprise

T

tabacaria f [tabakaree-a] tobacconist; tobacco store; tobacco goods; newsagent

tabaco m [tabakoo] tobacco

taberna f [tabehrna] pub

tabuleiro m [taboolayroo] tray

talheres mpl [tal-yehrish] cutlery

talho m [tal-yoo] butcher's shop

talvez [talvaysh] maybe, perhaps

talvez não [nowng] perhaps not

tamanho m [taman-yoo] size

também [tambayng] also, too, as well

eu também [ay-oo] so am I; so do I; me too

tampa f cap, lid

tampa do ralo f [doo raloo] plug (in sink)

tampões mpl [tampoyngsh] tampons

tanto [tantoo] so much

tanto faz [fash] it's all the same to me

tão [towng] so

tão ... como ... as ... as ...

tão ... quanto [kwantoo] as ... as

tão ... quanto possível

Ta

[pooseevil] as ... as possible
tapete m [tapayt] carpet
tarde f [tard] afternoon; late
à **tarde** in the afternoon
esta **tarde** [ehshta] this
afternoon
da **tarde** p.m.
três da **tarde** 3 p.m.
tarifa f [tareefa] charges
tasca f [tashka] small tavern
serving food
taxa de serviço f [tasha di
sirveesoo] service charge
te [ti] you; to you; yourself
teatro m [t-yatroo] theatre
tecido m [tiseedoo] cloth,
material
tecto m [tehtoo] ceiling
tejadilho m [tiJadeel-yoo] car
roof
tel. telephone
teleférico m [telefehrikoo] cable
car
telefonar [telefoonar] to call, to
phone
telefone m [telefohn]
telephone
telefone de cartão [di kartowng]
cardphone
telefone público [pooblikoo]
payphone
**Telefones de Lisboa e Porto
S.A.** telephone company for
Lisbon and Oporto
telefonista m/f [telefooneeshta]
operator
telemóvel m [telemovil] mobile
phone
televisão f [televizowng]

television
telhado m [til-yadoo] roof
tem [tayng] he/she/it has; you
have
tem ...? have you got any ...?,
do you have ...?
ele/ela tem de ... he/she must
...
têm [tay-ayng] you/they have
temos [taymoosh] we have
temos que ... [ki] we've got to
..., we must ...
temperatura f [taympiratoora]
temperature
tempestade f [taympishtad]
storm
tempo m [taympoo] time;
weather
a tempo on time
por quanto tempo? [poor
kwantoo] for how long?
tenda (de campismo) f [taynda
(di kampeeJmoo)] tent
tenho [tayn-yoo] I have; I am;
I have to
não tenho [nowng] I don't
have any
tenho de/que ... [di/ki] I
must ...
ténis m [tehnish] tennis
ténis de mesa [di mayza] table
tennis
tens [taynsh] you have
tensão f [taynsowng] tension;
voltage
tensão arterial alta [artir-yal]
high blood pressure
tentar [tayntar] to try
tépido [tehpidoo] lukewarm

ter [tayr] to have; to hold; to
be; to contain; to have to
ter de/que to have to
terça-feira [tayrsa fayra]
Tuesday
ter calor [tayr kalohr] to be
warm
terceiro [tirsayroo] third
terceiro andar m third floor,
(US) fourth floor
termas fpl [tehrmash] spa
terminado [tirminadoo] over;
finished
terminal m [tirminal] terminus
terminar [tirminar] to finish
termo m [tayrmoo] vacuum
flask
termómetro m [tirmohmitroo]
thermometer
terra f [tehrra] earth
terraço m [tirrasoo] terrace
terrível [tirreevil] terrible
tesoura f [tizohra] scissors
testa f [tehshta] forehead
testemunha m/f [tishtimoon-ya]
witness
teu [tay-oo], teus [tay-oosh]
your; yours
teve [tayv] he/she/it/you had
têxteis textiles
ti you
tia f [tee-a] aunt
tigela f [tijehla] dish, bowl
tijolo m [tijohloo] brick
tímido [teemidoo] shy
tinha [teen-ya] I/he/she/it/you
used to have
tinham [teen-yowng] you/they
used to have

tínhamos [teen-yamoosh] we
used to have
tinhas [teen-yash] you used to
have
tinta f [teenta] paint; tint
tinto [teentoo] red
tinturaria f [teentooraree-a] dry-
cleaner
tio m [tee-oo] uncle
típico [teepikoo] typical
tipo m [teepoo] sort, type, kind
tiragem f [tirajayng] collection;
edition; circulation
tirar to remove
tive [teev] I had
tivemos [tivaymoosh] we had
tiveram [tivehrowng] you/they
had
tiveste [tivehsht] you had
TLP telephone company for
Lisbon and Oporto
toalha f [twal-ya] towel
toalha de banho [di ban-yoo]
bath towel
toalha de cara [kara] flannel
toalha de mesa [mayza]
tablecloth
toalhas higiénicas fpl [twal-yaz
ij-yehnikash] sanitary towels
tocar [tookar] to touch
toda a gente [tohda a jaynt]
everyone
todas [tohdash] all; all of
them
todas as vezes [aj vayzish]
every time
todo [tohdoo] all; all of it
todo o dia/o dia todo [oo dee-
a] all day

todos [**toh**doosh] all; all of
them

todos os dias [**toh**dooz-ooJ dee-
ash] every day, daily

para todos suitable for all age
groups

toilette m [twal**eht**] toilet, rest
room

tolo [**toh**loo] silly

tomada f [too**mada**] socket;
plug; power point

tomada para a máquina de
barbear [ma**kina** di barb-**yar**]
shaving point

tomar [too**mar**] to take

o que vai tomar? [oo ki vī]
what'll you have?

tomar antes de se deitar to be
taken before going to bed

tomar a seguir às refeições to
be taken after meals

tomar banho [**ban**-yoo] to have
a bath

tomar banho de sol to
sunbathe

tomar conta de [**kohn**ta] to
look after, to take care of

tomar em jejum take on an
empty stomach

tomar ... vezes ao dia to be
taken ... times a day

tome lá [**tohm**] there you are

tónico m [**to**nikoo] toner

tonturas: sinto tonturas
[**seen**too ton**too**rash] I feel dizzy

topo: no topo de ... [**toh**poo di]
at the top of ...

toque (a campainha) ring (the
bell)

torcer [toor**sayr**] to sprain; to
twist

tornar-se [toor**narsi**] to become

torneira f [toor**nayra**] tap, faucet

tornozelo m [toornoo**zay**loo]
ankle

torre f [tohrr] tower

tosse f [tos] cough

tossir [too**seer**] to cough

tostão coin worth one tenth
of an escudo

totalmente [tootal**maynt**] totally;
altogether

touca de banho f [**toh**ka di ban-
yoo] bathing cap

tourada f [toh**rada**] bullfight

toureiro m [toh**ray**roo]
bullfighter

touro m [**toh**roo] bull

tóxico [**tok**sikoo] toxic,
poisonous

trabalhar [trabal-**yar**] to work

trabalho m [trabal-yoo] work

tradição f [tradi**sowng**] tradition

tradicional [tradis-yoonal]
traditional

tradução f [tradoo**sowng**]
translation

tradutor m [tradoot**ohr**],
tradutora f [tradoot**ohra**]
translator

traduzir [tradoo**zeer**] to translate

tragédia f [tra**Jehd**-ya] disaster

trajecto m [tra**Jeh**too] route

trancar [tran**kar**] to lock

tranquilo [tran**kwee**loo] peaceful

transferência f [transfi**rayns**-ya]
transfer

trânsito m [**tran**zitoo] traffic

trânsito condicionado traffic congestion

trânsito fechado road blocked

trânsito nos dois sentidos two-way traffic

trânsito proibido no thoroughfare, no entry

transmissão f [tranჂmisowng] transmission

traseiro (m) [trazayroo] bottom (of person); back

traumatismo m [trowmateeჂmoo] concussion

travão m [travowng] brake

travão de mão [di mowng] handbrake

travar to brake

travel-cheque m [shehk] traveller's cheque

travessa f [travehsa] tray

travessia f [travisee-a] crossing

trazer [trazayr] to bring

trazer de volta [dl] to bring back

três [traysh] three

trespassa-se premises for sale

treze [trayz] thirteen

trezentas [trizayntash], trezentos [trizayntoosh] three hundred

tribunal m [triboonal] court

tricotar [trikootar] to knit

trinta [treenta] thirty

tripulação f [tripoolasowng] crew

triste [treesht] sad

trocar [trookar] to change (money)

troco m [trohkoo] change (money)

trombose f [tromboz] thrombosis

trombose cerebral [siribral] stroke

trovão m [troovowng] thunder

trovoada f [troowwada] thunder

tu [too] you

tua [too-a], tuas [too-ash] your; yours

tubo de escape m [tooboo dishkap] exhaust pipe

tudo [toodoo] everything
é tudo [eh] that's all

tudo bem! [bayng] no problem!
tudo bem? how are you?

tudo incluído all-inclusive

túnel m [toonil] tunnel

turismo m [tooreeჂmoo] tourist information office

turista m/f [tooreeshta] tourist

U

UE [oo eh] EU

úlcera f [oolჂira] ulcer

último m [ooltimoo] last, latest

ultrapassar [ooltrapasar] to overtake, to pass

um [oong], uma [oo-ma] a, an; one

umas [oomash] some

uma vez [oo-ma vaysh] once

unha f [oon-ya] fingernail

União Europeia f [ooni-owng ay-ooroopay-a] European Union

unicamente para adultos for adults only

universidade f [oonivirsidad]

university
uns [oonsh] some
urgência f [oorJayns-ya] casualty, emergencies
urgente [oorJaynt] urgent
usar [oozar] to use
uso m [oozoo] use
uso externo for external use only
utensílios de cozinha mpl [ootaynseel-yoosh di koozeen-ya] cooking utensils
útil [ootil] useful

V

vaca f cow
vacina f [vaseena] vaccine
vacinação f [vasinasowng] vaccination
vagão m [vagowng] carriage (on train)
vagão restaurante [rishtowrant] dining car
vai he/she/it goes; you go
vais [vish] you go
vale m [val] valley
vale postal internacional international money order
válido [validoo] valid
válido até ... valid until ...
valioso [val-yohzoo] valuable
valor m [valohr] value
válvula f [valvoola] valve
vamos [vamoosh] we go
vamos! let's go!

vão [vowng] you/they go
varanda f balcony
varicela f [varisehla] chickenpox
vários [var-yoosh] several
vá-se embora! [vasi aymbora] go away!
vassoura f [vasohra] broom
vazio [vazee-oo] empty
vedação f [vidasowng] fence
vedado ao trânsito no thoroughfare
vegetariana (f) [viJitar-yana], **vegetariano (m)** [viJitar-yanoo] vegetarian
veículo m [vi-eekooloo] vehicle
veículos longos long vehicles
veículos pesados heavy vehicles
veio [vay-oo] he/she/it came, he/she/it has come; you came, you have come
vela f [vehla] spark plug; sail; candle
velejar [viliJar] to sail; sailing
velho [vehl-yoo] old
velocidade f [viloosidad] speed
velocidade máxima ... km/h maximum speed ... km/h
velocímetro m [vilooseemitroo] speedometer
vem [vayng] he/she/it comes; you come
vêm you/they come
venda f [vaynda] sale
à venda [vaynda] for sale
vendedor de jornais [di Jornish] newsagent, news vendor
vendem-se [vayndaynsi] for sale
vender [vayndayr] to sell

vende-se [**vayn**di-si] for sale
veneno m [vi**nay**noo] poison
venenoso [vini**noh**zoo] poisonous
venho [**vayn**-yoo] I come
vens [**vaynsh**] you come
vento m [**vayn**too] wind
ventoinha f [vayn**tween**-ya] fan (electrical)
ver [**vayr**] to look; to have a look; to see
Verão m [vi**rowng**] summer
verdade f [vir**dad**] truth
de verdade? [di] really?
verdadeiro [virda**day**roo] real; true
verde [**vayrd**] green
vergas fpl [**vayr**gash] wicker goods
verificar [viri**fikar**] to check
vermelho [vir**mayl**-yoo] red
verniz de unhas m [vir**neeJ doon**-yash] nail varnish
vespa f [**vaysh**pa] wasp
Véspera de Natal f [**veh**shpira di] Christmas Eve
véspera do dia de Ano Novo [**veh**shpira doo **dee**-a **da**noo **noh**voo] New Year's Eve
vestiário m [visht-**yar**-yoo] cloakroom, checkroom
vestido m [vish**tee**doo] dress
vestir [vish**teer**] to dress
vestir-se [vish**teer**si] to get dressed
veterinário m [vitiri**nar**-yoo] vet
vez f [**vaysh**] time
a próxima vez [**pro**sima] next time

a última vez [**oo**ltima] last time
esta vez [**eh**shta] this time
às vezes [aJ **vay**zish] sometimes
em vez [ayng] instead
em vez de ... [di] instead of ...
via (f) [**vee**-a] via; lane
via aérea: por via aérea by airmail
viagem f [v-ya**Jayng**] journey
viagem de negócios [di ni**gos**-yoosh] business trip
via intravenosa intravenously
viajar [v-ya**Jar**] to travel
via oral to be taken orally
via rápida dual carriageway, divided highway
via rectal per rectum
via superfície surface mail
vida f [**vee**da] life
videogravador m [veed-yoogravado**hr**] video recorder
vidraria f [vidra**ree**-a] glazier's
vidro m [**vee**droo] glass
viela f [v-**yeh**la] lane
viemos [v-**yay**moosh] we came, we have come
vieram [v-**yeh**rowng] you/they came, you/they have come
vieste [v-**yehsht**] you came, you have come
vim [**veeng**] I came, I have come
vimos [**vee**moosh] we come; we saw
vindima f [vin**dee**ma] grape harvest
vindo [**veen**doo] come

209

vinha f [**veen**-ya] vineyard

vinte [veent] twenty

vinte e um [**veen**ti-**oong**] twenty-one

viola f [v-**yola**] traditional Portuguese guitar

violação f [v-**yoolasowng**] rape

vir [veer] to come

virar [vee**rar**] to turn; to turn off

vir de carro [veer di **karroo**] to drive

vire à esquerda/direita [veer-ya shk**ayr**da/di**ray**ta] turn left/right

vírgula f [**veer**goola] comma; decimal point

visita f [vi**zee**ta] visit

visita guiada [vi**zee**ta gee-**a**da] tour

visitar [vi**zee**tar] to visit

visor m [vi**zohr**] viewfinder

vista f [**vee**shta] view

visto (m) [**vee**shtoo] visa; seen

visto que [**vee**shtoo ki] since

viu [vee-oo] you have seen

viúva f [v-**yoo**va] widow

viúvo m [v-**yoo**voo] widower

vivenda f [vi**vay**nda] villa

viver [vi**vayr**] to live

vivo [**vee**voo] bright; alive

vizinha f [vi**zeen**-ya], vizinho m [vi**zeen**-yoo] neighbour

voar [v-**war**] to fly

você [vo**say**] you

você primeiro [pri**mayr**oo] after you

vocês [vo**saysh**] you

de vocês [di] your; yours

volante m [**voo**lant] steering wheel

com volante à direita [kong] right-hand drive

volta: por volta de ... [poor] about ..., approximately ...

voltar to go back, to get back, to come back, to return

voltar a telefonar [voltar a tele**foo**nar] to ring back

volto já [**vol**too Ja] back in a minute

vomitar [voomi**tar**] to be sick, to vomit

voo m [**voh**-oo] flight

voo de ligação [di liga**sowng**] connecting flight

voo directo [di**reh**too] direct flight

voo doméstico [doo**mehsh**tikoo] domestic flight

voo fretado [fri**ta**doo] charter flight

voo regular [rigoo**lar**] scheduled flight

vou [voh] I go

voz f [vosh] voice

vulgar [**voo**lgar] ordinary

X

xadrez m [sha**draysh**] chess

xarope m [sha**rop**] cough medicine; cordial

Z

zangado [zanga**doo**] angry; mad

zona azul f [zohnazool] parking permit zone

zona de banhos swimming area under the surveillance of lifeguards

zona para peões pedestrian precinct

zona perigrosa danger zone

Menu Reader:
Food

Essential Terms

bread o pão [**pow**ng]
butter a manteiga [man**tay**ga]
cup a chávena [**sha**vena]
dessert a sobremesa [sobri**may**za]
fish o peixe [**pay**-ish]
fork o garfo [**gar**foo]
glass o copo [**ko**poo]
knife a faca
main course o prato principal [**pra**too prin**si**pal]
meat a carne [karn]
menu a ementa [e**may**nta]
pepper a pimenta [pi**may**nta]
plate o prato [**pra**too]
salad a salada
salt o sal
set menu a ementa fixa [e**may**nta **feek**sa]
soup a sopa [**soh**pa]
spoon a colher [kool-**yeh**r]
starter a entrada [**ayn**trada]
table a mesa [**may**za]

another ..., please outro/outra ..., por favor [**oh**troo – poor fa**voh**r]
excuse me! (to call waiter/waitress) se faz favor! [si fash]
could I have the bill, please? pode-me dar a conta, por favor?
  [**pod**-mi – poor fa**voh**r]

abóbora [aboboora] pumpkin

acepipes [asipeepish] hors d'œuvres

açorda de alho [asohrda dal-yoo] thick soup of bread and garlic

açorda de mariscos [di mareeshkoosh] thick soup of bread and shellfish

açorda de miolos [m-yoloosh] thick soup of bread and brains

açúcar [asookar] sugar

agriões [agr-yoyngsh] watercress

aipo [ipoo] celery

alcachofra [alkashohfra] artichoke

alface [alfas] lettuce

alheira [al-yayra] garlic sausage

alho [al-yoo] garlic

alho francês [fransaysh] leek

à lista [leeshta] à la carte

almoço [almohsoo] lunch

almóndegas [almohndigash] meatballs

alperces [alpehrsish] apricots

amêijoas [amayJwash] clams

amêijoas à Bulhão Pato [amayJwaza bool-yowng patoo] clams cooked with fresh coriander, garlic and olive oil

amêijoas na cataplana [amayJwash] clams, ham, sausages, onions, parsley, chillies and olive oil cooked slowly in a covered pan

ameixa [amaysha] plum

ameixas de Elvas [dehlvash] dried plums from Elvas

ameixas secas [saykas] prunes

amêndoas [amayndwash] almonds

amendoins [amayndweensh] peanuts

à moda de ... [di] ...-style

amoras [amorash] blackberries

ananás [ananash] pineapple

anchovas [anshohvash] anchovies

anho à moda do Minho [an-yon a moda doo meen-yoo] roast lamb served with rice

aniz [aneesh] aniseed

anona [anohna] custard apple

ao natural [ow natooral] plain

ao ponto [pohntoo] medium-rare

arroz [arrohsh] rice

arroz árabe [arrohz arab] fried rice with nuts and dried fruit

arroz à valenciana [valayns-yana] rice with chicken, pork and seafood

arroz branco [arrohJ brankoo] plain rice

arroz de cabidela [di kabidehla] rice cooked in birds' blood

arroz de frango [frangoo] rice with chicken

arroz de funcho [foonshoo] rice with fennel

arroz de mariscos [mareeshkoosh] a soupy dish of rice with mixed seafood

arroz de pato [patoo] rice with duck

arroz de polvo [pohlvoo] rice

with octopus
arroz doce [dohs] sweet rice dessert
asa [aza] wing
assado [asadoo] roasted
atum [atoong] tuna
atum assado [asadoo] baked tuna
avelãs [avilangsh] hazelnuts
aves [avish] poultry
azeitão [azaytowng] full fat soft goat's cheese
azeite [azayt] olive oil
azeitonas [azaytohnash] olives
azeitonas com pimentos [kong pimayntoosh] olives stuffed with pimentos
azeitonas recheadas [rish-yadash] stuffed olives

bacalhau [bakal-yow] dried salted cod
bacalhau à Brás [brash] dried cod with egg and potatoes
bacalhau à Gomes de Sá [gohmsh di] dried cod fried with onions, boiled eggs, potatoes and black olives
bacalhau assado [asadoo] roast dried cod
bacalhau à Zé do Pipo [zeh doo peepoo] dried cod with egg sauce
bacalhau com natas [kong natash] dried cod with cream
bacalhau dourado [dohradoo] dried cod baked in the oven
bacalhau grelhado [gril-yadoo] grilled dried cod

bacalhau na brasa [braza] barbecued dried cod
bacalhau na cataplana dried cod, onion, tomato, ham, coriander, prawns and cockles cooked slowly in a covered pan
banana flambée [flambay] flambéed banana
batata assada [batatasada] baked potato
batata murro [mooroo] small baked potato
batata palha [pal-ya] French fries
batatas [batatash] potatoes
batatas cozidas [koozeedash] boiled potatoes
batatas fritas [freetash] chips, French fries
batatas salteadas [salt-yadash] sautéed potatoes
baunilha [bowneel-ya] vanilla
bavaroise [bavarwaz] dessert made from egg whites and cream
bem passado [bayng pasadoo] well-done
berbigão [birbeegowng] shellfish similar to mussels
berinjela [bireenJehla] aubergine, eggplant
besugos [bizoogoosh] sea bream
beterraba [biterraba] beetroot
bifanas [beefanash] pork slice in a bread roll
bife [beef] steak
bife à cortador [koortadohr] thick tender steak

bife à portuguesa [poorloogayza] steak with mustard sauce and a fried egg

bife de alcatra [dalkatra] rump steak

bife de atum [datoong] tuna steak

bife de javali [di Javalee] wild boar steak

bife de pojadouro [pooJadohroo] type of beefsteak

bife de vaca [vaka] steak

bife de vaca com ovo a cavalo [kong ohvoo a kavaloo] steak with an egg on top

bife grelhado [gril-yadoo] grilled steak

bife tártaro [tartaroo] steak tartare

bifes de cebolada [beefsh di siboolada] thin slices of steak with onions

bifinhos de porco [beefeen-yooJ di pohrkoo] small slices of pork

bifinhos na brasa [braza] small slices of barbecued beef

bolacha [boolasha] biscuit, cookie

bola de carne [di karn] meatball

bolo [bohloo] cake

bolo de anjo [danJoo] angel cake

bolo de chocolate [shookoolat] chocolate cake

bolo de nozes [nozish] walnut cake

bolo inglês [inglaysh] sponge cake with dried fruit

bolo Rei [ray] ring-shaped cake (eaten at Christmas)

bolos e bolachas [bohlooz ee boolashash] cakes and biscuits/cookies

bomba de creme [bohmba di kraym] cream puff

borrego [boorraygoo] lamb

brioche [br-yosh] slightly sweet round bun

broa [broh-a] maize/corn bread or rye bread

broas [broh-ash] small maize/corn cakes (eaten at Christmas)

cabeça de pescada cozida [kabaysa di pishkada koozeeda] boiled head of hake

cabreiro [kabrayroo] goat's cheese

cabrito [kabreetoo] kid

cabrito assado [asadoo] roast kid

caça [kasa] game

cachola frita [kashola freeta] fried pig's heart and liver

cachorro [kashohrroo] hot dog

caldeirada [kaldayrada] fish stew

caldo [kaldoo] broth

caldo de aves [davish] poultry soup

caldo de carne [di karn] meat soup

caldo verde [vayrd] cabbage soup

camarões [kamaroyngsh] prawns

canela [kanehla] cinnamon

canja de galinha [kanJa di galeen-ya] chicken soup

caracóis [karakoysh] snails

caranguejo [karang**ay**Joo] crab

carapau [karap**ow**] mackerel

carapaus de escabeche [karap**ow**J dishkab**eh**sh] marinated mackerel

carapaus fritos [karap**ow**sh fr**ee**toosh] fried mackerel

caril [kar**ee**l] curry

carne [k**ar**n] meat

carne à jardineira [Jardin**ay**ra] meat and vegetable stew

carne de cabrito [di kab**ree**too] kid

carne de porco [di p**oh**rkoo] pork

carne de porco com amêijoas [kong am**ay**Jwash] pork with clams

carne de vaca [v**a**ka] beef

carne de vaca assada roast beef

carne de vaca guisada [g**ee**z**a**da] stewed meat

carne estufada [sht**oo**f**a**da] stewed meat

carneiro [karn**ay**roo] mutton

carneiro assado [as**a**doo] roast mutton

carne picada [pik**a**da] minced meat

carnes [k**ar**nish] meats

carnes frias [free-ash] selection of cold meats

caseiro [kaz**ay**roo] home-made

castanhas [kasht**an**-yash] chestnuts

cebola [sib**oh**la] onion

cenoura [sin**oh**ra] carrot

cerejas [sir**ay**Jash] cherries

chanfana de porco [sh**an**f**a**na di p**oh**rkoo] pork casserole

chantilly [shanti**lee**] whipped cream

charlottes [sh**ar**l**ot**sh] biscuits/cookies with fruit and cream

cherne [sh**ehr**n] sea bream

chocos [sh**oh**k**oo**sh] cuttlefish

chouriço [shoor**ee**soo] spiced sausage

choux [sh**oo**] cake made with choux pastry

churros [sh**oo**rrosh] long thin fritters

civet de lebre [s**ee**v**ay** di l**ehb**r] jugged hare

cocktail de camarão [k**ok**t**eh**l di kamar**ow**ng] prawn cocktail

codorniz [koodoorn**ee**sh] quail

codonizes fritas [koodoorn**ee**zish fr**ee**tash] fried quail

coelho [kw**ay**l-yoo] rabbit

coelho à caçadora [kasad**oh**ra] rabbit casserole with rice

coelho de escabeche [dishkab**eh**sh] marinated rabbit

coelho de fricassé [frikas**ay**] rabbit fricassee

coelho frito [fr**ee**too] fried rabbit

coêntros [kw**ay**ntroosh] coriander

cogumelos [kogoom**eh**loosh] mushrooms

cogumelos com alho [kong al-yoo] mushrooms with garlic

comida congelada [koom**ee**da konJil**a**da] frozen food

comidas [koomeedash] meals

compota stewed fruit

compota de laranja [di laranJa] marmalade

conquilhas [konkeel-yash] baby clams

consomme [konsoomay] consommé, clear meat soup

coração [koorasowng] heart

corações de alcachofra [koorasoyngsh dalkashohfra] artichoke hearts

corvina [koorveena] large saltwater fish

costela [kooshtehla] rib

costeleta [kooshtilayta] chop

costeletas de carneiro [kooshtilaytaJ di karnayroo] lamb chops

costeletas de porco [di pohrkoo] pork chops

costeletas fritas [freetash] fried chops

costeletas grelhadas [gril-yadash] grilled chops

courgettes com creme no forno [koorJehtsh kong kraym noo fohrnoo] baked courgettes/ zucchini served with cream

courgettes fritas [freetash] fried courgettes/zucchini

couve [kohv] cabbage

couve branca com vinagre [kong vinagr] white cabbage with vinegar

couve-flor [kohv flohr] cauliflower

couve-flor com molho branco no forno [kong mohl-yoo brankoo

noo fohrnoo] cauliflower in white sauce

couve-flor com natas [natash] cauliflower with cream

couve roxa [rohsha] red cabbage

couvert cover charge

couves de bruxelas [kohvsh di brooshehlash] Brussels sprouts

couves de bruxelas com natas [kong natash] Brussels sprouts with cream

couves de bruxelas salteadas [salt-yadash] sautéed Brussels sprouts

couves guisadas com salsichas [geezadash kong salseeshash] stewed cabbage with sausage

cozido [koozeedoo] boiled; stewed; poached; cooked (either in a sauce or with olive oil); stew

cozido à portuguesa [poortoogayza] stew made from chicken, sausage, rice, potatoes and vegetables

creme de cogumelos [kraym di kogoomehloosh] cream of mushroom soup

creme de mariscos [mareeshkoosh] cream of shellfish soup

crepe de camarão [krehp di kamarowng] prawn crêpe

crepe de carne [karn] meat crêpe

crepe de cogumelos

[kogoomehloosh] mushroom crêpe
crepe de espinafres [dishpinafrish] spinach crêpe
crepe de legumes [ligoomish] vegetable crêpe
crepe de pescada [pishkada] hake crêpe
crepes [krehpish] crêpes, pancakes
cru/crua [kroo/kroo-a] raw

damasco [damashkoo] apricot
dobrada [doobrada] tripe with chickpeas
doce [dohs] jam; any sweet dish or dessert
doce de amêndoas [damayndwash] almond dessert
doce de ovos [dovoosh] type of egg custard
doces regionais regional desserts
dose [doz] portion
dose para crianças [kr-yansash] children's portion
dourada [dohrada] dory (saltwater fish); browned, golden brown
dourado [dohradoo] browned, golden brown

éclair de café [ayklehr dih kafeh] coffee éclair
éclair de chantilly [shantilee] whipped cream éclair
éclair de chocolate [shookoolat] chocolate éclair
eirozes [ayrozish] eels

ementa [emaynta] menu
ementa fixa [feeksa] set menu
ementa turística [tooreeshtika] set menu
empada pie
empadão de carne [aympadowng di karn] large meat pie
empadão de peixe [paysh] large fish pie
encharcada [aynsharkada] dessert made from almonds and eggs
enguias [ayngee-ash] eels
enguias fritas [freetash] fried eels
ensopado de ... [aynsoopadoo di] ... stew
ensopado de borrego [boorraygoo] lamb stew
ensopado de enguias [dayngee-ash] eel stew
entradas [ayntradash] starters, appetizers
entrecosto [ayntrikohshtoo] entrecôte
entrecosto com amêijoas [kong amayJwash] entrecôte with clams
entrecosto frito [freetoo] fried entrecôte
ervas [ehrvash] herbs
ervilhas [irveel-yash] peas
ervilhas de manteiga [di mantayga] peas in butter
ervilhas reboçadas [riboosadash] peas in butter with bacon
escalope ao Madeira [shkalop ow madayra] escalope in Madeira wine

220

escalope de carneiro [di karnayroo] mutton escalope

escalope de porco [pohrkoo] pork escalope

escalopo panado [panadoo] breaded escalope

espadarte [shpadart] scabbard fish

espaguete à bolonhesa [shpageht a booloon-yayza] spaghetti bolognese

espargos [shpargoosh] asparagus

esparregado [shparrigadoo] stew made from chopped green vegetables

especiaria [shpic-yaree-a] spice

espetada de leitão [shpitada di laytowng] sucking pig kebab

espetada de rins [reensh] kidney kebab

espetada de vitela [vitehla] veal kebab

espetada mista [meeshta] mixed kebab

espinafre [shpinafr] spinach

espinafres gratinados [shpinafrish gratinadoosh] spinach with cheese sauce browned under the grill

espinafres salteados [salt-yadoosh] spinach sautéed in butter

estragão [shtragowng] tarragon

estufado [shtoofadoo] stewed

faisão [fizowng] pheasant

farinha [fareen-ya] flour

farófias [farof-yash] cream puff with filling made from egg whites, sugar and cinammon

farturas [fartoorash] long thin fritters

fatia [fatee-a] slice

fatias recheadas [fatee-ash rish-yadash] slices of bread with fried minced meat

favas [favash] broad beans

febras de porco [faybraJ di pohrkoo] thin slices of pork

feijão [fay.lowng] beans

feijoada [fayJwada] bean and meat stew

feijões [fayJoyngsh] beans

feijões verdes [vayrdish] French beans

fiambre [f-yambr] ham

fiambre caramelizado [karamileezadoo] glazed ham

fígado [feegadoo] liver

figos [feegoosh] figs

figos moscatel [mooshkatehl] moscatel figs

figos secos [saykoosh] dried figs

filete [feeleht] fillet

filete de bife com foie gras [di beef kong fwa gra] beef fillet with foie gras

filhozes [feel-yozish] sugary buns

folhado de carne [fool-yadoo di karn] meat in pastry

folhado de salsicha [salseesha] sausage roll

fondue de carne [fondoo di karn] meat fondue

fondue de chocolate [shookoolat] chocolate fondue

fondue de queijo [kayJoo] cheese fondue

framboesa [frambwayza] raspberry

frango [frangoo] chicken

frango assado [frangwasadoo] roast chicken

frango na púcara [pookara] chicken casserole with Port and almonds

frango no churrasco [noo shoorrashkoo] barbecued chicken

frango no espeto [nooshpaytoo] spit-roasted chicken

frito [freetoo] fried

frito de ... [di] fritter (usually filled with fruit)

fruta [froota] fruit

fruta da época [ehpooka] seasonal fruit

fumado [foomadoo] smoked

funcho [foonshoo] fennel

galantine de carne [galanteen di karn] cold meat roll

galantine de coelho [di kwayl-yoo] cold rabbit roll

galantine de galinha [galeen-ya] cold chicken roll

galantine de vegetais [viJitish] cold vegetable roll

galinha [galeen-ya] chicken

galinha de África [dafreeka] guinea fowl

galinha de fricassé [di frikasay] chicken fricassée

gambas [gambash] prawns

gambas grelhadas [gril-yadash] grilled prawns

ganso [gansoo] goose

garoupa [garohpa] fish similar to bream

gaspacho [gaspashoo] chilled vegetable soup

gelado [Jiladoo] ice cream

gelado de baunilha [di bowneel-ya] vanilla ice cream

gelado de frutas [frootash] fruit ice cream

geleia [Jilay-a] preserve

gengibre [JaynJeebr] ginger

gordura [goordoora] fat

grão [growng] chickpeas

grelhado [gril-yadoo] grilled

groselhas [groozehl-yash] redcurrants

guisado [geezadoo] stewed

hamburguer com batatas fritas [amboorgir kong batatash freetash] hamburger and chips/French fries

hamburguer com ovo [ohvoo] hamburger with an egg

hamburguer no pão [noo powng] hamburger in a roll

hortaliças [ortaleesash] green vegetables

hortelã [ortilang] mint

iogurte [yoogoort] yoghurt

iscas fritas com batatas [eeshkash freetash kong batatash] dish of fried liver and boiled potatoes

222

jantar [Jantar] evening meal, dinner; supper

jardineira [Jardinayra] mixed vegetables

lagosta [lagohshta] lobster

lagosta à Americana [amirikana] lobster with tomato and onions

lagosta thermidor [tirmeedohr] lobster thermidor

lagostim [lagooshteeng] saltwater crayfish

lampreia [lampray-a] lamprey

lampreia à moda do Minho [doo meen-yoo] marinated lamprey and rice, both cooked in the juices and blood of the lamprey

lampreia de ovos [dovoosh] dessert made from eggs and sugar in the shape of a lamprey

lanche [lansh] afternoon tea

laranja [laranJa] orange

lasanha [lasan-ya] lasagne

legumes [ligoomish] vegetables

leitão assado [laytowng asadoo] roast sucking pig

leitão da Bairrada [da birrada] sucking pig from Bairrada

leite [layt] milk

leite creme [kraym] light custard flavoured with cinammon

limão [limowng] lemon

língua [leengwa] tongue

língua de porco [di pohrkoo] pig's tongue

língua de vaca [vaka] ox tongue

llnguado [lingwadoo] sole

linguado à meunière [moon-yehr] sole dipped in flour and fried in butter

linguado frito [freetoo] fried sole

linguado grelhado [gril-yadoo] grilled sole

linguado no forno [noo fohrnoo] baked sole

lista de preços [leeshta di praysoosh] price list

lombo [lohmboo] loin

lombo de porco [di pohrkoo] loin of pork

lombo de vaca [vaka] sirloin

louro [lohroo] bay leaf

lulas [loolash] squid

lulas com natas [kong natash] stewed squid with cream

lulas fritas [freetash] fried squid

lulas guisadas [geezadash] stewed squid

lulas recheadas [rish-yadash] stuffed squid

maçã [masang] apple

maçã assada baked apple

macedónia de frutas [masidon-ya di frootash] fruit cocktail

maionese [mI-oonehz] mayonnaise

maionese de alho [dal-yoo] garlic mayonnaise

mal passado [pasadoo] rare

manjericão [manJirikowng] basil

manteiga [mantayga] butter

manteiga de anchova
[dansh**oh**va] anchovy butter

manteiga queimada [kaym**a**da]
butter sauce for fish

margarina [margar**ee**na]
margarine

marinada marinade

mariscos [mar**ee**shkoosh]
shellfish

marmelada [marmil**a**da] quince
jam

marmelos [marm**eh**loosh]
quinces

marmelos assados [marm**eh**looz
as**a**doosh] roast quinces

massa pasta

massa de fartos [di f**a**rtoosh]
choux pastry

meia desfeita [**may**-a dishf**ay**ta]
boiled dried cod, potatoes,
chickpeas and olive oil

meia dose [doz] half portion

mel [mehl] honey

melancia [milans**ee**-a]
watermelon

melão [mil**ow**ng] melon

melão com presunto [kong
priz**oo**ntoo] melon with ham

meloa com vinho do Porto/
Madeira [mil**oh**-a kong **vee**n-
yoo doo p**oh**rtoo/mad**ay**ra] small
melon with Port or Madeira
wine poured over it

melocotão [milookoot**ow**ng]
peach

merenda [mir**ay**nda] tea; snack

merengue [mir**ang**] meringue

mexilhões [mishil-y**oy**ngsh]
mussels

migas à Alentejana [m**ee**gaz a
alaynti**Ja**na] thick bread soup

mil folhas [meel **foh**l-yash]
millefeuille, custard slice, (US)
napoleon

miolos [m-y**o**loosh] brains

miolos com ovos [kong **o**voosh]
brains with eggs

míscaros [m**ee**shkaroosh]
mushrooms

moleja [mool**ay**Ja] soup made
from pig's blood

molho [m**oh**l-yoo] sauce

molho à Espanhola [shpan-**yo**la]
spicy onion and garlic sauce

molho ao Madeira [ow mad**ay**ra]
Madeira wine sauce

molho bearnaise [bayrn**eh**z]
béarnaise sauce

molho béchamel [baysham**eh**l]
béchamel sauce, white sauce

molho branco [**bran**koo] white
sauce

molho holandês [oland**ay**sh]
hollandaise sauce

molho mornay cheese sauce

molho mousseline [moosil**een**]
hollandaise sauce with
cream

molho tártaro [t**a**rtaroo] tartare
sauce

molho veloutée [viloot**ay**] white
sauce made from cream and
egg yolks

morangos [moor**a**ngoosh]
strawberries

morangos com chantilly [kong
shantil**ee**] strawberries and
whipped cream

morcela [moorsehla] black
pudding, blood sausage

mostarda [mooshtarda] mustard

mousse do chocolate [moos di
shookoolat] chocolate mousse

mousse de fiambre [f-yambr]
ham mousse

mousse de leite condensado
[layt kondaynsadoo] mousse
made from condensed milk

na brasa [braza] charcoal-
grilled

napolitanas [napoolitanash] long
flat biscuits/cookies

natas [natash] cream

natas batidas [bateedash]
whipped cream

nectarina [nektareena] nectarine

nêsperas [nayshpirash] loquats
(yellow fruit similar to a plum)

no churrasco [noo shoorrashkoo]
barbecued

no espeto [nooshpaytoo] spit-
roasted

no forno [fohrnn] baked

nozes [nozish] walnuts

noz moscada [noj mooshkada]
nutmeg

óleo [ol-yoo] oil

omeleta [omilayta] omelette

omeleta com ervas [kong
ehrvash] vegetable omelette

omeleta de cogumelos [di
kogoomehloosh] mushroom
omelette

omeleta de fiambre [f-yambr]
ham omelette

omeleta de queijo [kayJoo]
cheese omelette

omelete [omilayt] omelette

orelha de porco de vinaigrette
[orayl-ya di pohrkoo di vinagreht]
pig's ear in vinaigrette
dressing

ostras [ohshtrash] oysters

ovo [ohvoo] egg

ovo com maionese [kong mī-
oonehz] egg mayonnaise

ovo cozido [koozeedoo] hard-
boiled egg

ovo em geleia [ayng Jilay a] egg
in aspic

ovo escalfado [shkalfadoo]
poached egg

ovo estrelado [shtriladoo] fried
egg

ovo quente [kaynt] soft-boiled
egg

ovos mexidos [misheedoosh]
scrambled eggs

ovos mexidos com tomate
[kong toomat] scrambled eggs
with tomato

ovos verdes [vayrdish] eggs
stuffed with a mixture of
egg yolks, mayonnaise and
parsley

palha de ovos [pal-ya dovoosh]
egg pastries

panqueca [pankehka] pancake

pão [powng] bread

pão branco [brankoo] white
bread

pão de centeio [di sayntay-oo]
rye bread

pão de ló de Alfazeirão [law dalfazay-rowng] sponge cake

pão de ló de Ovar [dohvar] sponge cake

pão de milho [meel-yoo] bread made from maize flour, corn bread

pão integral [intigral] wholemeal bread

pão torrado [toorradoo] toasted bread

pargo [pargoo] sea bream

pargo assado [pargwasadoo] roast bream

pargo cozido [koozeedoo] bream cooked in a sauce or with olive oil

parrilhada [pareel-yada] grilled fish

passas [pasash] raisins

pastéis [pashteh-ish] pastries

pastéis de bacalhau [di bakal-yow] dried cod fishcakes

pastéis de carne [karn] puff-pastry patties filled with meat

pastéis de Chaves [shavish] thin dainty puff-pastry patties filled with meat

pastéis de nata custard tarts

pastéis de Tentúgal [tayntoogal] filo-pastry patties with an egg yolk and sugar filling, sprinkled with sugar

pastel [pashtehl] cake; pie

pastelinhos de bacalhau [pashtileen-yoosh di bakal-yow] fishcakes made from dried cod

pataniscas [pataneeshkash]

dried cod fritters

pataniscas de miolos [di m-yoloosh] brain fritters

paté de aves [patay davish] pâté made from chicken, duck or goose liver

paté de coelho [di kwayl-yoo] rabbit pâté

paté de fígado [feegadoo] liver pâté

paté de galinha [galeen-ya] chicken pâté

paté de lebre [lehbr] hare pâté

pato [patoo] duck

pato assado [asadoo] roast duck

pato com laranja [kong laranJa] duck à l'orange

peixe [paysh] fish

peixe espada [shpada] swordfish

peixe espada de escabeche [dishkabehsh] marinated swordfish

peixinhos da horta [paysheen-yoosh da orta] French bean fritters

pepino [pipeenoo] cucumber

pequeno almoço [pikaynoo almohsoo] breakfast

pequeno almoço continental [kontinayntal] continental breakfast

pêra [payra] pear

pêra abacate [abakat] avocado

pêra bela helena [behlaylayna] pear in chocolate sauce

percebes [pirsehbish] shellfish similar to barnacles

perdiz [pirdeesh] partridge

perdizes de escabeche [pirdeeziJ dishkabehsh] marinated partridge

perdizes fritas [pirdeezish freetash] fried partridge

perdizes na púcara [pirdeeziJ na pookara] partridge casserole

perna [pehrna] leg

perna de carneiro assada [di karnayroo] roast leg of lamb

perna de carneiro entremeada [ayntrim-yada] stuffed leg of lamb

perninhas de rã [pirneen-yash di rang] frogs' legs

peru [piroo] turkey

peru assado [asadoo] roast turkey

peru de fricassé [di frikasay] turkey fricassée

peru recheado [rish-yadoo] stuffed turkey

pescada [pishkada] hake

pescada cozida [koozeeda] hake cooked in a sauce or with olive oil

pescadinhas de rabo na boca [pishkadeen-yash di raboo na bohka] fried whiting served with their tails in their mouths

pêssego [paysigoo] peach

pêssego careca [karehka] nectarine

petiscos [piteeshkoosh] savouries

picante [pikant] hot, spicy

pimenta [pimaynta] pepper

pimenta preta [prayta] black pepper

pimentos [pimayntoosh] peppers, capsicums

piperate [peepirat] pepper stew

piri-piri [peeree-peeree] seasoning made from chillies and olive oil

polvo [pohlvoo] octopus

porção [poorsowng] portion

porco [pohrkoo] pork

porco à alentejana [alayntijana] pork cooked with clams

prato [pratoo] dish; course

prato do dia [doo dee-a] today's special

prato especial da casa [shpis-yal da kaza] speciality of the house

prato principal [prinsipal] main course

prego [prehgoo] thin slice of steak in a bread roll

prego no fiambre [noo f-yambr] steak sandwich with sliced ham

prego no pão [noo powng] steak sandwich

prego no prato [pratoo] steak, usually served with a fried egg

presunto [prizoontoo] ham

pudim de ovos [poodeeng dovoosh] egg pudding

pudim flan [flang] crème caramel

pudim molotov [molotof] crème caramel with egg whites

puré de batata [pooray di] mashed potatoes

puré de castanhas [kashtan-yash] chestnut purée

p.v. (preço variado) [praysoo var-yadoo] price varies

queijadas de Sintra [kayJadaJ di seentra] small tarts with a filling made from milk, eggs, sugar and vanilla

queijo [kayJoo] cheese

queijo curado [kooradoo] dried matured hard white cheese

queijo da Ilha [eel-ya] strong cheese from the Azores flavoured with pepper

queijo da Serra [sehrra] goat's cheese from Serra da Estrela

queijo de cabra [di] goat's cheese

queijo de ovelha [dovayl-ya] sheep's cheese

queijo de Palmela [palmehla] small white mild dried cheese

queijo de Serpa [sehrpa] small strong dried goat's cheese

queijo fresco [frayshkoo] medium-firm mild cheese

queijos [kayJoosh] cheeses

rabanadas [rabanadash] bread dipped in beaten egg and fried, then sprinkled with sugar and cinammon

raia [rī-a] skate

refeição [rifaysowng] meal

refeição ligeira [liJayra] snack, light meal

remoulade [rimoolad] dressing with mustard and herbs

requeijão [rikayJowng] curd cheese

rillete [ree-eht] potted pork meat

rins [reensh] kidneys

rins ao Madeira [reenz ow madayra] kidneys cooked in Madeira wine

rissóis [riso-ysh] deep-fried meat patties

rissol [risol] deep-fried meat patty

rissol de camarão [di kamarowng] prawn rissole

robalo [roobaloo] rock bass

rojões [rooJoyngsh] cubes of pork

rolo de carne [rohloo di karn] meat loaf

rosmaninho [rooJmaneen-yoo] rosemary

sabayon [saba-yohng] dessert made from egg yolks and white wine

sal salt

salada salad

salada de agriões [dagr-yoyngsh] watercress salad

salada de alface [dalfas] green salad

salada de atum [datoong] tuna salad

salada de chicória [di shikor-ya] chicory salad

salada de frutas [frootash] fruit salad

salada de lagosta [lagohshta] lobster salad

salada de ovas [dovash] fish roe salad

calada de tomate [di toomat] tomato salad

salada mista [meeshta] mixed salad

salada russa [roosa] Russian salad, salad of diced vegetables in mayonnaise

salgado [salgadoo] savoury, salty

salmão [salmowng] salmon

salmão fumado [foomadoo] smoked salmon

salmonete [salmoonayt] red mullet

salmonetes grelhados [salmoonaytsh gril-yadoosh] grilled red mullet

salsa parsley

salsicha [salseesha] sausage

salsichas de cocktail [salseeshaJ di koktehl] cocktail sausages

salsichas de peru [piroo] turkey sausages

salsichas de porco [pohrkoo] pork sausages

salteado [salt-yadoo] sautéed

sandes [sandish] sandwich

sandes de fiambre [di f-yambr] ham sandwich

sandes de lombo [lohmboo] steak sandwich

sandes de paio [pī-oo] sausage sandwich

sandes de presunto [prizoontoo] ham sandwich

sandes de queijo [kayJoo] cheese sandwich

sandes mista [meeshta] mixed sandwich, usually ham and cheese

santola spider crab

santola gratinada [gratinada] spider crab with cheese sauce browned under the grill

sapateira [sapatayra] spider crab

sarda mackerel

sardinha [sardeen-ya] sardine

sardinhas assadas [sardeen-yaz asadash] roast sardines

selecção de queijos [silehsowng di kayJoosh] selection of cheeses

sobremesas [sobrimayzash] desserts

solha [sohl-ya] flounder

solha assada no forno [noo fohrnoo] baked flounder

solha frita [freeta] fried flounder

solha recheada [rish-yada] stuffed flounder

sonho [sohn-yoo] type of doughnut

sopa [sohpa] soup

sopa à alentejana [alayntiJana] bread soup with a poached egg on top

sopa de agriões [dagr-yoyngsh] watercress soup

sopa de alho francês [dal-yoo fransaysh] leek soup

sopa de camarão [kamarowng] prawn soup

sopa de caranguejo [karang**ay**Joo] crab soup

sopa de cebola gratinada [sib**ohla**] French onion soup with melted cheese on top

sopa de cogumelos [kogoom**eh**loosh] mushroom soup

sopa de espargos [dish**pa**rgoosh] asparagus soup

sopa de feijão verde [fay**Jow**ng vayrd] green bean soup

sopa de grão [gr**ow**ng] chickpea soup

sopa de lagosta [lag**oh**shta] lobster soup

sopa de legumes [lig**oo**mish] vegetable soup

sopa de mariscos [mar**ee**shkoosh] shellfish soup

sopa de ostras [d**oh**shtrash] oyster soup

sopa de panela [di pan**eh**la] egg-based dessert

sopa de pão e coentros [powng ee kw**ay**ntroosh] bread and coriander soup

sopa de pedra [**peh**dra] thick vegetable soup

sopa de peixe [paysh] fish soup

sopa de rabo de boi [r**a**boo di boy] oxtail soup

sopa de tartaruga [tartar**oo**ga] turtle soup

sopa do dia [doo d**ee**-a] soup of the day

sopa dourada [doh**ra**da] egg-based dessert

sopa e cozido [**soh**pī kooz**ee**doo] meat stew

sopa juliana [**soh**pa Jool-yana] vegetable soup

sopas [**soh**pash] soups

soufflé de camarão [soo**flay** di kamar**ow**ng] prawn soufflé

soufflé de chocolate [shookoola**t**] chocolate soufflé

soufflé de cogumelos [kogoom**eh**loosh] mushroom soufflé

soufflé de espinafres [dishpinafrish] spinach soufflé

soufflé de peixe [paysh] fish soufflé

soufflé de queijo [kay**J**oo] cheese soufflé

soufflé gelado [Jil**a**doo] ice-cream soufflé

tarte de amêndoas [tart dam**ay**ndwash] almond tart

tarte de cogumelos [di kogoom**eh**loosh] mushroom quiche

tarte de limão [lim**ow**ng] lemon tart

tarte de maçã [mas**a**ng] apple tart

taxa de serviço [**ta**sha di sirv**ee**soo] service charge

tempero da salada [taymp**ay**roo da sal**a**da] salad dressing

tomar [too**ma**r] fresh soft goat's cheese

tomate [too**ma**t] tomato

tomates recheados [too**ma**tish rish-ya**doo**sh] stuffed tomatoes tomilho [toomeel-yoo] thyme

toranja [tooranja] grapefruit

torrada [toorrada] toast

torresmos [toorray.lmoosh] small fried rashers of bacon

torta tart

torta de maçã [masang] apple pie

torta de nozes [di nozish] walnut tart

tortilha [toorteel-ya] Spanish-style omelette with potato

tosta [toshta] toasted sandwich

tosta mista [meeshta] toasted ham and cheese sandwich

toucinho do céu [tooseen-yoo doo seh-oo] kind of dessert made from eggs, sugar and almonds

tripas [treepash] tripe

tripas à moda do Porto [treepaza moda doo pohrtoo] tripe with beans and vegetables

trufas de chocolate [troofaJ di shookoolat] chocolate truffles

truta [troota] trout

truta assada no forno [noo fohrnoo] baked trout

truta cozida [koozeeda] trout cooked in a sauce or with olive oil

truta frita [freeta] fried trout

uvas [oovash] grapes

uvas brancas [oovaJ brankash] green grapes

uvas moscatel [mooshkatehl] muscatel grapes

uvas pretas [oovaJ praytash] black grapes

veado assado [v-yadoo asadoo] roast venison

vieiras recheadas [v-yayrash rish-yadash] scallops filled with seafood

vinagre [vinagr] vinegar

vinagre de estragão [dishtragowng] tarragon vinegar

vitela [vitehla] veal

Menu Reader:
Drink

Essential Terms

beer a cerveja [sirvayJa]
bottle a garrafa
brandy o brandy
coffee o café [kafeh]
  a cup of ... uma chávena de ... [ooma shavena di]
gin o gin [Jeeng]
  gin and tonic um gin-tónico [oong Jeeng tonikoo]
glass o copo [kopoo]
  a glass of ... um copo de ... [oong kopoo di]
milk o leite [layt]
mineral water a água mineral [agwa]
orange juice o sumo de laranja [soomoo di laranJa]
port o vinho do Porto [veen-yoo doo pohrtoo]
red wine o vinho tinto [teentoo]
rosé rosé [roozay]
soda (water) a soda
soft drink a bebida não alcoólica [bibeeda nowng alko-oleeka]
sugar o açúcar [asookar]
tea o chá [sha]
tonic (water) a água tónica [agwa]
vodka o vodka
water a água [agwa]
whisky o whisky [weeshkee]
white wine o vinho branco [veen-yoo brankoo]
wine o vinho [veen-yoo]
wine list a lista dos vinhos [leeshta dooJ veen-yoosh]

another ..., please outro/outra ..., por favor [ohtroo – poor favohr]

açúcar [asookar] sugar

água mineral [agwa mineral] mineral water

aguardente [agwardaynt] clear spirit/brandy (literally: 'firewater'), distilled from wine or grape skins

aguardente de figo [feegoo] fig brandy

aguardente de pêra [di payra] brandy with a pear or pears in the bottle

aguardentes bagaceiras [agwardayntish bagasayrash] clear spirit/brandy distilled from grape skins

aguardentes velhas [vehl-yash] matured brandies

aguardentes velhas ou preparadas [vehl-yaz oh preparadash] brandies matured in oak

álcool [alko-ol] alcohol

amêndoa amarga [amayndwa amarga] bitter almond liqueur

aperitivo [apiriteevoo] aperitif

bagaço [bagasoo] clear spirit/ brandy (literally: 'firewater'), distilled from grape skins

Bairrada [birrada] region producing fruity red wines

batido de leite [bateedoo di layt] milkshake

bebida [bibeeda] drink

bica [beeka] small black espresso-type coffee

branco [brankoo] white

bruto [brootoo] extra-dry

Bual [boo-al] medium-sweet Madeira wine

Bucelas® [boosehlash] crisp dry white wine from the Estremadura area

cacau [kakow] cocoa

café [kafeh] small black espresso-type coffee

café com leite [kong layt] white coffee, coffee with milk

café com pingo [peengoo] espresso with brandy

café duplo [dooploo] two espressos in the same cup

café glacé [glasay] iced coffee

café instantâneo [inshtantan-yoo] instant coffee

caneca [kanehka] half-litre

capilé [kapileh] drink made from water, sugar and syrup

carapinhada de café [karapeen-yada di kafeh] coffee drink with crushed ice

carapinhada de chocolate [shookoolat] chocolate drink with crushed ice

carapinhada de groselha [groozehl-ya] redcurrant drink with crushed ice

carapinhada de morango [moorangoo] strawberry drink with crushed ice

carioca [kar-yoka] small weak black coffee

cerveja [sirvayJa] beer

cerveja branca [branka] lager

cerveja de pressão [di prisowng] draught beer

235

cerveja preta [prayta] bitter, dark beer

chá [sha] tea

chá com leite [kong layt] tea with milk

chá com limão [limowng] lemon tea

chá com mel [mehl] tea with honey

chá de limão [di limowng] infusion of hot water with a lemon rind

chá de lucialima [loos-yaleema] herb tea

chá de mentol mint tea

chá de tília [teel-ya] linden blossom tea

champanhe [shampan-yi] champagne

chocolate glacé [shookoolat glasay] iced chocolate

chocolate quente [kaynt] hot chocolate

cidra [seedra] cider

cimbalino [simbaleenoo] small espresso

clarete [klarayt] claret

Colares [koolarish] table wine from the Colares region

com gás [kong gash] carbonated

com gelo [Jayloo] with ice, on the rocks

conhaque [koon-yak] cognac, brandy

Constantino® [konshtanteenoo] Portuguese brandy

cubo de gelo [kooboo di Jayloo] ice cube

Dão® [downg] red table wine from the Dão region

descafeinado [dishkafaynadoo] decaffeinated

doce [dohs] sweet (usually very sweet)

espumante [shpoomant] sparkling

espumantes naturais [shpoomantish natoorīsh] sparkling wine made by the champagne method

expresso [shprehsoo] espresso

figo [feegoo] fig brandy

galão [galowng] large weak milky coffee, served in a tall glass

garoto [garohtoo] small coffee with milk

garrafa bottle

garrafeira [garrafayra] aged red wine set aside by the producer in years of exceptional quality

gasoso [gazohzoo] fizzy

gelo [Jayloo] ice

ginja [JeenJa], ginjinha [JeenJeen-ya] brandy with sugar and cherries added

imperial [eempir-yal] regular glass size for drinking beer (about ¼ litre)

italiana [ital-yana] half a very strong espresso

jarro [Jarroo] jug

Lagoa® [lagoh-a] table wine
from the Algarve

leite [layt] milk

licor [likohr] liqueur; sweet
flavoured spirit

Licor Beirão® [bayrowng]
cognac with herbs

licor de medronho [di midrohn-
yoo] berry liqueur

licor de ovo [dohvoo] advocaat

licor de pêras [di payrash] pear
liqueur

licor de whisky [weeshkee]
whisky liqueur

limonada [limoonada] fresh
lemon juice with water and
sugar

lista de preços [leeshta di
praysoosh] price list

lista dos vinhos [dooJ veen-
yoosh] wine list

Macieira® [masi-ayra]
Portuguese brandy

Madeira [madayra] wine-
producing region; sweet and
dry fortified wines

maduro [madooroo] mature

Malvasia [malvasee-a] Malmsey
wine, a sweet heavy Madeira
wine

Mateus Rosé® [matay-oosh
roozay] sweet rosé wine

mazagrin [mazagrang] iced
coffee with lemon

meia de leite [may-a di layt]
large white coffee

meia garrafa half-bottle

meio seco [may-oo saykoo]
medium-dry (usually fairly
sweet)

morena [moorayna] mixture of
lager and bitter

moscatel [mooshkatehl]
muscatel wine

não alcoólico [nowng alko-
oleekoo] non-alcoholic

pingo [peengoo] small coffee
with milk

ponche [pohnsh] punch

pré-pagamento pay in advance

região demarcada wine-
producing region subject to
official controls

Reguengos [rigayngoosh] table
wine from Alentejo

reserva [rizehrva] aged wine set
aside by the producer in years
of exceptional quality

Sagres® [sagrish] popular
brand of lager

Sagres Europa® [sagriz ay-
ooropa] brand of lager

Sagres Preta® [prayta] dark
beer resembling British
brown ale

saquinhos de chá [sakeen-yooJ
di sha] teabags

seco [saykoo] dry

selo de garantia seal of
guarantee

sem gás [sayng gash] still

237

sem gelo [Jayloo] without ice
Sercial [sirsee-al] the driest
  variety of Madeira wine
sirva gelado served chilled
sirva-se à temperatura
  ambiente serve at room
  temperature
sirva-se fresco serve cool
sumo de laranja [soomoo di
  laranJa] orange juice
sumo de lima [leema] lime juice
sumo de limão [limowng] lemon
  juice
sumo de maçã [masang] apple
  juice
sumo de tomate [toomat]
  tomato juice
Sumol® [soomol] fizzy fruit
  juice
Super Bock® brand of lager

tarifas de consumo price list
Tavel® [tavehl] rosé wine
tinto [teentoo] red
Tri Naranjus® [treenaranJoosh]
  brand name for a range of
  fruit drinks

Valpaços® [valpasoosh] table
  wine from Trás-os-Montes
velha [vehl-ya] old, mature
velhíssima [vehl-yeesima] very
  old (spirits)
Verdelho [virdayl-yoo] a
  medium-dry Madeira wine
vermute [vermoot] vermouth
vinho [veen-yoo] wine
vinho branco [brankoo] white
  wine

vinho da casa [kaza] house
  wine
vinho da Madeira [madayra]
  Madeira wine
vinho de aperitivo [dapiriteevoo]
  aperitif
vinho de mesa [di mayza] table
  wine
vinho de Xerêz [shiraysh] sherry
vinho do Porto [doo pohrtoo]
  port
vinho espumante [shpoomant]
  sparkling wine
vinho moscatel [mooshkatehl]
  muscatel wine
vinho rosé [roozay] rosé wine
vinho tinto [teentoo] red wine
vinho verde [vayrd] young,
  slightly sparkling white, red,
  or rosé wine produced in the
  Minho

whisky de malte [weeshkee di
  malt] malt whisky

xarope [sharop] cordial,
  concentrated juice
xarope de groselha [di groozehl-
  ya] redcurrant cordial
xarope de morango [moorangoo]
  strawberry cordial

How the Language Works

Pronunciation

In this phrasebook, the Portuguese has been written in a system of imitated pronunciation so that it can be read as though it were English, bearing in mind the notes on pronunciation given below:

a	as in hat
ay	as in may
eh	as in get
g	as in goat
i	as in it
ī	as the 'i' sound in might
J	as the 's' sound in pleasure
o	as in not
oh	like the exclamation oh
oo	as in boot
ow	as in now

In words such as **não** [nowng] and **bem** [bayng], the final 'g' in the pronunciation signifies a nasal sound and should barely be sounded.

Letters given in bold type indicate the part of the word to be stressed.

Abbreviations

adj	adjective
f	feminine
fam	familiar
m	masculine
pl	plural
pol	polite
sing	singular

Nouns

All nouns in Portuguese have one of two genders: masculine or feminine. Generally speaking, those ending in -o are masculine:

> o sapato
> oo sap**a**too
> the shoe

Nouns ending in **-or** are masculine. To make the corresponding feminine, add **-a**:

> o professor
> oo proofes**ohr**
> the (male) teacher

> a professora
> a proofes**ohr**a
> the (female) teacher

Nouns ending in **-a**, **-ade** or **-ão** are usually feminine (although there are exceptions):

> a cama
> a k**a**ma
> the bed

> a cidade
> a sid**a**d
> the city

> a pensão
> a payns**ow**ng
> the boarding house

A small number of nouns ending in **-a** and **-e** (usually professions) can be either masculine or feminine:

> o/a guia
> oo/a g**ee**-a
> the tourist guide

> o/a intérprete
> oo/a int**eh**rprit
> the interpreter

Plural Nouns

The plurals of nouns are formed according to the rules below.

For nouns ending in a vowel, add **-s**:

> a empregada
> a aympreg**a**da
> the waitress

> as empregadas
> az aympreg**a**dash
> the waitresses

To obtain the plural of nouns ending in -ão, remove the -ão and add -ões:

a pensão   as pensões
a payns**ow**ng   ash paynso**oy**ngsh
the guesthouse   the guesthouses

To obtain the plural of nouns ending in -l, remove the -l and add -is:

o hotel   os hotéis
oo oht**eh**l   ooz oht**eh**-ish
the hotel   the hotels

To obtain the plural of nouns ending in -m, remove the -m and add -ns:

o homem   os homens
oo **oh**mayng   ooz **oh**mayngsh
the man   the men

For nouns ending in other consonants, the plural is formed by adding -es:

o condutor   os condutores
oo kondoot**ohr**   oosh kondoot**ohr**ish
the driver   the drivers

uma mulher   umas mulheres
ooma mool-y**ehr**   **oo**mash mool-y**ehr**ish
a woman   some women

Articles

The words for articles in Portuguese depend on the number (singular or plural) and gender of the noun.

The Definite Article

The definite article (the) is as follows:

	singular	plural
masculine	o [oo]	os [oosh]
feminine	a [a]	as [ash]

o livro	os livros
oo **lee**vroo	ooJ **lee**vroosh
the book	the books

a piscina	as piscinas
a pishs**ee**na	ash pishs**ee**nash
the swimming pool	the swimming pools

When the definite article is used in combination with **a** (to), **de** (of), **em** (in, on) or **por** (by), it changes as follows:

	o	a	os	as
a +	ao	à	aos	às
	ow	a	owsh	ash
de +	do	da	dos	das
	doo	da	doosh	dash
em +	no	na	nos	nas
	noo	na	noosh	nash
por +	pelo	pela	pelos	pelas
	p**i**loo	p**i**la	p**i**loosh	p**i**lash

vamos ao museo	perto do hotel
va**mooz** ow moos**ay**-oo	p**eh**rtoo doo oht**ehl**
let's go to the museum	near the hotel

The Indefinite Article

The indefinite article (a, an, some) also changes according to the gender and number of the accompanying noun:

	singular	plural
masculine	um [oong]	uns [oonsh]
feminine	uma [**oo**ma]	umas [**oo**mash]

um selo	**uns selos**
oong **say**loo	oonsh **say**loosh
a stamp	some stamps
uma rapariga	**umas raparigas**
ooma rapar**ee**ga	**oo**mash rapar**ee**gash
a girl	some girls

When the indefinite article is used in combination with **em** (in, on) it changes as follows:

masculine	**em** + **um** = **num** [noong]
feminine	**em** + **uma** = **numa** [**noo**ma]

gostava de ir numa viagem ao Brasil
goosht**a**va deer **noo**ma v-ya**Jay**ng ow braz**ee**l
I'd like to go on a trip to Brazil

Adjectives and Adverbs

Adjectives must agree in gender and number with the noun they refer to. In the English-Portuguese section of this book, all adjectives are given in the masculine singular. Unlike English, Portuguese adjectives usually follow the noun.

The feminine singular of the adjective is formed by changing the masculine endings as follows:

masculine	feminine
-o	-a
-or	-ora
-ês	-esa

um cozinheiro estupendo	**uma cozinheira estupenda**
oong koozeen-**yay**roo shtoop**ay**ndo	**oo**ma koozeen-**yay**ra shtoop**ay**nda
a wonderful cook	a wonderful cook
um senhor encantador	**uma senhora encantadora**
oong sin-y**oh**r aynkantad**oh**r	**oo**ma sin-y**o**ra aynkantad**o**ra
a nice man	a nice woman

um rapaz inglês	**uma rapariga inglesa**
oong rap**az** ingl**ay**sh	**oo**ma rapar**ee**ga ingl**ay**za
an English boy	an English girl

For other types of adjective, the feminine form is the same as the masculine:

um homem agradável	**uma mulher agradável**
oong **oh**mayng agrad**a**vil	**oo**ma mool-y**eh**r agrad**a**vil
a nice man	a nice woman

Note that the adjective **mau** (bad) is irregular: the feminine is **má**.

The plurals of adjectives are formed in the same way as the plurals of nouns, by adding an **-s**, an **-es** or changing **-l** to **-is**:

o preço alto	**os preços altos**
oo pr**ay**soo **a**ltoo	oosh pr**ay**sooz **a**ltoosh
the high price	the high prices
uma taxa alta	**as taxas altas**
ooma t**a**sha **a**lta	ash t**a**shaz **a**ltash
a high rate	the high rates
um homem agradável	**uns homens agradáveis**
oong **oh**mayng agrad**a**vil	oonz **oh**mayngz agrad**a**vay-ish
a nice man	some nice men

When the adjective ends in **-ês**, the **ê** is replaced by **e** in the plural:

um rapaz inglês	**uns rapazes ingleses**
oong rap**az** ingl**ay**sh	oonsh rap**a**ziz ingl**ay**zish
an English boy	some English boys

Comparatives

The comparative is formed by placing **mais** (more) or **menos** (less) in front of the adjective or adverb and **que** (than) after it:

bonito	**mais bonito**
boon**ee**too	mīʒ boon**ee**too
beautiful	more beautiful

quente	**menos quente**
kaynt	m**ay**noosh kaynt
hot	less hot

este hotel é mais/menos caro que o outro
aysht oht**ehl** eh mīsh/m**ay**noosh k**a**roo ki oo **oh**troo
this hotel is more/less expensive than the other one

tem um quarto mais barato?
t**ay**ng oong kw**a**rtoo mīʒ bar**a**too
do you have a cheaper room?

pode falar mais devagar, por favor?
pod fal**a**r mīʒ div**a**gar poor fav**oh**r
could you speak more slowly please?

Superlatives

Superlatives are formed by placing one of the following before the adjective: **o/a mais** or **os/as mais** (depending on the noun's gender and number):

qual é o mais divertido?
kwal**eh** oo mīʒ divirt**ee**doo
which is the most entertaining?

o dia mais quente	**o carro mais rápido**
oo d**ee**-a mīsh kaynt	oo k**a**rroo mīsh r**a**pidoo
the hottest day	the fastest car

The following adjectives have irregular comparatives and superlatives:

bom	good	**melhor**	better	**o melhor**	the best
bong		mil-y**or**		oo mil-y**or**	
grande	big	**maior**	bigger	**o maior**	the biggest
grand		mī-**or**		oo mī-**or**	

mau	bad	pior	worse	o pior	the worst
mow		p-yor		oo p-yor	
pequeno	small	menor	smaller	o menor	the smallest
pik**ay**noo		min**or**		oo min**or**	

Note that **mais pequeno** (smaller) is also used.

'As ... as ...' is translated as follows:

> **Lisboa está tão bonita como sempre!**
> liJb**oh**-a shta towng boon**ee**ta k**oh**moo saympr
> Lisbon is as beautiful as ever!

The superlative form ending in **-íssimo** indicates that something is 'very/extremely ...' without actually comparing it to something else:

lindo	lindíssimo
l**ee**ndoo	lind**ee**simoo
beautiful	very beautiful

Adverbs

There are two ways to form an adverb. If the adjective ends in -o, take the feminine and add **-mente** to form the corresponding adverb:

exacto	exactamente
iz**a**too	izatam**ay**nt
accurate	accurately

If the adjective ends in any other letter, add **-mente** to the basic masculine form:

feliz	felizmente
fil**ee**sh	filiЈm**ay**nt
happy	happily

Possessive Adjectives

Possessive adjectives, like other Portuguese adjectives, agree with the noun in gender and number:

	singular		plural	
	masculine	feminine	masculine	feminine
my	**o meu**	**a minha**	**os meus**	**as minhas**
	oo **may**-oo	a **meen**-ya	ooJ **may**-oosh	aJ **meen**-yash
your	**o teu**	**a tua**	**os teus**	**as tuas**
(sing, fam)	oo **tay**-oo	a **too**-a	oosh **tay**-oosh	ash **too**-ash
his/her/its,	**o seu**	**a sua**	**os seus**	**as suas**
your, their	oo **say**-oo	a **soo**-a	oosh **say**-oosh	ash **soo**-ash
our	**o nosso**	**a nossa**	**os nossos**	**as nossas**
	oo **no**soo	a **no**sa	ooJ **no**soosh	aJ **no**sash

A more formal way of translating 'your' is:

	singular	plural
masculine	**do senhor**	**dos senhores**
	doo sin-**yohr**	doosh sin-**yoh**rish
feminine	**da senhora**	**das senhoras**
	da sin-**yo**ra	dash sin-**yo**rash

See page 250 for when to use this.

a tua casa	**as suas pastilhas**
a **too**-a **ka**za	ash soo-ash pash**teel**-yash
your house	his/her/your/their tablets
a sua mala	**os nossos amigos**
a **soo**-a **ma**la	oJ **no**sooz ame**ee**goosh
his/her/your/their suitcase	our friends

If when using **o seu, o sua** etc, it is unclear whether you mean 'his', 'her', 'your' or 'their', you can use the following after the noun instead:

dele	[dayl]	his
dela	[**deh**la]	her
deles	[**day**lish]	their (m)
delas	[**deh**lash]	their (f)
de vocês	[di vos**aysh**]	your (pl)

o dinheiro dela	o dinheiro dele	o dinheiro de vocês
oo deen-**yay**roo de**h**la	oo deen-**yay**roo dayl	oo deen-**yay**roo di vos**ay**sh
her money	his money	your money

Possessive Pronouns

To translate 'mine', 'yours', 'theirs' etc, use one of the following forms. Like possessive adjectives, possessive pronouns must agree in gender and number with the object or objects referred to:

	singular		plural	
	masculine	feminine	masculine	feminine
mine	**meu**	**minha**	**meus**	**minhas**
	m**ay**-oo	m**ee**n-ya	m**ay**-oosh	m**ee**n-yash
yours (sing, fam)	**teu**	**tua**	**teus**	**tuas**
	t**ay**-oo	t**oo**-a	t**ay**-oosh	t**oo**-ash
his/hers,	**seu**	**sua**	**seus**	**suas**
yours, theirs	s**ay**-oo	s**oo**-a	s**ay**-oosh	s**oo**-ash
ours	**nosso**	**nossa**	**nossos**	**nossas**
	n**o**soo	n**o**sa	n**o**soosh	n**o**sash

A more formal way of translating 'yours' is:

	singular	plural
masculine	**do senhor**	**dos senhores**
	doo sin-y**oh**r	doosh sin-y**oh**rish
feminine	**da senhora**	**das senhoras**
	da sin-y**o**ra	dash sin-y**o**rash

See the section on subject pronouns for when to use this.

Generally, possessive pronouns are used with the definite article.

esta é a sua chave e esta é a minha
ehshteh a **soo**-a shavee **eh**shteh a m**ee**n-ya
this is your key and this is mine

este carro não é o seu
aysht **ka**rroo nowng eh oo **say**-oo
this car is not yours

If when using **seu**, **sua** etc, it is unclear whether you mean 'his', 'hers', 'yours' or 'theirs', you can use the following after the noun instead:

dele	[dayl]	his
dela	[dehla]	hers
deles	[daylish]	theirs (m)
delas	[dehla]	theirs (f)
de vocês	[di vosaysh]	yours (pl)

não é dele, é dos amigos dele
nowng eh dayl eh dooz am**ee**gooJ dayl
it's not his, it's his friends'

Personal Pronouns

Subject Pronouns

eu	[**ay**-oo]	I
tu	[too]	you (sing, fam)
ele	[ayl]	he, it
ela	[**eh**la]	she, it
você	[vos**ay**]	you (sing, pol)
nós	[nosh]	we
eles	[aylsh]	they (m)
elas	[**eh**lash]	they (f)
vocês	[vos**ay**sh]	you (pl)

Tu is used when speaking to one person and is the familiar form generally used when speaking to family, close friends and children.

Você and **vocês** are more formal and are used to address people you don't know well. They take the third person forms of verbs: **você** takes the same form as 'he/she/it'; **vocês** takes the same form as 'they'.

There is another way of saying 'you', which is used to address complete strangers or in formal situations. These forms all take the third person of the verb, i.e. the same as 'he/she/it' for the singular and 'they' for the plural:

	singular	plural
masculine	**o senhor**	**os senhores**
	oo sin-y**oh**r	oosh sin-y**oh**rish
feminine	**a senhora**	**as senhoras**
	a sin-y**o**ra	ash sin-y**o**rash

(Note that **Senhor** also means 'Mr' and **Senhora** means 'Mrs'.)

a senhora é a mãe da Rita?
a sin-y**o**ra eh a mayng da r**ee**ta
are you Rita's mother?

In Portuguese the subject pronoun is usually omitted:

não sabem	**está cansado**
nowng s**a**bayng	sht**a** kans**a**doo
they don't know	he is tired

But it may be retained for emphasis or to avoid confusion:

sou eu!	**somos nós!**
soh **ay**-oo	s**oh**mooɹ nosh
it's me!	it's us!

eu pago as sandes e você paga as cervejas
ay-oo p**a**gwash sandsh ee vos**ay** p**a**gash sirv**ay**ɹash
I'll pay for the sandwiches and you pay for the beers

ele é inglês e ela é americana
ayl**eh** ingl**ay**z ee **eh**leh amirik**a**na
he's English and she's American

Object Pronouns

object pronoun added to verb

me	[mi]	me
te	[ti]	you (sing, fam)
o	[oo]	him, it, you (sing, pol)
a	[a]	her, it, you (sing, pol)
você	[vos**ay**]	you (sing, pol)
nos	[noosh]	us
os	[oosh]	them (m), you (mpl)
as	[ash]	them (f), you (fpl)
vocês	[vos**ay**oh]	you (pl)

object pronoun used with prepositions

mim	[meeng]	me
ti	[tee]	you (sing, fam)
ele	[ayl]	he, it
ela	[**eh**la]	she, it
você/si	[vos**ay**/see]	you (sing, pol)
nós	[nosh]	we
eles	[**ay**lsh]	them (m)
elas	[**eh**lash]	them (f)
vocês	[vos**ay**sh]	you (pl)

The object pronouns (as listed in the first table above) generally follow the verb:

pode ajudar-me?	comprei-as
pod aJood**a**rmi	kompr**ay**-ash
can you help me?	I bought them

But note the word order in the following:

não o vi
nowng oo vee
I didn't see him

The object pronouns (as listed in the right-hand column of the table above) are used after prepositions:

para você	com ele
para vos**ay**	kong ayl
for you	with him

sem ela	depois de você
sayng **eh**la	dip**oh**-ish di vos**ay**
without her	after you

isso é para mim	isso é para ti/si
eesoo eh **pa**ra meeng	**ee**soo eh **pa**ra tee/see
that's for me	that's for you

After the preposition **com** (with), **mim**, **ti** and **si** change as follows:

comigo	contigo	consigo
koom**ee**goo	kont**ee**goo	kons**ee**goo
with me	with you	with you

If you are using an indirect object pronoun to mean 'to me', 'to you' etc (although 'to' might not always be said in English), you generally use the following:

me	[mi]	to me
te	[ti]	to you (sing, fam)
lhe	[l-yi]	to him, to her, to you (sing, pol)
o/a	[oo/a]	to it
nos	[noosh]	to us
lhes	[l-yish]	to them, to you (pl)

comprei-lhe flores	pedi-lhe um favor
kompr**ayl**-yi fl**oh**rish	pid**eel**-yi oong fav**ohr**
I bought flowers for him/her	I asked him/her a favour

importa-se de lhe pedir que ...?
imp**o**rtasi di l-yi pid**eer** ki
could you ask him/her to ...?

Reflexive Pronouns

These are used with reflexive verbs like **lavar-se** 'to wash (oneself)', i.e. where the subject and the object of the verb are one and the same person:

me	[mi]	myself
te	[ti]	yourself (fam)
se	[si]	himself, herself, itself, yourself (pol), themselves, yourselves, oneself
nos	[noosh]	ourselves

apresentar-se to introduce oneself

apresento-me: chamo-me Richard
aprisay**n**toomi: sha**moo**mi Richard
may I introduce myself? my name's Richard

divertir-se to enjoy oneself

divertimo-nos multo na festa
divir**tee**moonooɔ mwee**ng**too na fe**h**shta
we enjoyed ourselves a lot at the party

Demonstratives

The English demonstrative adjective 'this' is translated by **este**. 'That' is translated either by **esse** or **aquele**. **Esse** refers to something nearby. **Aquele** refers to something further away.

Like other adjectives, demonstrative adjectives agree with the noun they qualify in gender and number but they are positioned in front of the noun. Their forms are:

masculine singular			feminine singular		
este	esse	aquele	esta	essa	aquela
aysht	ays	ak**ayl**	**eh**shta	**eh**sa	ake**h**la

masculine plural			feminine plural		
estes	esses	aqueles	estas	essas	aquelas
ayshtish	**ay**sish	ak**ay**lish	**eh**shtash	**eh**sash	ake**h**lash

este restaurante	esse camareiro	aquela praia
aysht rishtow**r**ant	ays kamar**ay**roo	ak**eh**la pr**ī**-a
this restaurant	that waiter	that beach
		(in the distance)

The demonstrative pronouns 'this one', 'that one', 'those', 'these' etc are the same as demonstrative adjectives in Portuguese:

queria estes/esses/aqueles
kir**ee**-a **ays**htish/**ay**sish/ak**ay**lish
I'd like these/those/those (over there)

However, a neuter form also exists which is used when no specific noun is being referred to:

isto	isso	aquilo
eeshtoo	**ee**soo	ak**ee**loo
this	that	that (over there)

isso não é justo	o que é isto?
eeso nowng eh j**oo**stoo	oo ki eh **ee**shtoo
that's not fair	what is this?

Verbs

The basic form of the verb given in the **English-Portuguese** and **Portuguese-English** sections is the infinitive (e.g. to drive, to go etc). There are three verb types in Portuguese which can be recognized by their infinitive endings: -ar, -er, -ir. For example:

amar	[amar]	to love
comer	[koom**ay**r]	to eat
partir	[part**ee**r]	to leave

Present Tense

The present tense corresponds to 'I leave' in English. To form the present tense for the three main types of verb in

Portuguese, remove the **-ar**, **-er** or **-ir** and add the following
endings:

amar to love

am-o	[amoo]	I love
am-as	[amaзh]	you love (sing, fam)
am-a	[ama]	he loves, she loves, you love (sing, pol)
am-amos	[amamoosh]	we love
am-am	[amowng]	they love, you love (pl)

comer to eat

com-o	[kohmoo]	I eat
com-es	[kohmish]	you eat (sing, fam)
com-e	[kohmi]	he eats, she eats, you eat (sing, pol)
com-emos	[komaymoosh]	we eat
com-em	[kohmayng]	they eat, you eat (pl)

partir to leave

part-o	[partoo]	I leave
part-es	[partsh]	you leave (sing, fam)
part-e	[part]	he leaves, she leaves, it leaves, you leave (sing, pol)
part-imos	[parteemoosh]	we leave
part-em	[partayng]	they leave, you leave (pl)

Some common verbs are irregular:

dar to give

dou	[doh]	I give
dás	[dash]	you give (sing, fam)
dá	[da]	he gives, she gives, it gives, you give (sing, pol)
damos	[damoosh]	we give
dão	[downg]	they give, you give (pl)

ir to go

vou	[voh]	I go
vais	[vīsh]	you go (sing, fam)
vai	[vī]	he/she/it goes, you go (sing, pol)
vamos	[vamoosh]	we go
vão	[vowng]	they go, you go (pl)

pôr to put

ponho	[pohn-yoo]	I put
pões	[poyngsh]	you put (sing, fam)
põe	[poyng]	he/she/it puts, you put (sing, pol)
pomos	[pohmoosh]	we put
põem	[poh-ayng]	they put, you put (pl)

ter to have

tenho	[tayn-yoo]	I have
tens	[tayngsh]	you have (sing, fam)
tem	[tayng]	he/she/it has, you have (sing, pol)
temos	[taymoosh]	we have
têm	[tay-ayng]	they have, you have (pl)

vir to come

venho	[vayn-yoo]	I come
vens	[vayngsh]	you come (sing, fam)
vem	[vayng]	he/she/it comes, you come (sing, pol)
vimos	[veemoosh]	we come
vêm	[vay-ayng]	they come, you come (pl)

The first person singular (the 'I' form) of the following verbs is irregular:

dizer	to say	digo	[deegoo]
fazer	to do, to make	faço	[fasoo]
saber	to know	sei	[say]
sair	to go out	saio	[sī-oo]
poder	to be able	posso	[posoo]

See page 265 for the present tense of the verbs **ser** and **estar**.

Past Tense:

Preterite Tense

The preterite is the tense most commonly used to express a completed action that has taken place in the past. To form the preterite tense for the three main types of verb in Portuguese, remove the -ar, -er or -ir and add the following endings:

am-ei	[amay]	I loved
am-aste	[amasht]	you loved (sing, fam)
am-ou	[amoh]	he loved, she loved, you loved (sing, pol)
am-ámos	[amamoosh]	we loved
am-aram	[amarowng]	they loved, you loved (pl)

com-i	[komee]	I ate
com-este	[komaysht]	you ate (sing, fam)
com-eu	[komay-oo]	he ate, she ate, it ate, you ate (sing, pol)
com-emos	[komaymoosh]	we ate
com-eram	[komayrowng]	they ate, you ate (pl)

part-i	[partee]	I left
part-iste	[parteesht]	you left (sing, fam)
part-iu	[partee-oo]	he left, she left, it left, you left (sing, pol)
part-imos	[parteemoosh]	we left
part-iram	[parteerowng]	they left, you left (pl)

The following verbs are irregular in the preterite:

dizer to say

disse	[dees]	I said
disseste	[disehsht]	you said (sing, fam)
disse	[dees]	he said, she said, you said (sing, pol)
dissemos	[disaymoosh]	we said
disseram	[disehrowng]	they said, you said (pl)

fazer to do

fiz	[feesh]	I did
fizeste	[fiz**eh**sht]	you did (sing, fam)
fez	[faysh]	he did, she did, it did, you did (sing, pol)
fizemos	[fiz**ay**moosh]	we did
fizeram	[fiz**eh**rowng]	they did, you did (pl)

ter to have

tive	[teev]	I had
tiveste	[tiv**eh**sht]	you had (sing, fam)
teve	[tayv]	he had, she had, it had, you had (sing, pol)
tivemos	[tiv**ay**moosh]	we had
tiveram	[tiv**eh**rowng]	they had, you had (pl)

vir to come

vim	[veeng]	I came
vieste	[v-yehsht]	you (sing, fam)
veio	[**vay**-oo]	he came, she came, it came, you came (sing, pol)
viemos	[v-y**ay**moosh]	we came
vieram	[v-y**eh**rowng]	they came, you came (pl)

The verbs **ser** (to be) and **ir** (to go) are irregular and have the same form in the preterite:

fui	[fwee]	I was; I went
foste	[fohsht]	you were (sing, fam); you went (sing, fam)
foi	[f**oh**-i]	he/she/it was, you were (sing, pol); he/she/it went, you went (sing, pol)
fomos	[f**oh**moosh]	we were; we went
foram	[f**oh**rowng]	they were, you were (pl, pol); they went, you went (pl)

quem te disse isso?	**conhecemos o seu pai ontem**
kayng ti dees **ee**soo	kon-yes**ay**mooz oo **say**-oo pī **oh**ntayng
who told you that?	we met your father yesterday

compámos um carro no ano passado

kompr**amooz** oong **karr**oo noo **a**noo pas**a**doo

we bought a car last year

See page 265 for the preterite tense of the verbs **ser** and **estar**.

Imperfect Tense

This tense is used to express what was going on regularly over an indefinite period of time and is often translated by 'used to + verb'. It is formed as follows:

amar to love

am-ava	[am**a**va]	I used to love
am-avas	[am**a**vash]	you used to love (sing, fam)
am-ava	[am**a**va]	he/she used to love, you used to love (sing, pol)
am-ávamos	[am**a**vamoosh]	we used to love
am-avam	[am**a**vowng]	they used to love, you used to love (pl)

comer to eat

com-ia	[kom**ee**-a]	I used to eat, I was eating etc
com-ias	[kom**ee**-ash]	you used to eat (sing, fam)
com-ia	[kom**ee**-a]	he/she/it used to eat, used to eat (sing, pol)
com-íamos	[kom**ee**-amoosh]	we used to eat
com-iam	[kom**ee**-owng]	they used to eat, you used to eat (pl)

partir to leave

part-ia	[part**ee**-a]	I used to leave, I was leaving etc
part-ias	[part**ee**-ash]	you used to leave (sing, fam)
part-ia	[part**ee**-a]	he/she/it used to leave, used to leave (sing, pol)
part-íamos	[part**ee**-amoosh]	we used to leave
part-iam	[part**ee**-owng]	they used to leave, you used to leave (pl)

todas as quartas-feiras saíamos para dar um passeio

tohdazash kw**a**rtash f**ay**rash sa-**ee**-amoosh p**a**ra dar oong pass**ay**-oo

every Wednesday we used to go for a walk, every Wednesday
   we went for a walk

sempre chegávamos cedo ao emprego

s**ay**mpr shig**a**vamoosh s**ay**dwow aympr**ay**goo

we always arrived early at work

One useful irregular verb in the imperfect tense is:

ter to have

tinha	[**teen**-ya]	I used to have
tinhas	[**teen**-yash]	you used to have (sing, fam)
tinha	[**teen**-ya]	he/she/it used to have,
		you used to have (sing, pol)
tínhamos	[**teen**-yamoosh]	we used to have
tinham	[**teen**-yowng]	they used to have,
		you used to have (pl)

See page 265 for the imperfect tense of the verbs **ser** and
estar.

Future Tense

To form the future tense in Portuguese (I will do, you will
do etc), add the following endings to the infinitive. The same
endings are used whether verbs end in **-ar**, **-er** or **-ir**:

amar to love

amar-ei	[amar**ay**]	I will love
amar-ás	[amar**a**sh]	you will love (sing, fam)
amar-á	[amar**a**]	he will love, she will love,
		you will love (sing, pol)
amar-emos	[amar**ay**moosh]	we will love
amar-ão	[amar**ow**ng]	they will love, you will love (pl)

voltarei mais tarde

voltar**ay** m**ee**sh tard

I'll come back later

The immediate future can also be translated by **ir** + infinitive:

> **vamos comprar uma garrafa de vinho tinto**
> va**moosh** komprar **oo**ma ga**rra**fa di **veen**-yoo **teen**too
> we're going to buy a bottle of red wine

> **irei buscá-lo**
> i**ray** boosh**ka**loo
> I'll fetch him, I'll go and fetch him

In Portuguese, as in English, the future can sometimes be expressed by the present tense:

> **o seu avião parte à uma**
> oo **say**-oo av-**yowng** parte **noo**ma
> your plane takes off at one o'clock

However, Portuguese often uses the present tense where the future would be used in English:

> **dou-lhe oitocentos escudos**
> d**oh**l-yi oh-ito**sayn**tooz shk**oo**doosh
> I'll give you eight hundred escudos

The following verbs are irregular in the future tense:

dizer to say

dir-ei	[di**ray**]	I will say
dir-ás	[di**rash**]	you will say (sing, fam)
dir-á	[di**ra**]	he will say, she will say, you will say (sing, pol)
dir-emos	[di**ray**moosh]	we will say
dir-ão	[di**rowng**]	they will say, you will say (pl)

fazer to do

far-ei	[fa**ray**]	I will do
far-ás	[fa**rash**]	you will do (sing, fam)
far-á	[fa**ra**]	he will do, she will do, it will do, you will do (sing, pol)
far-emos	[fa**ray**moosh]	we will do
far-ão	[fa**rowng**]	they will do, you will do (pl)

See page 266 for the future tense of the verbs **ser** and **estar**.

Use of the Past Participle

There are two auxiliary verbs in Portuguese: **ter** (more commonly used) and **haver**. These two combine with the past participle to make a compound form of the past tense.

To form the past participle, remove the infinitive endings and add the endings **-ado** or **-ido** as indicated below:

infinitive	past participle	
amar	am-ado	[amadoo]
comer	com-ido	[komeedoo]
partir	part-ido	[parteedoo]

ela já tinha comprado o bilhete
ehla Ja **tee**n-ya kompra**d**oo oo bil-**yay**t
she had already bought the ticket

Some further examples using the past participle:

este livro foi comprado em Lisboa
aysht **lee**vroo **foh**-i kompradoo ayng liJb**oh**-a
this book was bought in Lisbon

temos comido bem	**ela deve ter partido ontem**
taymoosh kom**ee**doo bayng	**eh**la dehv tayr part**ee**doo **oh**ntayng
we've been eating well	she should have left yesterday

Some verbs have irregular past participles:

fazer to do, to make	feito	[**fay**too]
abrir to open	aberto	[a**beh**rtoo]
dizer to say	dito	[**dee**too]
pôr to put	posto	[**poh**shtoo]
ver to see	visto	[**vee**shtoo]
vir to come	vindo	[**vee**ndoo]
satisfazer to satisfy	satisfeito	[satish**fay**too]

The Verb 'To Be'

There are two verbs 'to be' in Portuguese: **ser** and **estar**. They are conjugated as follows:

Present Tense

ser

sou	[soh]	I am
és	[ehsh]	you are (sing, fam)
é	[eh]	he is, she is, it is, you are (sing, pol)
somos	[**soh**moosh]	we are
são	[sowng]	they are, you are (pl)

estar

estou	[shtoh]	I am
estás	[shtash]	you are (sing, fam)
está	[shta]	he is, she is, it is, you are (sing, pol)
estamos	[sht**a**moosh]	we are
estão	[shtowng]	they are, you are (pl)

Preterite Tense (I was etc)

ser		estar	
fui	[fwee]	estive	[shteev]
foste	[fohsht]	estiveste	[shtiv**eh**sht]
foi	[**foh**-i]	esteve	[shtayv]
fomos	[**foh**moosh]	estivemos	[shtiv**ay**moosh]
foram	[**foh**rowng]	estiveram	[shtiv**eh**rowng]

Imperfect Tense (I used to be etc)

ser		estar	
era	[**eh**ra]	estava	[sht**a**va]
eras	[**eh**rash]	estavas	[sht**a**vash]
era	[**eh**ra]	estava	[sht**a**va]
éramos	[**eh**ramoosh]	estávamos	[sht**a**vamoosh]
eram	[**eh**rowng]	estavam	[sht**a**vowng]

Future Tense (I will be etc)

ser   estar

serei	[siray]	estarei	[shtaray]
serás	[sirash]	estarás	[shtarash]
será	[sira]	estará	[shtara]
seremos	[siraymoosh]	estaremos	[shtaraymoosh]
serão	[sirowng]	estarão	[shtarowng]

Ser

Ser indicates an inherent quality, a permanent state or charac-
teristic, i.e. something which is unlikely to change:

a neve é branca
a nehv eh branka
snow is white

Ser is also used with occupations, nationalities, the time and
to indicate possession:

somos escoceses   **minha mãe é professora**
sohmoosh shkoosayzish   meen-ya mayng eh proofesohra
we are Scottish   my mum is a teacher

este é o nosso carro   **são cinco da tarde**
ayshteh oo nosoo karroo   sowng seenkoo da tard
this is our car   it's five o'clock in the afternoon

Estar

Estar, on the other hand, is used to describe the temporary or
passing qualities of something or someone:

estou zangado contigo   **estou cansado**
shtoh zangadoo konteegoo   shtoh kansadoo
I'm angry with you   I'm tired

este café está frio
aysht kafeh shta free-oo
this coffee is cold

Notice the difference between the following two phrases:

Isabel é muito bonita	**Isabel está muito bonita (hoje)**
Izab**ehl** eh m**wee**ngtoo bon**ee**ta	Izab**ehl** shta m**wee**ngtoo bon**ee**ta (ohJ)
Isabel is very pretty	Isabel looks pretty (today)

Negatives

To express a negative in Portuguese, to say 'I don't want', 'it's not here' etc, place the word **não** in front of the verb:

percebo	**não percebo**
pirs**ay**boo	nowng pirs**ay**boo
I understand	I don't understand
gosto deste gelado	**não gosto deste gelado**
g**o**shtoo daysht Jil**a**doo	nowng g**o**shtoo daysht Jil**a**doo
I like this ice cream	I don't like this ice cream
aluguei-o aqui	**não o aluguei aqui**
aloog**ay**-oo ak**ee**	nowng oo aloog**ay** ak**ee**
I rented it here	I didn't rent it here
vão cantar	**não vão cantar**
vowng kant**a**r	nowng vowng kant**a**r
they're going to sing	they're not going to sing

Unlike English, Portuguese makes use of double negatives with words like 'nothing/anything' or 'nobody/anybody':

não há ninguém aqui	**não comprámos nada**
nowng a ning**ay**ng ak**ee**	nowng kompr**a**moosh n**a**da
there's nobody here	we didn't buy anything

não sabemos nada dela
nowng sab**ay**moosh n**a**da d**eh**la
we don't know anything about her

To say 'there's no ...', 'I've no ...' etc, make the accompanying verb negative:

não há vinho		**não tenho fósforos**
nowng a **vee**n-yoo		nowng **tayn**-yoo **fosh**fooroosh
there's no wine		I've no matches

To say 'not him', 'not her' etc, just use the personal pronoun followed by **não**:

nós, não	**ela, não**	**eu, não**
noJ nowng	**eh**la nowng	**ay**-oo nowng
not us	not her	not me

Imperative

The imperative form of the verb is used to give commands. To form the imperative, remove the **-ar**, **-er** or **-ir** from the infinitive and add these endings:

	tu	você	vocês
amar to love	**ama**	**am**-e	**am**-em
	ama	**a**mi	a**mayng**
comer to eat	**come**	**com**-a	**com**-am
	kohm	**koh**ma	**koh**mowng
partir to leave	**parte**	**part**-a	**part**-am
	part	**par**ta	**par**towng

coma devagar
kohma diva**gar**
eat slowly

When you are telling someone not to do something, use the forms above and place **não** in front of the verb:

não me interrompa, por favor	**não beba álcool!**
nowng mintirr**oh**mpa poor fa**vohr**	nowng **bay**ba **a**lko-ol
don't interrupt me, please	don't drink alcohol!

não venha esta noite
nowng **vayn**-ya **eh**shta n**oh**-it
don't come tonight

por favor, não fale tão rápido (to one person)
poor favohr nowng fali towng rapidoo
please, don't speak so fast

por favor, não falem tão rápido (to several people)
poor favohr nowng falayng towng rapidoo
please, don't speak so fast

Pronouns are added to the end of the imperative form:

acorde-me às oito, por favor
akordimi azoh-itoo poor favohr
wake me up at eight o'clock, please

ajude-me, por favor
aJoodimi poor favohr
help me please

However, when the imperative is negative, pronouns are placed in front of it:

não as deixe aqui
nowng aJ daysh akee
don't leave them here

Questions

Often the word order remains the same in a question, but the intonation changes, the voice rising at the end of the question:

queres dançar?
kehrish dansar
do you want to dance?

fica longe?
feeka lohnJ
is it far?

Dates

Use the numbers on page 40 to express the date.

um de Setembro [oong di sitaymbroo] the first of September
dois de Dezembro [doh-iJ di dizaymbroo] the second of
  December
vinte-e-um de Janeiro [veenti-oong di Janayroo] the twenty first
  of January

Days

Monday segunda-feira [sigoonda fayra]
Tuesday terça-feira [tayrsa fayra]
Wednesday quarta-feira [kwarta fayra]
Thursday quinta-feira [keenta fayra]
Friday sexta-feira [sayshta fayra]
Saturday sábado [sabadoo]
Sunday domingo [doomeengoo]

Months

January Janeiro [Janayroo]
February Fevereiro [fivrayroo]
March Março [marsoo]
April Abril [abreel]
May Maio [mī-oo]
June Junho [Joon-yoo]
July Julho [Jool-yoo]
August Agosto [agohshtoo]
September Setembro [sitaymbroo]
October Outubro [ohtoobroo]
November Novembro [noovaymbroo]
December Dezembro [dizaymbroo]

Time

what time is it? que horas são? [k-yorash sowng]
one o'clock uma hora [ooma ora]
two o'clock duas horas [doo-az orash]
it's one o'clock é uma hora [eh ooma ora]
it's two o'clock são duas horas [sowng doo-azorash]
it's three o'clock são três horas [trayzorash]
five past one uma e cinco [oomi seenkoo]
ten past two duas e dez [doo-azi dehsh]
quarter past one uma e um quarto [oomi-oong kwartoo]
quarter past two duas e um quarto [doo-azi-oong]
half past ten dez e meia [dehz ee may-a]
twenty to ten dez menos vinte [dehJ maynooJ veent]
quarter to ten dez menos um quarto [dehJ maynooz oong kwartoo]
at eight o'clock às oito horas [azoh-itoo orash]
at half past four às quatro e meia [ash kwatroo ee may-a]
2 a.m. duas da manhã [doo-aJ da man-yang]
2 p.m. duas da tarde [tard]
6 a.m. seis da manhã [saysh da man-yang]
6 p.m. seis da tarde [tard]
noon meio-dia [may-oo dee-a]
midnight meia-noite [may-a noh-it]
an hour uma hora [ooma ora]
a minute um minuto [oong minootoo]
two minutes dois minutos [doh-iJ minootoosh]
a second um segundo [oong sigoondoo]
a quarter of an hour um quarto de hora [kwartoo dora]
half an hour meia hora [may-a ora]
three quarters of an hour três quartos de hora [traysh kwartoosh
   dora]

Numbers

0	zero [**zeh**roo]	80	oitenta [oh-it**ayn**ta]
1	um [oong]	90	noventa [noo**vayn**ta]
2	dois [**doh**-ish]	100	cem [sayng]
3	três [traysh]	101	cento e um [**sayn**twee oong]
4	quatro [kw**a**troo]		
5	cinco [**seen**koo]	120	cento e vinte [veent]
6	seis [saysh]	200	duzentos [doo**zayn**toosh],
7	sete [seht]		duzentas [doo**zayn**tash]
8	oito [**oh**-itoo]	300	trezentos [tri**zayn**toosh],
9	nove [nov]		trezentas [tri**zayn**tash]
10	dez [dehsh]	400	quatrocentos
11	onze [ohnz]		[kwatro**sayn**toosh],
12	doze [dohz]		quatrocentas
13	treze [trayz]		[kwatro**sayn**tash]
14	catorze [kat**ohr**z]	500	quinhentos [keen-**yayn**toosh], quinhentas
15	quinze [keenz]		[keen-**yayn**tash]
16	dezasseis [diza**saysh**]	600	seiscentos
17	dezassete [diza**seht**]		[saysh**sayn**toosh],
18	dezoito [diz**oh**-itoo]		seiscentas
19	dezanove [diza**nov**]		[saysh**sayn**tash]
20	vinte [veent]	700	setecentos
21	vinte e um [**veen**ti-oong]		[sete**sayn**toosh],
22	vinte e dois [**veen**ti **doh**-ish]		setecentas [sete**sayn**tash]
23	vinte e três [**veen**ti traysh]	800	oitocentos
30	trinta [**treen**ta]		[oh-itoo**sayn**toosh],
31	trinta e um [**treen**ti-oong]		oitocentas
32	trinta e dois [**treen**tī **doh**-ish]		[oh-itoo**sayn**tash]
40	quarenta [kwar**ayn**ta]	900	novecentos
50	cinquenta [sinkw**ayn**ta]		[nove**sayn**toosh],
60	sessenta [ses**ayn**ta]		novecentas
70	setenta [set**ayn**ta]		[nove**sayn**tash]
		1,000	mil [meel]

2,000	dois mil [**doh**-ish]
5,000	cinco mil [**seen**koo]
10,000	dez mil [dehsh]
1,000,000	um milhão [mil-**yow**ng]

um is used with masculine nouns:

> **um carro**
> oong karroo
> one car

uma is used with feminine nouns:

> **uma bicicleta**
> **oo**ma bisikle**h**ta
> one bike

With multiples of a hundred, the -as ending is used with feminine nouns:

> **trezentos homens**
> tri**zayn**tooz **oh**mayngsh
> 300 men

> **quinhentas mulheres**
> keen-**yayn**taJ mool-**yeh**rish
> 500 women

Ordinals

1st	primeiro [prim**ay**roo]
2nd	segundo [sig**oon**doo]
3rd	terceiro [tir**say**roo]
4th	quarto [**kwar**too]
5th	quinto [**keen**too]
6th	sexto [**saysh**too]
7th	sétimo [**seh**timoo]
8th	oitavo [oh-i**tav**oo]
9th	nono [**noh**noo]
10th	décimo [**deh**simoo]

Conversion Tables

1 centimetre = 0.39 inches	1 inch = 2.54 cm
1 metre = 39.37 inches = 1.09 yards	1 foot = 30.48 cm
1 kilometre = 0.62 miles = 5/8 mile	1 yard = 0.91 m
	1 mile = 1.61 km

km	1	2	3	4	5	10	20	30	40	50	100
miles	0.6	1.2	1.9	2.5	3.1	6.2	12.4	18.6	24.8	31.0	62.1

miles	1	2	3	4	5	10	20	30	40	50	100
km	1.6	3.2	4.8	6.4	8.0	16.1	32.2	48.3	64.4	80.5	161

1 gram = 0.035 ounces	1 kilo = 1000 g = 2.2 pounds

g	100	250	500	1 oz = 28.35 g
oz	3.5	8.75	17.5	1 lb = 0.45 kg

kg	0.5	1	2	3	4	5	6	7	8	9	10
lb	1.1	2.2	4.4	6.6	8.8	11.0	13.2	15.4	17.6	19.8	22.0

kg	20	30	40	50	60	70	80	90	100
lb	44	66	88	110	132	154	176	198	220

lb	0.5	1	2	3	4	5	6	7	8	9	10	20
kg	0.2	0.5	0.9	1.4	1.8	2.3	2.7	3.2	3.6	4.1	4.5	9.0

1 litre = 1.75 UK pints / 2.13 US pints

1 UK pint = 0.57 litre	1 UK gallon = 4.55 litre
1 US pint = 0.47 litre	1 US gallon = 3.79 litre

centigrade / Celsius   °C = (°F - 32) x 5/9

°C	-5	0	5	10	15	18	20	25	30	36.8	38
°F	23	32	41	50	59	64	68	77	86	98.4	100.4

Fahrenheit   °F = (°C x 9/5) + 32

°F	23	32	40	50	60	65	70	80	85	98.4	101
°C	-5	0	4	10	16	18	21	27	29	36.8	38.3